THE WORLD IN A LIFE

THE LIVES OF PEOPLE and the unfolding of earth-shaking events inspire us to love history. We live in a global age where big concepts such as "globalization" often tempt us to forget the "people" side of the past. The titles in *The World in a Life* series aim to revive these meaningful lives. Each one shows us what it felt like to live on a world historical stage and even to shape the world's destiny.

The lives of most individuals are full of activity and color and even passion and violence. The people examined in *The World in a Life* series often faced outsized challenges, but they usually met the great events of their day energetically. They lived amidst enormous change, as we often do. Their lives show us how to navigate change and to find solutions. They made fateful decisions, often with much soul-searching or—as often—on the spur of the moment and even intuitively. We have much to learn from these fateful past lives.

Their actions, however, were filled with complexity. Biographies in this series give a "nutshell" explanation of how important paradoxes and dilemmas have been in the stories of individuals operating on the world stage. Their lives become windows onto the complicated trends, events, and crises of their time, providing an entry point for a deeper understanding of a particular historical era. As such events and crises unfolded, these historical figures also faced crises in their personal lives. In the intertwined dramas of the personal and political, of the individual and the global, we come to understand the complexities of acting on the world stage and living in world history.

BONNIE G. SMITH

SIMONE de BEAUVOIR

SERIES EDITOR: Bonnie G. Smith, *Rutgers University*

THE WORLD IN A LIFE

SIMONE de BEAUVOIR

CREATING A FEMINIST EXISTENCE IN THE WORLD

SANDRINE SANOS

New York   Oxford
OXFORD UNIVERSITY PRESS

Oxford University Press is a department of the University of Oxford.
It furthers the University's objective of excellence in research,
scholarship, and education by publishing worldwide.

Oxford New York
Auckland   Cape Town   Dar es Salaam   Hong Kong   Karachi
Kuala Lumpur   Madrid   Melbourne   Mexico City   Nairobi
New Delhi   Shanghai   Taipei   Toronto

With offices in
Argentina   Austria   Brazil   Chile   Czech Republic   France   Greece
Guatemala   Hungary   Italy   Japan   Poland   Portugal   Singapore
South Korea   Switzerland   Thailand   Turkey   Ukraine   Vietnam

For titles covered by Section 112 of the US Higher Education
Opportunity Act, please visit www.oup.com/us/he for the
latest information about pricing and alternate formats.

Published in the United States of America by
Oxford University Press
198 Madison Avenue, New York, NY 10016
http://www.oup.com

Library of Congress Cataloging-in-Publication Data

Names: Sanos, Sandrine.
Title: Simone de Beauvoir : creating a feminist existence in the world /
  Sandrine Sanos.
Description: Oxford ; New York : Oxford University Press, 2016. | Includes
  index.
Identifiers: LCCN 2015037222 | ISBN 9780190278090
Subjects: LCSH: Beauvoir, Simone de, 1908–1986. | Authors, French--20th
  century--Biography. | Feminists--France--Biography.
Classification: LCC PQ2603.E362 Z8754 2016 | DDC 848/.91409--dc23 LC
record available at http://lccn.loc.gov/2015037222

Printing number: 9 8 7 6 5 4 3 2 1

Printed in the United States of America
on acid-free paper

CONTENTS

LIST OF ILLUSTRATIONS AND MAPS

ACKNOWLEDGMENTS

I WOULD LIKE TO THANK friends and colleagues who have read portions of the manuscript for their insightful advice and enthusiastic encouragement: Flora Bernard, Darcie Fontaine, Daniel Lee, Claudia Peppel (who introduced me to Alice Schwarzer's documentary), and especially Natasha Crawford and Laura Muñoz for reminding me of the importance of the biographical. I would also like to thank my parents, Louise and Serge Sanos, for their unwavering support as always. I am also especially grateful to Judy Coffin for sharing her work on Beauvoir with me and for our conversations regarding Beauvoir's politics. I would like to thank TAMU-CC students Veronica Guzman-Hays and Lynn Jaworski-Besanceney for their assistance at critical moments of the project. Working in different libraries in the United States and France was, at times, challenging: I would like to thank Brenton Day for making sure I could get my hands on all of Beauvoir's works at all times. I owe much to Charles Cavaliere, Julieta Cardenas, and the editorial and production team at Oxford University Press for the consideration and care they brought to this biography. Finally, I am extremely grateful to Sarah Fishman, University of Houston; Marc Matera, University of California, Santa Cruz and Elisa Camiscioli, Binghamton University without whom the manuscript would not have taken shape, and especially to Bonnie Smith who first suggested I write about Beauvoir and whose encouragement, attentive eye, and wise counsel as I tried to tell this story proved invaluable.

ABOUT THE AUTHOR

SANDRINE SANOS is a cultural and intellectual historian of modern Europe, educated in France, the United Kingdom, and the United States. Her scholarship and teaching focus on twentieth-century France and its empire, specifically the intersections of gender and sexuality, the relation of aesthetics and politics, and the question of violence, war, exile, and feminist theory. Her book, *The Aesthetics of Hate: Far-Right Intellectuals, Antisemitism and Gender in 1930s France* was published in 2012 by Stanford University Press. She has also written about European film and French literature and received awards for her teaching and scholarship. Her current work examines the cultural representation of violence, displacement, and gender in France between 1954 and 1967.

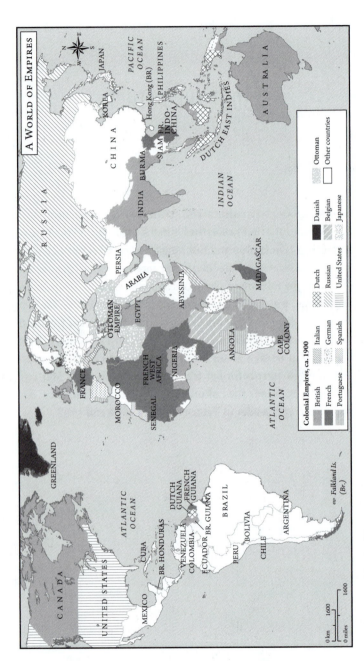

MAP 1. A WORLD OF EMPIRES

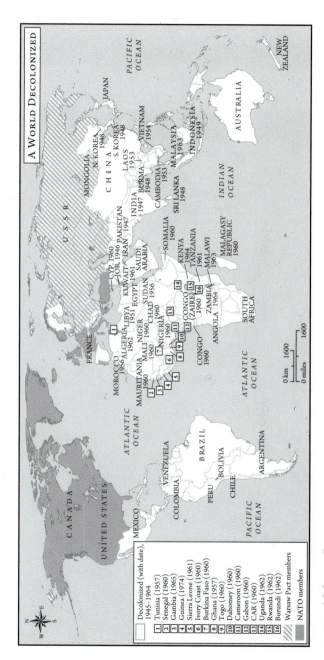

MAP 2. A WORLD DECOLONIZED

SIMONE de BEAUVOIR

INTRODUCTION

IN 1970, A TWENTY-EIGHT-YEAR-OLD West German feminist and freelance journalist, Alice Schwarzer, traveled to Paris to meet and interview the worldwide famous novelist and philosopher Simone de Beauvoir. In 1973, she released a documentary film about Beauvoir.[1] The documentary shows the sixty-four-year-old Beauvoir in all kinds of situations: immaculately dressed while reading newspapers in a Rome café, having lunch with enthusiastic younger French feminists, or discussing the meaning of her four-decades-long intellectual and personal relationship with equally world-famous French philosopher Jean-Paul Sartre. In the documentary, Beauvoir explains how she is a feminist and what that means to her. That last image is the one most people have of Beauvoir to this day: a feminist icon and worldwide celebrity. However, as Schwarzer explained decades later, Beauvoir's work is "a classic every woman and man claims to know—but, in fact, the smallest number had actually read her."[2] Indeed, Beauvoir's public image, reputation, and fame seem frozen in time. They are actually the legacy of the last fifteen years of her life (when she became a prominent feminist activist who wrote, demonstrated, and appeared on TV). They do not do justice to the long and complicated life she led, the intellectual and political trajectory she followed, and the many issues she spoke about in her letters, diaries, and in print. Just as Beauvoir had once explained about her philosophy, her life was always embedded in the world.

Beauvoir's life is also more complex than she let on in her work. Beauvoir had always promised her readers that her writings, especially her memoirs, were dedicated to revealing the

1

truth about her life and her perception of the world. She some-times grew impatient with readers who, she felt, did not under-stand her but never fully dispelled readers' assumptions that her fiction was a barely veiled autobiography. Some of her most famous works are her memoirs where readers believed she pro-vided a window into her life and the world she lived in. But, like any writer, she dramatized and rearranged. She sometimes left things out, especially when it came to her personal life (even though she wrote often and frankly about her relationships and friendships). Her vision of the world was a very personal and sub-jective one. That was not a problem for Beauvoir. As a novelist, she believed she was in the business of transforming what she ex-perienced and imagined into literature. As a philosopher, she was intimately convinced individuals must always strive to examine how they exist in the world, how they are shaped by the world in which they exist, and how they must challenge and question their situation and the world.

Beauvoir was also a prolific writer. Over the course of almost fifty years, she published philosophy, novels, short stories, politi-cal essays, memoirs, diaries, and newspaper articles. She edited one of the most notable postwar leftist magazines, *Modern Times* (*Les Temps Modernes*). She supported and championed other writers who have become important literary voices. She was in-volved in some of the most significant events and political devel-opments of the twentieth century, either as participant or witness.

Those events shaped her thought. She had been enjoying the carefree life of a young female professional and aspiring novelist in Paris when World War II broke out. The war was a shock but, following the Nazi occupation, Beauvoir lived her life like most other French citizens, neither resisting the Nazis nor helping those persecuted by the Nazis and the authoritarian French gov-ernment. The immediate postwar period brought recognition as a novelist, she traveled, and became part of a vibrant circle of politically engaged intellectuals who believed in social justice, revolution, and working to end oppression and violence. She came to politics only in the late 1950s as she saw the ravages of the Algerian War of Independence and wrote against torture and in support of Algerians seeking independence from French colonialism. She spent the next two decades, further immersed in politics, traveling the world, to Latin America, North America, North Africa, East Asia, and the Middle East, always hoping a socialist regime could bring a better world. She was now famous, along with her long-time intellectual companion, Jean-Paul Sartre. They were photographed and filmed everywhere they went. She wrote about all the big events that shook France and the world: from the Algerian War, to the Chinese Revolution, the Vietnam War, the May '68 student uprisings, the Israeli-Palestinian conflict, and much more. Finally, in the 1970s, she found herself swept up by the energy and commitment of a new generation that demanded a more radical politics. Some of these were feminists and Beauvoir embraced the life of a feminist activist, putting her name, reputation, and influence behind feminist causes.

All the while, Beauvoir was driven by one important principle, how to attain freedom and liberate oneself from oppression. She wrote about all of these. This was not an easy task: Beauvoir was not always concerned with politics. Her political involvement evolved throughout the course of her life. She experienced hope, excitement, enthusiasm, but also disillusion, disappointment, and even despair in the face of political trials and tribulations. She tried to fight injustice and oppression but, at times, could not escape the limits of her position as privileged intellectual. Schwarzer said it well when she explained that Beauvoir is fascinating because of the "intersection of project, life, and political engagement" that was "intertwined until the very end."[3] This is why Beauvoir is such a captivating figure. She was, in many ways, an exceptional woman, at the forefront of some of the most important issues of the twentieth century. At the same time, she was also of her times, and her actions, writings, and blind spots reflected that. Still, as a witness, actor, and intellectual, she inspired many readers then and now.

But what does it mean to read Beauvoir, then and now? Beauvoir's works have been read worldwide. Still, readers have not always grasped the full extent of her many interests, and there have been many misunderstandings. For a long time, she was believed to be a second-rate philosopher who had merely copied her companion's, Jean-Paul Sartre, ideas. That caricature has been challenged in the last thirty-five years, mostly by feminist thinkers and philosophers who have taken her work seriously. That misunderstanding was also the result of a strange situation. Beauvoir wrote a huge amount through the course of her life. However, as Schwarzer said, most people have only read a few of her works. In the 1970s, French feminists turned to Beauvoir as an intellectual reference and a political model, but few had read her 1949 almost thousand-page two-volume book on the condition of women, *The Second Sex*. Readers who have loved her memoirs have not necessarily read her novels. Those who know her literature have not read her journalism and essays. To others, she is first and foremost a political commentator and her other literary and philosophical writings are less important. Beauvoir is an icon read in fragments.

Even worse, for decades, the reception of her work was hampered by inadequate and misleading translations. This is especially the case for the American translation of Beauvoir's *The Second Sex*. In the 1960s and 1970s, many American feminist activists and scholars discovered feminism by reading Beauvoir. However, they were reading a truncated and inaccurate translation. *The Second Sex* was published in English in 1953 only four years after its French release. It was a huge bestseller. But readers had no idea of what was missing from the text they were reading. Its translator took it upon himself to "simplify" Beauvoir's prose. In doing so, he took out all the philosophical references and concepts that were central to Beauvoir's demonstration. He also took out evidence of the extensive research Beauvoir had done, the "documentation of women's lived experience" she used as evidence, and depoliticized the text.[4] As feminist scholar Toril Moi has noted, "there are mistakes and omissions on every page," and 15 percent of the original text was cut.[5] After over two decades of asking for a new translation, *The Second Sex* was reissued with an updated translation in 2011.

In the last fifteen years, many have rediscovered Beauvoir. New translations and collections of previously untranslated works have been published.[6] An entire generation of feminist philosophers and scholars are commenting on and engaging with Beauvoir's thought. Beauvoir's work remains very much alive and is seen by many as especially relevant to contemporary issues. In the same way, it is time to learn of Beauvoir's place in the world, the ways in which (as she explained) her life was always embedded in the world, and how it shaped her life and writings. In short, we must learn how Beauvoir crafted a "feminist existence in the world."

Note: All translations from the French in the text are my own. However, for English readers, references to the English publications have been included, unless the works were unavailable in English.

CHAPTER 1

"THE DUTIFUL DAUGHTER": OBLIGATIONS, HOPES, AND POSSIBILITIES, 1909–1939

SIMONE DE BEAUVOIR WROTE ONCE that a "woman writer is not a housewife who writes, but someone whose entire existence is devoted to writing." She insisted that "this life is as good as any other."[1] Beauvoir felt it was her destiny to be an author. She was born at the beginning of the twentieth century, when women's lives were changing and new possibilities were emerging. Nonetheless, a "woman who writes" was still a rare affair in France and elsewhere. There had been female writers whose novels were celebrated and widely read, but they were exceptional and unconventional figures. In the nineteenth century, Aurore Dupin published novels, literary criticism, and memoirs under the male pseudonym of Georges Sand. She was famous for wearing male attire in public; shocked Parisian society with her affair with a much younger lover, the poet Alfred de Musset; and was friends with some of the most well-known authors of the time, such as novelist Gustave Flaubert. Born three years before Sand's death, Colette was another controversial figure: she was a musical performer and started her writing career with successful short novels about a rebellious young woman, Claudine. She consistently transgressed conventional norms of behavior with her unabashed freedom, marriages, lesbian affairs, and most importantly, was recognized as a "woman of genius" after World War I, thanks to her 1920 novel, *Chéri*. Beauvoir's unconventional life followed in these novelists' footsteps. Beauvoir read their works as a teenager as she discovered the world of books. She read voraciously and widely from her parents' library. Every novel enchanted her. It was literature that gave Beauvoir a sense that other worlds existed. Years later, as Beauvoir wrote about her childhood, she explained that, thanks to novels, she "was able to free herself from her childhood to enter a complicated, adventurous, and unexpected world."[2] Literature allowed her to leave behind the role of the "dutiful daughter" that had been expected of her in order to forge a different path.

COMING INTO THE WORLD

When Beauvoir was born in Paris in 1908, Europe had entered the "modern age." Across the Continent and in Britain, Europeans now owned bicycles, and homes boasted sewing machines. In offices, typewriters and lamps appeared. In factories, electricity allowed longer working hours. The first airplane was flown in 1903 and, a few years later, cars zoomed through cities, even though only the wealthy could afford them. Cities grew and technology changed the nature of life. Beauvoir's parents experienced these changes. In fact, her family's fate mirrored that of changes in French society. Her parents, at first glance, seemed to be rather typical of the bourgeois Catholic class that had emerged in the previous century. From the outside, they appeared respectable, their lives rather unremarkable. Her father, Georges-Bertrand de Beauvoir, had studied law. His professional life followed a conventional path—the one he chose over his long-harbored desire to become an actor. On the other hand, her mother, Françoise, seemed well-suited to this uneventful bourgeois life. She came from a profoundly Catholic and wealthy provincial family. A life devoted to respectable and religious domesticity was expected of middle-class housewives, and Beauvoir's mother embraced that role. Simone and her younger sister Hélène, born two years after Simone, seemed at first destined to a life similar to their mother's. But the Great War that consumed France changed both daughters' fates.

Beauvoir was only a child when the war broke out in 1914. In a context of virulent nationalism and imperial competition, European nations eagerly and swiftly went to war. Leaders imagined the war would be quick, and ordinary citizens chanted patriotic songs as they rallied behind their governments. Austria-Hungary and Germany faced off against Great Britain, France, and Russia. Soon the world was engulfed in what became a long, bloody, and devastating conflict. The war meant little to young Simone, unlike the millions of adult French men and women who suffered through it. She recalled being a young child unthinkingly mimicking the patriotism of adults around her and destroying her doll because it displayed a "Made in Germany" label.

Her father was called for service but was soon demobilized because of his poor health. This unexpected development probably saved his life. Hundreds of thousands died horrible unheroic deaths in muddy trenches where they had spent long months interrupted by the noise of bombs that might mutilate them. Unending artillery gun attacks meant certain death, and the constant fear of a gas attack required men to sleep with a gas mask next to their makeshift beds. At the same time, trench warfare encouraged an unusual sense of camaraderie among soldiers. It seemed class boundaries no longer mattered, and that soldiers across enemy lines had more in common with one another than they had with those they had left behind. The experience of the front haunted many after the war.

It was not just men who were affected by the war. Both working-class and middle-class women on the home front toiled in factories and had taken their fathers', husbands', and brothers' jobs in order to sustain the war effort. All citizens—men and women—were called upon to help. This was "total war."

All disagreements among political parties and labor unions were suspended. In France, this was called the "Sacred Union" (*union sacrée*). When the armistice was signed in 1918, almost forty million men had been killed or wounded throughout Europe. More than a million and a half French men had died in trenches. France was the Western European nation to have lost the most lives in proportion to its overall population. Countries like Russia had seen more deaths, but no Western European nation was as affected as France was. The war therefore shaped much of the social, cultural, and political world of interwar France.

The war changed French society and, it also had a profound effect on Beauvoir's family. By 1918, most European countries had to rebuild because of the physical devastation and psychological effects of this conflict. Another world had emerged. Her family struggled to maintain its bourgeois status: the family fortune had been lost during the war, and Beauvoir's father was unsuccessful in the various business ventures he took on afterward. They moved to a smaller apartment. Her parents started arguing. Their loss of wealth decisively influenced how the two girls were raised. As their father told them, they would have to find independent means of income. There were to be no dowries (as was the practice for middle-class families marrying their daughters) for the Beauvoir sisters, and they therefore could not aspire to the traditional future of young bourgeois housewives. Instead, they would have to work. This proved a saving grace for the young Simone who loved her studies and yearned to escape the stifling environment of her politically conservative family and distance herself from the overbearing Catholic faith of her mother.

One of her first transformations occurred while still a child: she stopped believing in religion. This may have been a less radical choice than Beauvoir thought at the time. In contrast to her pious mother, her father had never been a committed Catholic, and Beauvoir gladly followed suit, eventually renouncing her faith.[3] She first started seeing priests as "impostors" then, emboldened by her skepticism, biblical stories soon became fables in her eyes.[4] Literature replaced religion. Beauvoir remained an atheist her entire life. She was not alone in leaving Catholicism behind. Her turn away from religion was symptomatic of the secularization of French society that had been underway since the nineteenth century and that drove much of France's republican

FRIENDSHIP. *Simone de Beauvoir (right) and her best friend Elisabeth Lacoin (left), or "Zaza" (1925).*

political culture. Those who, like Beauvoir, came of age in the first half of the twentieth century challenged the Catholic norms that had structured their parents' generation. Many of the intellectuals she later associated with, Jean-Paul Sartre especially, were equally skeptical of faith and religion. They tried to formulate a political and ethical vision of the world grounded in humanist and secular principles. The war had challenged the place of God. Now only the human individual could be thought of as the foundation of a meaningful world where inequities, injustice, and oppression would, one day, be eradicated. That goal sustained many young intellectuals. This was the first of the many personal transformations Beauvoir underwent throughout her life.

EMBRACING KNOWLEDGE, CHOOSING PHILOSOPHY

As Beauvoir entered her teens, she continued to study at the private Catholic girls' school where she spent her days with her beloved friend Elisabeth Lacoin, nicknamed Zaza, dreaming and debating with her about what the future had in store for them. While she read novels at home and trained her mind to arduous and rigorous exercises at school, Beauvoir remained unaware of the changes around her that were shaping the nature of education. She both directly and indirectly benefited from the educational reforms that were taking place as she was moved through the ranks of the French school and university system. In 1924, when Beauvoir was sixteen, separate secondary education for boys and girls was ended. Schools everywhere in France now welcomed both boys and girls in the same classrooms. Beauvoir did not experience this directly as she remained in the private girls-only Cours Désir, but she was nonetheless able to enjoy new opportunities. High school diplomas (*baccalauréat*) were now the same for boys and girls, and the preparatory classes to France's elite institutions were now open to women. She successfully graduated in 1925, followed by many other young girls. The proportion of women earning high school diplomas jumped from 6 percent in 1914 to 36 percent in 1939. These young women could now enter university, and the proportion of female university students doubled in a decade, increasing from 20 percent in 1920 to 40 percent in 1930. Beauvoir was one of them. She chose to study philosophy at the oldest and most prestigious French university, La Sorbonne. By the time of France's defeat to Germany in the Second World War in 1940, women made up a third of all university students. Many of these women took up white-collar jobs; others became high-school professors, as Beauvoir did.

Among her fellow students, Beauvoir seemed unusually gifted. Only two years after graduating from high school, she successfully completed a degree (*licence*) in philosophy at the Sorbonne. Philosophy was, at the time, the most revered of all disciplines. It was considered the most challenging and bestowed the greatest prestige upon its practitioners. Beauvoir's choice was a bold and ambitious one: philosophy was an unusual choice for a woman then. Beauvoir later explained it had attracted her precisely because it promised to "fulfill her desire to know the world in its totality."[5] To know the world in its entirety was an impossible ambition, but one that appealed to the young Simone who believed everything was within reach. She spent the following years preparing to pass the *agrégation*—an incredibly arduous and competitive exam that allowed students to become part of France's educational elite. This highly selective exam (in the sciences and the humanities) allowed those who passed to teach in high schools and universities, which were public institutions. It was also considered a mark of intellectual excellence and, since the nineteenth century, many well-known thinkers and politicians had been "agrégés." While preparing for her exams, she met a group of students who introduced her to a different and exciting life and to a world of ideas that she had not previously imagined. She spent her days talking and reading with aspiring philosophers Jean-Paul Sartre and his friend Paul Nizan. They welcomed her into their group, affectionately referring to her by the playful nickname a male friend had given her that stuck with her for life: Castor, the French word for "beaver," an allusion to her name.[6] These were exciting times especially since, with Sartre, Beauvoir felt she had met her intellectual match with whom she could share everything. He also became her first lover. That meeting was decisive for both and changed the course of her life.

Though an integral part of the group, Beauvoir remained an oddity among these young men. She claimed she never felt any different because she was a woman. But being a woman did affect her situation. Unlike her contemporaries, she was not allowed to attend the prestigious École normale supérieure (ENS), which trained the greatest minds of France and its future leaders. Most of the well-known French philosophers of the twentieth century have passed through it, including Sartre, Nizan, and Maurice Merleau-Ponty. In the 1920s, however, it was still closed to women. Despite this exclusion, Beauvoir managed to earn second place at the *agrégation*, just behind Sartre. A professor who reviewed their exams recalled, years later, that the exam committee had long hesitated between them. After much deliberation, they opted for the familiar. They decided to rank Sartre, who was sitting for the exam for the second time and was two years older, first. Beauvoir was second. In 1930, at the age of twenty-two, Beauvoir was the youngest-ever student in France to successfully pass this exam. Her professional and literary life had begun.

A PROVINCIAL CAREER

Becoming an engaged intellectual in the public eye was not yet Beauvoir's ambition—and nor was it even possible for her in 1930. Literature was her passion. Becoming a recognized novelist was what she aspired to. But Beauvoir first had to follow the course set for her by her education: passing the *agrégation* required teaching for five years in high schools before one was able to move to another profession. She also had to earn a living, and so she took a position teaching philosophy in a high school. In doing so, she left behind her success in a mostly male preserve and joined the ranks of growing numbers of young middle-class women entering governmental institutions (like schools) and the service industry. The female workforce in France had steadily been growing. Already in 1906, women had made up almost 38 percent of the French labor force, though mostly in domestic work and lesser paid positions. In the early twentieth century, 20 percent of married women worked. This was the highest proportion in Western Europe. During World War I, many women had been mobilized to work in order to sustain the war effort, taking jobs in munitions and industrial factories. At the close of the war, circumstances changed the nature of work, and women had to leave these jobs. Beauvoir's situation was slightly different. She was part of the growing number of middle-class women entering white-collar jobs.

Her life as a teacher appeared, at first, to be a disappointment. While she enjoyed teaching, the daily routine of being a professor

TEACHING. *Simone de Beauvoir and her students at the secondary school of Mongrand in Marseille (1931).*

proved uneventful and even rather dull. Even more disappointing, she had had to leave Paris for a position in a small town. She experienced this as a forced exile she resented, for it meant leaving her lover, friends, and the cultural life she loved. Beauvoir was assigned two different provincial posts: first in the South of France, in the bustling port town of Marseilles in 1931, and the following year in Rouen which, to her relief, was closer to Paris. She remained unexcited by the routine demands of high school life. Teaching, however, showed Beauvoir something she did enjoy for the rest of life: mentoring young adults, especially young women. She relished training the most talented of her students, and she often became friends with them. Her students remembered her as an energetic and gifted speaker who seemed to improvise her classes and was unafraid of introducing her students to what was then considered unorthodox and even scandalous topics.[7] In some of her classes, she taught the ideas of the great Viennese psychoanalyst Sigmund Freud.[8] This was considered rather daring as Freud's ideas had only slowly made their way into the French intellectual and educational world, even though Germany and England had debated these texts since the late nineteenth century. Equally bold was her decision to teach the novels of André Gide. Gide was, by then, a celebrated novelist.[9] But, to many people on the right and far-right, his celebration of homosexuality, Protestant origins, and later, flirtation with communism, made him into a depraved figure whose ideas should be shunned. Beauvoir thus blended her own tastes with the requirements of the official philosophy curriculum her students had to master.

Beauvoir did not only display a complete disregard for conventions in the content of her classes. She was also to disregard openly the conventions a young middle-class female professional was supposed to embody at that time. One student, Jacqueline, whom she taught at the bourgeois *lycée Molière* in a sedate upper-class neighborhood of Paris described a young and "brilliant" professor who seemed distant from them and carried an "aura of scandal around her."[10] That aura of scandal students whispered to one another about came from the knowledge that Beauvoir was a friend of the up-and-coming controversial philosopher Jean-Paul Sartre. They were not married and "lived a very free life."[11] Beauvoir lived in hotels and worked in cafés. These bustling public places became her office; she occasionally met some of her students, graded exams, and began writing her novels and essays at a café table. In many ways, in the eyes of these young women, Beauvoir embodied the figure of the "New Woman" that emerged after World War I and caused heated debates in France at the time.

A NEW WOMAN?

To many, it seemed the world had been turned upside down in the aftermath of the Great War. In the early 1920s, when Beauvoir was coming of age, she was a young woman still ensconced in the habits of her middle-class, conservative, and Catholic upbringing. When she became a professor several years later, it was her lifestyle that scandalized. At the same time, another type of young woman shocked observers with her bobbed hair, shorter than ankle-length hemlines, cigarette smoking, and presence in the Parisian night clubs where jazz was played and alcohol flowed freely. Of course, this was hardly the case of the majority of French women. But, in Paris, these middle-class young women who seemed to disregard all social conventions struck observers. They were soon given a name: the "New Woman." In magazines, fashion plates, articles, and commentaries, they represented the freedom and excitement of the new that many young people yearned for after four long, dreary, and terrible war years. To others, they embodied the decadence that had come as a result of this conflict, in short, no less than the end of civilization. One novel epitomized these trends: *The Boyish Woman* (*La Garçonne*) published in 1922 by an established but second-rate novelist, Victor Margueritte. The novel was a huge bestseller: it sold over a million copies. One prominent right-wing novelist and veteran of the war, Pierre Drieu La Rochelle, famously exclaimed that this novel showed how this "civilization no longer has clothes, no longer has churches, no longer has theaters, no longer has paintings, no longer has books, no longer has sexes."[12] For Drieu La Rochelle, the transgression of gender norms that these young women embodied was a sure sign of the undoing of French civilization. The fact that so many across the political spectrum felt compelled to comment on and debate the merits of the New Woman shows how, as society was changing, French people felt especially concerned about the preservation of gender roles as a measure of the greatness of a society.

When writing about her youth, Beauvoir claims that she had not been one of these sexually liberated young women who smoked, went out late at night, and embraced both lesbian and heterosexual relationships. She explains that, in the early 1930s, she was still enslaved by "sexual taboos" and that women who were perceived as "too easy" or "too free" shocked her.[13] But that would be too simple. It was also not quite true. In other ways, Beauvoir had already joined the ranks of these New Women. For Beauvoir, becoming an adult, a free-thinking and independent individual, as well as a recognized author, had meant leaving behind the stifling constraints of her upbringing. After all, the memoir of her youth is structured around the tragic story of her best friend, Zaza, who symbolized the effects on young women of unfair expectations and frustrated desires and hopes. In her first memoir about her childhood and youth, Beauvoir interpreted Zaza's untimely death from meningitis as the price for Beauvoir's freedom. Zaza had not freed herself. Her world had suffocated her, and her death had not been simply brought about by illness: it was also the consequence of her family's desire to arrange her marriage. Beauvoir's memoir was the story of her emancipation from the role of "dutiful daughter," which Zaza had unsuccessfully tried to rebel against. Refusing these expectations meant refusing marriage and a life of middle-class domesticity uncomplicated by independence and politics. Despite her claims that, in the early 1930s, she had still not liberated herself from the moral and social conventions of her bourgeois upbringing, her life was, in many ways, as unconventional as *La Garçonne*'s heroine.

Beauvoir quickly rejected the bourgeois life that seemed the lot of young middle-class women. Her family's economic downturn had already allowed Beauvoir greater freedom because it had meant she would have to work. She yearned for independence and autonomy, having decided as a teenager she would devote her life to "intellectual labors."[14] Independence for a woman required financial autonomy, which her teaching position provided. Still, even if she was now a philosophy teacher with her own income, her family upbringing demanded that she marry—rather quickly or she would become a "dried fruit" as her father often joked—and begin having children. Bourgeois matrimony and motherhood were expected of Beauvoir, and this is what she refused most fervently. In the 1930s, rejecting bourgeois conventions meant rejecting that model of domesticity and motherhood. And, if one hoped to be "modern," then one must challenge most social and moral conventions. That principle drove Beauvoir.

Beauvoir therefore eagerly accepted the unorthodox proposal Sartre made when they were still students preparing to pass the *agrégation*: he argued their relationship should oppose the bourgeois conventions they had both been raised to follow. He suggested they enter into an agreement. Their relationship, he explained, was unique and impossible to rival. It was "necessary." They would be bound together by that "necessary love" but should remain free to engage in "contingent relationships" during their time together without jeopardizing the emotional and intellectual bond between them.[15] Their relationship should therefore not be based on bourgeois monogamy. At the same time, it would preserve their special intellectual and emotional bond. This would be the basis of a two-year renewable contract. Beauvoir agreed. They were committed to "freedom" as an ideal. Refusing middle-class norms and practicing freedom required them to reimagine personal and private relationships. That contract lasted long beyond the initial two years, despite moments of uncertainty, frustration, and that both of them engaged in other meaningful erotic and emotional partnerships. Most important, that initial conversation inaugurated a lifelong companionship characterized by transparency and unvarnished honesty. Beauvoir and Sartre promised to tell each other everything (and usually did) just as they read everything the other wrote. Rejecting bourgeois conjugal monogamy was one important step toward the freedom they wanted to achieve.

Beauvoir's early years of her relationship with Sartre in the 1930s were an exciting time when both tried to live out this principle. This unconventional life would have shocked their families (Beauvoir's mother certainly did not agree), but they were not alone in contesting traditional notions of marriage, monogamy, and sexuality. Sex was on people's minds in those years. While politicians and social scientists worried about the depopulation of France and its low birth rate (a fact many blamed on emancipated *garçonnes*), advice manuals encouraged married heterosexual couples to consider sexual satisfaction a necessary foundation for a successful marriage. Others theorized that homosexuality was not a perversion but a fact of nature. People (much like Beauvoir) began reading Freud who had theorized that sexuality was an unavoidable human feature. Freud shocked many when he asserted that sexuality structured much of the individual's psychic and emotional life. It was a provocative claim. It also proved an inspiration for many. The surrealists, a Parisian group of radical avant-garde artists, took up Freud's principles and explored them in their writings, paintings, and photographs. Sex, they believed, was neither to be feared nor repressed but revealed as the origin of humans' engagement in the world. One talented but little-known artist on the margins of this group, the Jewish lesbian author, Claude Cahun, began translating the work of British doctor and social reformer Havelock Ellis whose studies of human sexuality influenced many across Europe. In 1929, Cahun's translation of Ellis's 1897 study of homosexuality was published, the same year that Beauvoir wrote that she and Sartre decided to embrace "radical freedom."[16] While Beauvoir seemed unaware of these publications and did not pay much attention to the surrealists in the early 1930s, her unconventional erotic life echoed what many other Parisian radical and nonconformist intellectuals and artists pursued.

Beauvoir's relationship with Sartre was the foundation of a rich and vibrant circle of friends who filled the lives of these two aspiring writers: friends became lovers who remained friends once sex and love had dissipated. As a philosophy teacher, Beauvoir met many talented and promising young women who were, predictably, enthralled by Beauvoir. Admiration mingled with desire and, in those years, Beauvoir began relationships with several young women she had first met in the classes she taught. Some of these short-lived "contingent" affairs led to lifelong friendships: Beauvoir had a brief affair with Olga Kosakiewicz, who had been a student of hers in Rouen in the early 1930s. Olga's sister, Wanda, became Sartre's lover. Another one of Beauvoir's former students, Bianca Bienenfeld, also fell in love with both Beauvoir and Sartre. Yet another young man Jacques-Laurent Bost, who had been a student of Sartre's, became Beauvoir's lover in the late 1930s. Olga, Bianca, and Jacques remained lifelong friends. While they experienced such contingent relationships, Sartre and Beauvoir remained committed to each other, writing almost daily to each other about the trials and tribulations of their different affairs. In those years, these relations could be tempestuous, especially since Sartre and Beauvoir always upheld their relationship above others. They also showed how differently Beauvoir and Sartre lived their lives from most ordinary people.

To Beauvoir and Sartre, friendship was as important as familial and conjugal relationships, if not more. Beauvoir explained that friendship "is a delicate construction" that requires nurturing and organization.[17] She added, "it can sustain sharing but it also demands a certain exclusivity. Every single combination that we made up—of three of us, four even—had a distinctive character." She concluded that "it was important not to sacrifice the diversity of these friendships."[18] Despite her inconsistencies and occasional betrayals, Beauvoir tried to remain true to this principle, and these occasional lovers became a different kind of family Sartre and Beauvoir forged where the ties of friendship were as powerful as the bonds of kinship.

Still, forging such a path was not an easy affair for Beauvoir and many women like her. The figure of the New Woman could be seen everywhere and was much debated. But it was still more myth than reality for many French women, especially outside Paris. In fact, even if a small number of women embraced new professions, cut their hair, and lived unconventionally, most were still expected to remain housewives and mothers. At the same time as young men and women challenged the world they had inherited, others were intent on preserving, even restoring, a society they felt had been shaken to its foundations by the war. Legislators, critics, and political leaders explained it was urgent to "restore" motherhood since, in their eyes, women's role as mothers was one of the cornerstones of a nation that needed rebuilding. This task was especially urgent because French people, many political leaders complained, were no longer having children. French birth rates had indeed been declining since the mid-nineteenth century. To conservative commentators, the situation had become urgent after the devastation of the war. With the deaths of over a million men, how could France restore its political greatness if it was lacking healthy and fit male citizens? A number of laws designed to encourage women to be proper mothers were passed. On July 31, 1920, the government passed a law that made abortion and birth control illegal. That law would not be struck down for another forty-five years. Beauvoir speaks little of these matters in her memoirs. She did not seem interested. Being a middle-class professional allowed her some escape from these norms and to defy these laws. Though aware of the limits placed on women's lives, Beauvoir appears to have taken that privilege (denied many other women) for granted.

In 1930, Beauvoir was an independent professional woman earning her own income, living alone, unmarried, with a rather unconventional erotic life. Yet, she believed her life was unique and did not identify with any form of political movement devoted to challenging the constraints that weighed on women. Despite the political restrictions imposed on French women, feminism as a political movement or set of ideas meant little to her. Beauvoir did not care much about her lack of political rights then: unlike other European nations such as England, Germany, and Sweden which had granted their female citizens the vote at the end of World War I, France still denied women access to politics. They could not vote, and their bodies were regulated and controlled. French women were still under the strict conditions set by the 1804 Napoleonic code. An 1884 law had made divorce legal but only in cases of adultery (wives were more limited in grounds for divorce), conviction for a serious crime, or serious bodily or mental harm. Fathers and husbands remained the uncontested authority at the head of households. The French feminist movement had also receded from public view and was no longer a substantial political force. Beauvoir crafted her life in this context. Still, despite the ways in which her life contradicted the norms of her middle-class upbringing, and the conservative gender ideals that many wished to reaffirm, she did not openly challenge the political constraints imposed on her. Instead, as a promising young philosophy teacher aspiring to become a novelist, she began thinking about issues that she, time and time again, turned to in her work; namely, the conditions of freedom, and the ways in which individuals' sense of self was forged in relation to others.

THE MEANING OF FREEDOM

Freedom was a philosophical ideal that, like Sartre, Beauvoir vowed early on to make her lifelong practice. But what did freedom mean to Beauvoir then? In the interwar years, freedom meant doing what she wanted and enjoying the novelty and excitement that Paris had to offer. Because she was stuck in what she considered the drudgery and boredom of her provincial teaching position, Beauvoir sought every opportunity to return to Paris. She taught only sixteen hours a week and was thus able to hop on a train as soon as her classes were done. It is true that, in the 1920s and 1930s, Paris was a city bustling with excitement, so much so that contemporaries renamed that period "the crazy years." Beauvoir wrote in 1929: "Paris seemed to me the center of the world"; she "was healthy; had plenty of leisure activities; and [she] had met a companion who was eager to travel with [her] and walked side by side in the same paths with greater assurance" than her.[19] She loved staying out all night or choosing to stay in bed all day, and eating out as she wished; in short, following her moods in everything.

Her memoirs tell the story of these exciting nights: jazz clubs, bars, and cafés were the places Beauvoir and Sartre spent their time. Bars had evocative, American-sounding names, like the Vikings or the Jungles, where they drank cocktails with fancy names. Like many other Parisians, they rushed to listen to Josephine Baker, the new star of Paris nights. The African-American singer's scantily clad performance at the Revue du Bal Nègre, in a "banana skirt" to the beat of her jazz orchestra, enthralled many and made her famous. Along with Baker's performance, it was the new music of jazz, recently arrived from America, that provided the flavor and tone of Parisian nights. Beauvoir loved dancing and regularly attended the famous Left Bank "dance halls." She and Sartre went from bar to bar where they met other artists and intellectuals, like the painters Robert and Sonia Delaunay, and drank until two or three in the morning. "Evenings were spent railing against human stupidity, against the corruption of society, against fashionable art and literature," wrote Beauvoir. They invented crazy and impossible schemes to express their refusal of conventions, such as planning "to rent the Eiffel tower in order to have bright neon letters spelling 'shit.'"[20] Beauvoir confessed these schemes were usually not her own, but she enjoyed these conversations and being part of this group of rebellious and en-thusiastic friends. She "loved the smoke, the jingling of glasses," around her, and "the noise of these excited voices" that carried on in streets as the city fell asleep.[21] She "did not need much alcohol to feel tipsy," since life itself enchanted her and she could not get enough of her new-found freedom. She felt that she "had so much to learn, that any experience taught [her] something."[22]

The excitement of these Parisian years also lay in the fact that the "city of lights" attracted many intellectuals, authors, and art-ists who flocked to it. Other unconventional and exciting figures visited the cafés where Beauvoir worked and the bars where she spent her evenings. Paris was home to a thriving cultural and in-tellectual life that surrounded Beauvoir even if she did not always directly partake in it. It created an atmosphere and, for the aspir-ing novelist that she was, a world full of promise. On the Left Bank, her regular haunts were also home to the surrealists who, led by iconoclast and World War I veteran André Breton, tried to uproot the foundations of a staid and exhausted Western bour-geois world. They were joined by many expatriates and exiled au-thors who had found refuge there: some came from Russia or Eastern Europe, like painters Sonia Delaunay and Tamara de Lempicka; others had traveled from the United States. The mod-ernist novelist Gertrude Stein who moved to Paris in 1903 with her partner, Alice B. Toklas, was famous for her literary salon where the avant-garde and the nonconformists met, from painters Pablo Picasso and Henri Matisse to writers Ernest Hemingway or F. Scott Fitzgerald. Entrance to Stein's Saturday gatherings was sought after by many. Beauvoir did not experience this exclusive world of exiled and expatriate writers and artists.

Neither was she aware of the many other lesser known intel-lectual and artistic gatherings that took place throughout Paris, such as the Nardal sisters' salon. Paulette and Jane Nardal were from Martinique, a French colony. Paulette was the first black Martinican woman to attend the prestigious Sorbonne university in 1920. Both sisters were journalists and writers. They were also fluent in French and English, a rare occurrence in interwar France. In Paris they brought together the Antillean writers seeking to define a black identity escaping and challenging French colonial racism (which became known as *négritude*—implying the valorization of "blackness" against a long history of imperial racism and assimilation) with the numerous African-American writers and artists who came to France in order to escape American racial segregation. Compared to America, France seemed color-blind. It promised equality and hospitality, especially since Parisians were especially enthralled by African and African-American culture. This was, after all, the time of "afrophilia" (even if many often problematically conflated both Africans and African-Americans, as they did for jazz). Harlem Renaissance writers like Langston Hughes, and later Richard Wright, met French *Négritude* writers such as the Martinican Aimé Césaire, Senegalese Léopold Sédar Senghor, and Guyanese Léon-Gontran Damas.[23] For many who came from afar, Paris was the place to be and an exhilarating refuge. Beauvoir was one of those young people who wanted to experience this excitement, even if her world remained somewhat small. She was certainly blissfully ignorant of endeavors like the Nardal sisters' salon and writings and those they welcomed. She had not yet learned to look beyond her immediate circle and to the world around her.

THE PRIMACY OF LITERATURE

This was the world that Beauvoir joined in the early 1930s. She read widely, went to the theater, and, most of all, hoped to become a writer in her own right. With Sartre, she had decided to devote herself seriously to this task. Literature and philosophy consumed them. Their only concern was to discuss "themselves, their relation, their lives, and their books to come."[24] They enjoyed their freedom from conventions and obligations, and eagerly embraced their bohemian life. But, as Beauvoir noted years later, they refused to see that their freedom was a privilege allowed by the "good fortune" of their bourgeois class and elite education. They did not worry about money because they had some. Their teaching jobs provided them with the income needed to enjoy their freedom and independence. Unlike many intellectuals, writers, and even artists around them, they "had little interest in public and political events."[25] The world only existed for them as it provided the backdrop to their sole ambition: to become recognized authors and, maybe even, attain literary fame.

It is true that, as Beauvoir recognized years later, politics and the outside world concerned them little. Her indifference is especially striking since the 1930s were a tumultuous decade where new ideologies emerged, mass movements of people dominated the streets and the news, and the threat of war loomed large. When Sartre went to Berlin in 1933 thanks to a fellowship, he was only concerned with studying the philosophy of Edmund Husserl and Martin Heidegger and seemed to pay little attention to the new Nazi regime, which had just come to power with Adolf Hitler as its undisputed leader. In his letters to Beauvoir, Sartre hardly mentioned what was happening around him in Berlin—as if nothing existed but philosophy. Sartre and Beauvoir also did not pay much attention to Mussolini's fascist Italy, just as they felt relatively indifferent to communism and the Soviet Union. In fact, when Mussolini declared train fares would be discounted by 70 percent to encourage tourists to visit the great 1932 "Fascist Revolution Exhibit," they both decided to visit Italy and spent two weeks in Florence.[26] (Annual summer trips to Italy became their ritual.) As the 1930s unfolded and situations seemed to worsen as fascism, militarism, and diplomatic tensions developed between European nations, Beauvoir remained blissfully unconcerned with international politics. The Spanish Civil War erupted in 1936, opposing the republican Popular Front to Franco's fascist forces. She would say, years later, that this is when "history seized her," but, in fact, at the time if "the Spanish tragedy dismayed" her, it still felt remote from her Parisian life.[27] Unlike others who joined republican voluntary military forces or clamored for the

French government to support Spanish republicans against authoritarian fascism, Beauvoir looked on from afar. She was "scared by what was happening in Germany" but did not do much beyond "feeling indignant at the world's injustice."[28]

Domestic politics also concerned her little. Demonstrations, riots, and strikes were a common occurrence in those years. Politics became especially volatile, with scandals and affairs regularly featured on the front page of newspapers. The failed coup against the parliamentary regime in February 1934, which had mobilized veterans and far-right leagues and ended in a face-off between leftist and rightist militants, did not influence her or Sartre's life. She was happy when the Popular Front left-wing coalition came to power in France in May 1936 but remained content to enjoy her Parisian nights as she had done before, even if far-right and quasi-fascist militia and youth groups started fighting with communists in those same streets. Most happened around the cafés where she spent her days. Years later, when Beauvoir told the story of these youthful years, she proved unforgiving toward her earlier apolitical self. She explained that, as a young woman, she had only held one strong political conviction: she hated the far-right and what she called its blend of "violence and stupidity."[29] Her and Sartre's politics were ill-defined then: as Beauvoir described it, they were "anticapitalist but not Marxist"; they celebrated individualism and rejected bourgeois conventions the way "anarchists" did; they embraced "the power of pure conscience," rejected religion, and were firmly "antispiritual."[30] Their political principles were well meaning, abstract, and vague. In short, as Beauvoir reflected decades later, she said they were still "petit-bourgeois," that is, small minded in their vision of the world, absorbed by selfish concerns, and myopic as they could not see how their passion for philosophy and literature was part and parcel of a larger world where people suffered and oppression dominated. In fact, she said they were idealists who had not escaped their social and economic class.[31]

Rather than politics, Beauvoir immersed herself in the literary world. She started thinking about writing a novel. She was influenced by American literature: the works of John Dos Passos and Ernest Hemingway made a great impression on her because they showed her how to develop a subjective point of view. Beauvoir felt, at first, ill-suited for the life of a writer, and sitting down to develop a work of fiction was laborious. Sartre who was, at the same time, reading Heidegger and working on his own philosophical texts, encouraged her. She had drafted a few things in the early 1930s while teaching. Now, in 1935, she set out to write a collection of short stories that she entitled *When Things of the Spirits Come First* (*Quand prime le spirituel*). Though the title borrowed from a well-respected contemporary Catholic philosopher's work, Jacques Maritain, these stories attacked the confining strictures of bourgeois Catholic society in 1920s France. Each story focused on a female character, highlighting the ways in which young women were caught up, oppressed, and fooled by what the world asked them to be. One story fictionalized the tragic fate of her dear friend Zaza, who could not escape the puritan conventions her family foisted upon her. Another talked about the dull horror of being a teacher in a small-town high school. The heroines were not necessarily sympathetic. They could not come to terms with the reality of their lives nor were they able to face the hypocrisy of the world they lived in. Here, Beauvoir tackled some of the most important philosophical themes that she and Sartre were trying to work out; namely, the ways one could live one's life in "bad faith," the conditions of one's freedom, and the meaning of life in a godless world where religion actively participated in oppression, especially that of women. She also wrote from her own experience. When she sent it to the two most prestigious Parisian publishing houses, Gallimard and Grasset, in 1937, her collection was roundly rejected. (It was published forty years later.) Being a published author remained an elusive dream for Beauvoir, while Sartre enjoyed success and recognition with the publication in 1938 of his first novel, *Nausea* (*La nausée*). Nonetheless, as politics raged around her, she sat down and began drafting her first novel.

CONCLUSION: DARKER HORIZONS

Beauvoir wrote, "it is arbitrary to slice up one's life."[32] Yet, she identified two dates that mattered to her and marked two important moments in her life: 1929 and 1939. 1929 had been a "momentous year": it meant the "end of her studies, financial emancipation, leaving the paternal house, the end of youthful friendships and her meeting with Sartre."[33] A new era had begun for her, and her hopes and ambitions seemed closer, more real, than when she had dreamt of them as a young girl. By 1939, much had changed. Sartre had found fame with his first novel, *Nausea* (*La Nausée*), fictionalizing the vagaries of Antoine Roquentin. Beauvoir had read every draft, commented, and suggested edits (as she would for the rest of their lives). Despite an earlier rejection, it was finally published in 1938. Some Catholic and right-wing critics found its content shocking; others misread the book as a bleak and pessimistic story. Most, however, praised the novel. Sartre had become a legitimate and recognized author. He had been asked to write for the prestigious literary magazine, *New French Review* (*Nouvelle Revue Française*).[34] On the other hand, her own manuscript had been rejected, and she was still working on her first novel. Being an author still seemed remote. While they had spent much of the decade seemingly unconcerned by what took place around them, politics had become unavoidable by then. War was on the horizon. Sartre was increasingly tense. Beauvoir felt anguish overcoming her, but also, as she admitted, she was at a loss as to what could be done. Fierce pacifism was their only consistent commitment. The 1938 Munich Agreement, seemingly placating Hitler's expansionist ambitions, had briefly reassured her. Yet news everywhere seemed to predict an impeding conflict that most, in Europe, wanted to avoid; it was only twenty years after that global and bloody war. Pessimism had replaced the excitement, utopian ideas, and hopeful promises of her early Parisian life.

CHAPTER 2

| LIVING THROUGH THE WAR: |
RESPONSIBILITIES AND
CHOICES, 1939–1944

THE YEAR 1939 WAS A turning point for Beauvoir. She wrote, "Suddenly, History fell upon [her] and [she] exploded." She added, perhaps melodramatically, that she "found [her]self scattered to the four corners of the earth, connected to each and all."[1] It is true few could have predicted what took place over the next five years. When the Nazis invaded Poland in September 1939, England and France responded quickly and, two days later, declared war on Germany. War had begun. Men were mobilized. Beauvoir recalls her anxiety at the knowledge that both Sartre and her then lover, young budding intellectual Jacques-Laurent Bost, were risking their lives. The lack of news caused her incredible anguish. She stayed in Paris, like many others, and waited. At first, she wrote, "war seemed to be nowhere."[2] In the first few months, little seemed to take place, so much so that some started speaking of "the phony war." However, in the spring of 1940, news trickled in of the devastating offense by the German army. Few French citizens expected the sudden and shameful military defeat that would ensue. Within only six weeks, the French army was defeated, and France officially capitulated to Germany on June 25, 1940. On July 10, a new regime was declared: "The French State" (l'État

Français). Along with a million and half French soldiers who had been captured (almost five million men had been mobilized in 1939–1940), Sartre joined a million and half soldiers who were transferred to German POW camps over the summer. He was sent to a camp in Trier on the eastern border of Germany. At the same time, Parisians panicked at the news that the German army was marching toward Paris. Civilians started fleeing Paris, to the dismay of the government, which was unprepared for such an evacuation. Beauvoir dramatized that incident in *The Blood of Others*, which she wrote and published in 1945. The "exodus," as it became known, meant thousands of people flooding roads and trains, with suitcases, belongings, "mattresses, bicycles." Panicked and anxious, "cartloads of refugees slowly marched, carrying entire villages with them." People slept in makeshift tents at night, fearful that German airplanes might bomb them. Chaos ruled and the world felt like a "strange madness."[3] Upon the news of France's capitulation, many chose to return to Paris. Like Hélène, one of the protagonists of *The Blood of Others*, Beauvoir, who had fled Paris, decided to return upon hearing the news of France's defeat and of a new regime governing France. What else was there to do? Where else to go? The only hope was that this occupation would not last long.

The French parliament voted full powers to World War I hero, Marshal Philippe Pétain, a conservative patriarch who seemed to offer comfort and certainty to the French people in these unpredictable times. The Third Republic had died, and Pétain soon exclaimed on French radios that "Family, Work, and Fatherland" were the order of the day, replacing the Republican motto "Liberty, Equality, Fraternity," which dated from the French Revolution. Beauvoir felt "nauseous" upon hearing Pétain's speech but also relieved that all French soldiers were now safe. The new regime's ideology called for returning to a conservative order that represented everything that Beauvoir hated: she wrote that, the "stupidity that had been the leitmotiv of her childhood (family, virtuous purity) now darkened the whole of the country."[4]

This new regime, which was officially the French state, was given the name Vichy in reference to the small spa-town where political and military authorities had retreated. France was divided into two main zones: an Occupied zone, overseen by German military authorities with Paris at its center, and an Unoccupied zone under the rule of this new government (there were five more with different administrative status). The country was now split in two. Unlike other occupied countries whose governments had gone into exile, the French government was a legal one, established with Nazi approval. The Occupation had begun.

1940: A STRANGE WORLD

The Occupation meant different things to different people. On the one hand, little seemed to have changed. Like many of her fellow Parisians, Beauvoir tried to return to her prewar routine: she still spent her evenings in her familiar haunts, the Left Bank

A STRANGE WORLD. *A Paris café during the Nazi Occupation, Right Bank near the Moulin Rouge cabaret (Oct. 20, 1940).*

Café de Flore, which Germans avoided. Yet everything had been turned upside down. Beauvoir wrote that she felt "disoriented" as if she now lived in a foreign country.[5] The vibrant city of Paris that had been one of Europe's cultural capitals now offered a very different sight: swastikas hung from buildings. German street names reminded Parisians they were occupied. "Every morning, Germans paraded down the Champs-Elysées in full uniforms with military bands and flags flying."[6] Beauvoir stopped going to her favorite night clubs because they were "invaded by Germans." The popular "bal nègre" was closed, cinemas were shut down, and a curfew was imposed.[7] Buses and metros were restricted. Bicycles replaced cars.[8] The streets of Paris became eerily empty. Parisians were consumed with how to deal with the particularly harsh winter of 1940. Oil, electricity, and coal were scarce, and many, like Beauvoir, could not heat their bedrooms and had to sleep bundled up in ski trousers and sweaters.

The Occupation affected the texture and rhythms of everyday life: heat, transport, and food became obsessions for many French people. The government oversaw the distribution of food and basic necessities. It established food rationing and price controls. Food shortages were nonetheless frequent, and only a quarter of the French population had enough to eat. Much of daily life was therefore spent trying to secure food. Beauvoir wrote that she was often hungry. Daily food rations were meager, dropping at some point to a thousand calories a day. Cities were no longer desirable places to live. Anyone with personal access to the countryside was better off. Peasants and farmers fared the best because of their access to agricultural products. Especially in the wintertime, "the search for adequate food supplies occupied every French family's time, drained its income, and became a daily obsession."[9] Beauvoir was no different. Her memoir provides accounts of her obsessions with finding and cooking food: the woman who had refused domesticity now developed a "rigorous organization" of supplies and meals and started cooking whatever she could get her hands on, with sometimes "humorous" consequences since supplies could be rotten or full of maggots. The woman who lived in hotels, worked in cafés, and aspired to become a writer found herself beaming with pride at the ingenuity with which she cooked the limited supplies she had acquired. Bribery, corruption, and a thriving black market soon became the norm, though some considered this unethical and a violation of the spirit of resistance to the Occupation regime. Food was indeed a political issue: according to the government, trying to avoid these restrictions amounted to disobedience and treason.[10]

Beauvoir said she experienced the first year of Nazi Occupation in a daze. With Sartre still a prisoner of war and many of her friends exiled or in hiding, she felt isolated and lonely. Paris seemed to have become a world populated only by women. Despite her horror at the new regime and Nazi presence, she was not involved in any political network. Those actively resisting Nazism were only a small clandestine minority at the beginning. They were mostly leftists who, before the war, had already been involved in antifascist and anti-Nazi politics. There were also foreign and French Jews who were acutely aware of Nazi antisemitic policies and suspicious of Vichy and those who had sought refuge in France from the 1930s onward—Spanish republicans, Poles, Armenians, and other Eastern Europeans. Like many of her fellow citizens, Beauvoir did not seek out any active underground political resistance. She did not own a radio and could not listen to the BBC, the only station that offered news outside the propaganda of German-controlled press and of the rabidly antisemitic and pro-Vichy newspapers that proliferated in these years. In the early years of the Occupation, Germany seemed invincible. Though many tried to keep a semblance of normalcy, things had definitely changed.

The Vichy regime was intent on remaking French society. Most of its leaders believed that France had been defeated because, in the last twenty years, it had fallen prey to what they held to be "decadent" and corrupting forces: parliamentary democracy, socialism, communism, unchecked individualism, secularization, reversed gender roles, and sexual freedom—all at the expense of family and the nation. This is what the far-right had railed against in the interwar period. The Vichy regime borrowed from them, Catholic conservatives, and even some fascist sympathizers to bring these beliefs to life. It promoted a "National Revolution" destined to restore France to its rightful place. Only order in politics, authority in society, and hierarchy in family would regenerate the French "organic community."[11] The new government immediately took measures to purge society of its "undesirable" elements and enforce these conservative values in both public and private. Over the next few years, it tightened control over women's lives: all married women who were civil servants were fired, a law prohibited divorce in the first three years of marriage, large families were encouraged, and, in 1942, abortion was made a "crime against the nation" punishable by death. Political organizations were suppressed, newspapers were censored, and civil servants had to declare their loyalty to this new regime. Being a schoolteacher meant Beauvoir was a civil servant and, like many others, she had to sign a document in September 1940 declaring that she was neither Jewish nor a Freemason. This was the condition for her to keep her job as philosophy teacher. As an unmarried woman, she had escaped other restrictions against female civil servants (married women were no longer allowed to work for the state). Beauvoir could have resisted or resigned but, at the time, was neither ready nor committed to do so. Instead, she later explained that she found it "disgusting to sign but no one refused," justifying her choice by insisting, "there was no other way."[12]

One of Vichy's early legislative acts showed its leaders' political aims: as soon as it was in place, it began targeting those who were foreign or considered not French enough. In July 1940, children of foreign parents were now second-class citizens. Immigrants and refugees who had been naturalized from 1927 onward were stripped of their citizenship. Foreign refugees who had tried to escape fascist Italy, Nazi Germany, and the Spanish Civil War were especially targeted. In fact, almost fifteen thousand people lost their nationality during the Vichy years. Among these immigrants and refugees, six thousand were Jewish.[13] This was no accident. Antisemitism was, from the beginning, at the heart of this new conservative and authoritarian order. It had a long history in France and seemed to engulf the country at the end of the nineteenth century when a series of scandals rocked the Third Republic and divided French public opinion, especially around the infamous late nineteenth-century Dreyfus Affair. Even then, however, the government had not persecuted its Jewish citizens. For the first time since the French Revolution, a French government enacted discriminatory and repressive antisemitic laws against its own citizens and those it had welcomed. While Beauvoir tried to get by like the majority of French people, she felt horrified by the violence of the government's antisemitic propaganda, which she said "scared" her.[14] Her feelings were, in fact, ambivalent. She hated Nazism but it felt distant and "foreign" to her. She was especially enraged and disgusted by Pétain's speeches and the emergence of new types: *collaborators*, that is, people eager to collaborate with the Nazi regime, and *collaborationists*, those who wanted to turn France into a fascist country.[15] But, aside from this overarching disgust, Beauvoir commented little on the situation despite a quickly worsening situation.

Anti-Jewish sentiment surged in the first few years of the occupation. It ultimately spared no one. There were almost 350,000 Jews in France. Half of them were refugees from Germany and Eastern Europe, and many were stateless. France's Algerian colony was also home to another 110,000 Jews who had lived there for generations. Antisemitism was encouraged and fueled by the government. Radio and newspapers freed from the legal restrictions against hate speech now spouted anti-Jewish sentiment daily. The Vichy government demanded that all those who were Jewish register with French authorities and, on its own initiative, passed decrees mimicking German anti-Jewish statutes. On October 3, 1940, the government issued a statute excluding

French Jews from civil service, the army, and "professions that influence people": they could no longer work in the film industry, the press, and in teaching jobs. The aim was to exclude Jews, many of whom were citizens, from social and economic life. Beauvoir was horrified by this officially sanctioned antisemitism. She had never adopted the Catholic conservative anti-Jewish sentiments that bourgeois men like her father had exhibited. Like so many other French people, however, she was not directly affected and did nothing to publicly protest these measures. Her memoirs of those years, *The Prime of Life* (*La force de l'âge*), note these developments but do not dwell on them. In this, Beauvoir was again no different than most of her fellow citizens: in 1940, most paid little attention to these measures. After all, it seemed to most that all kinds of people were persecuted by the regime. Anyone "judged dangerous to internal security" could be fired and arrested and, by June 1941, almost five thousand communist activists and sympathizers had been arrested. Parisians did not know about the internment camps in the South of France and its Algerian colony where, at the end of 1940, almost sixty thousand people were detained. Among them were foreign Jews but also French citizens who were communists, former members of volunteer brigades fighting fascists in Spain, and anti-fascist Spaniards who had found refuge in France in the late 1930s.[16]

Those who were not directly persecuted instead focused on their daily lives. Beauvoir felt slightly ashamed of her inertia, but she justified it by explaining she found "nothing else to do than to live, survive, while waiting for something better." In 1940, she, like others, "did not want to admit the triumph of the Reich" but neither did they "dare to hope for its defeat." To justify her passive indifference, Beauvoir maintained years later that "this was an ambiguous period."[17] To her dismay, she learned that her friend Paul Nizan, a young intellectual who had embraced communism, had died at the front. She was relieved by Olga and Bost's return to Paris.[18] Days went by, and as Beauvoir negotiated this strange new life, she felt she needed something to anchor her days. She turned to philosophy and writing to avoid the anxiety, boredom, and restlessness of her lonely days. Writing was for her "an act of faith and of hope."[19] She began spending her spare days at the Bibliothèque Nationale where she started reading German philosophy. Immersing herself in difficult texts provided her both with a refuge from daily life and a way to begin thinking about the meaning of what was happening to her and those around her.

1941: SARTRE'S RETURN AND THE RETURN OF POLITICS

The paradox of the Occupation years is that politics seeped into Beauvoir's life at the moment when writing became her entire existence and she achieved the literary recognition she had been yearning for. First, she had to face the murky world of life under German occupation. The months following France's defeat had been lonely and difficult. She had managed nonetheless. Beauvoir was overjoyed when Sartre was able to return to Paris, liberated from his prisoner of war camp thanks to a "fake" medical certificate. But Sartre had changed too. When he returned at the end of March 1941, Beauvoir was surprised, shocked even, by what seemed to be his "rigid moralism." His camp experience had radicalized his politics: he disapproved of her occasional use of the black market and reproached her for having signed the document professing she was neither Jewish nor Freemason.[20] (Although Sartre did not publicly protest the exclusion from the university of some of his philosophy colleagues who were Jewish.) During his time at the German POW camp, he had found a brotherhood of antifascist sympathizers and experienced the fraternity of political resistance. He told Beauvoir he needed to act and that they needed to resist this new political situation. Beauvoir was skeptical. Her experience had been different: How do you find ways to resist a regime that seems to have reached every area of life? This is the question that the Occupation raised for many ordinary citizens, as well as intellectuals and writers: Should one resist? What did resistance mean?

It is true that intellectual and cultural life had also radically changed. The Nazis imposed censorship on publications, the press, and cultural affairs. Writers and intellectuals considered ideological enemies of the Nazis or responsible for the decadence of French life in the last twenty years were blacklisted. The director of France's most prestigious literary magazine, *The New French Review* (*La Nouvelle Revue Française*), Jean Paulhan, was replaced with the far-right and fascist sympathizer, Pierre Drieu La Rochelle. Those who, in the 1930s, had been in the antirepublican opposition now dominated the intellectual and literary scene and sought to "clean up" France according to their nationalist, authoritarian, antisemitic, and xenophobic principles. Beauvoir watched this with baffled rage. She says she was disgusted when she glimpsed the front page of collaborationist writer Robert Brasillach's newspaper, *I Am Everywhere* (*Je Suis Partout*), and his vociferous editorials asking for all "enemies" to the regime to be arrested, especially Jews. To her, the editorial team intent on attacking Jews, Freemasons, foreigners, and communists, as if they were the scourge of the world, appeared to suffer from "collective paranoia" obsessed only by the desire to denounce everything.[21] But their words only amplified the Vichy government's actions, which, in the spring of 1941, further limited Jewish life and embarked on the "Aryanization" of property belonging to Jews.

Sartre and Beauvoir had not been especially concerned or involved in politics before the war. That indifference to politics still somewhat shaped their attitudes during the Occupation, and the ways they conceived of political activism and resistance. In those years, they remained on the margins of efforts and initiatives on the part of many politically engaged intellectuals across the political spectrum. While some writers and journalists eagerly joined ranks with the Nazis to bring about a new world order, a minority came together in 1941 to create an intellectual organization designed to mobilize writers into a national front that would clandestinely publish and work against Nazism and Vichy collaboration, the National Committee of Writers

(*Comité National des Écrivains*). Under its aegis, clandestine newspapers were created and published in the free zone: there was the communist *French Letters* (*Les lettres françaises*), edited by the National Committee of Writers founder Jean Paulhan; *Struggle* (*Combat*) that Albert Camus would run from 1943 onward; and a surprising number of others with evocative names such as *Liberation* (*Libération*), *Defense of France* (*Défense de la France*), or *The Independent* (*Le Franc Tireur*). All were set up in 1941, once the shock of French defeat had passed, and the true nature of the Vichy regime had revealed itself. Neither Sartre nor Beauvoir belonged to these resistance networks. They were not asked to join. For some on the left or in resistance groups, their brand of individualism and prewar indifference to politics remained suspect. Sartre was a newcomer to the literary scene, and Beauvoir had never been published. Still, energized by what he had witnessed in the POW camp in which he had been interned, Sartre convinced the somewhat skeptical Beauvoir they must craft their own intellectual resistance.

Sartre's first suggestion was to create an intellectual resistance group he named Socialism and Freedom (Socialisme et Liberté). Its aim was not to defeat Germany; after all, in the early years of the war, the Nazi army seemed invincible. Instead, the idea was to bring together intellectuals, writers, and university students to devise anti-German pamphlets and leaflets that they would distribute. The aim was to work against German propaganda in order to disrupt the Occupation status quo and subvert Nazi and collaborationist ideology. Projects of this nature were carried out by others, though not in France. For instance, the surrealist Claude Cahun who had moved to the island of Jersey in 1937, which was invaded by the Nazis in 1940, distributed anonymous leaflets written in German, with her partner Suzanne Malherbe. They were signed "the Soldier Without Name" and were designed to create confusion and disorder among the Nazi occupiers. Sartre and Beauvoir were at once more ambitious and less practical. The idea was to remedy the "political impotence" they experienced. They also had less to risk, unlike Cahun who was Jewish and a lesbian and who was ultimately arrested, tortured, and imprisoned by the Gestapo. Beauvoir was investigated in December 1941 by the authorities after the mother of one of her former students had lodged a complaint against her for "incitement to debauchery," but the inquest concluded there was no cause to prosecute. On the surface, for government authorities, Sartre and Beauvoir were not a threat. In 1941, their intellectual resistance project remained rather vague; its aims little defined beyond attempting to subvert Nazi propaganda and did not require any direct or dangerous action. They were, at first, a small group of friends, including Maurice Merleau-Ponty. They held meetings where there were heated discussions as to how to "act." And, at times, this project involved almost fifty writers, university professors and students.[22] Sartre, however, did not try to contact others who might help, guide, or advise him on how best to carry out such "intellectual resistance." Instead, he convinced Beauvoir to first seek out some of France's recognized literary figures to secure legitimacy for their project.

In order to garner support, Sartre and Beauvoir decided to go to the Unoccupied southern zone and reach out to the prominent intellectual André Malraux, who had become famous for his involvement in the antifascist republican Popular Front forces fighting Franco during the Spanish Civil War. In the 1930s, Malraux was the epitome of the engaged intellectual. The other person they wanted to visit was the aging great writer André Gide, whose novels Beauvoir taught in her classes. In August 1941, they set off for the South of France from Paris on a train with their bicycles in what was a rather surreal endeavor. Neither Beauvoir nor Sartre seemed to have noticed the irony of their enterprise: they could travel freely, unperturbed, unlike many others who were directly persecuted or fearful for their lives, in the midst of German occupation, at a time when things had worsened and "Germans no longer spoke of friendship but had become threatening."[23] They crossed the checkpoints separating the Occupied from the

Unoccupied zone with relative ease. Beauvoir recalls her trip as a strangely idyllic time where she felt "free."[24] They biked to Marseilles and found both men who met their request with disbelief and skepticism. After all, neither Sartre nor Beauvoir had experience in political organization nor been involved in politics before the war. Socialism and Freedom was a resounding failure (and Beauvoir would admit as much twenty years later). While political prisoners and foreign Jews sat in camps scattered throughout the South of France and the Vichy government passed another set of decrees excluding French Jews from public life, they finished their holidays.

Upon their return to Paris at the end of the summer, Sartre remained undeterred. He contacted communist groups who, at the time, seemed the only ones prepared and organized. Communists had been opposing fascists since the 1930s. They also benefited from a preexisting organization, structure, and discipline. Despite his eagerness to act, Sartre was to them no more than a bourgeois intellectual who had little experience in clandestine and militant work, and they remained suspicious of him. Sartre and Beauvoir's attempt at resistance had failed, so they settled into an uneasy life that illustrated the many shades of gray that characterized most French people's lives. She wrote that they "were trying to keep hope but the horizon was dark."[25] They spent much of the rest of 1941 in their Left Bank cafés (the only places that were consistently lit and warm) with other intellectuals they had met and who became lifelong friends, such as philosopher Maurice Merleau-Ponty or the Italian artist Alberto Giacometti. Beauvoir said little in her memoirs of ongoing arrests around them. Sartre decided to write plays that would convey his critique of the current political situation. According to Beauvoir, he imagined speaking to an audience where every single person would be connected to another through a "community of situation."[26] Meanwhile, Beauvoir continued writing, focused on publishing her first novel.

Publication in the Occupied zone was a delicate enterprise and a political choice. The Nazis now oversaw cultural affairs with the help of the fiercest collaborationists such as Drieu La Rochelle or Sartre's former ENS classmate, Robert Brasillach. Beauvoir explained that the National Committee of Writers had offered guidelines: one should refuse writing in newspapers in the Occupied zone. Doing so from the Unoccupied zone was acceptable. However, things were murky for those who had stayed in Paris, at the heart of the Occupied zone: What about writing in those newspapers and magazines the Nazis tolerated? Could that offer the possibility of some form of covert resistance? The National Committee of Writers further instructed that publishing in the Unoccupied zone was allowed but, in the Occupied zone, it depended upon the content of the book. While some writers and authors decided to stop publishing altogether, or wrote only in Resistance newspapers, Beauvoir and Sartre remained in Paris where they decided they would work from within and embed their political critique in their published works.

Beauvoir kept busy: she was finishing the novel she had begun in 1938 in the wake of her unsuccessful collection of short stories. She titled it *She Came to Stay (L'Invitée)*.[27] Beauvoir's works had some autobiographical dimension, often composed once she felt she "was becoming different from the one [she] was describing in the novel."[28] They were not a roadmap to her life but allowed her to fictionalize the issues that preoccupied her. She took on the subject of her and Sartre's relationship with Olga Kosakiewicz, their former student and a friend, now in a relationship with Beauvoir's former lover, Jacques-Laurent Bost. The novel tells the story of the triangular relationship between the narrator, Françoise, with Pierre and Xavière, and the difficulties of jealousy, betrayal, and equality. The face-off between the women is resolved when Françoise murders Xavière, thinking that she had finally made a choice. Murdering Xavière had been the accomplishment of her "will." She "had chosen herself" over others.[29] That resolution echoed the epigraph Beauvoir had chosen for the novel, taken from Hegel's work, namely that "one conscience always wants the annihilation of the other." It was an attempt to work out in fictional form the philosophical issues of freedom and dependence on others that Beauvoir was interested in. The novel was also potentially scandalous since literature was expected by the Vichy regime to embody conservative moral values. Here, the personal also evoked the larger situation in which most French citizens found themselves: a murky world where people had to contend with a dangerous foreign occupier, helped by a regime that those like Beauvoir and Sartre regarded with contempt, rage, and disgust, and that was complicit in oppressing its own citizens.

1942: A FATEFUL TURNING POINT

When the new year came, only bleak and worsening news reached civilians. The Nazi army was expanding in all directions, seemingly impossible to defeat. It was also moving into North Africa with the hope of conquering Egypt. In Southeast Asia, Japan had conquered the Philippines, Indonesia, and Singapore. The French and British empires were imperiled. At the same time, the German army's move into Russia in June 1941 had brought the Soviet Union into the war. The Japanese attack on the American fleet at Pearl Harbor in December had also thrown the United States into this conflict. This was now a global war that engulfed most areas of the world and almost all of its most powerful nations. Despite the strengthening of the Allied forces, victory appeared uncertain. Still, resistance movements committed to weakening the Nazi occupation sprang up across Europe, including France. However, they could do little to slow down the expansion of the Nazi empire and its genocidal project. Beauvoir simply kept on recording in her memoirs how her daily life unfolded.

By 1942, most of Western and Eastern Europe was under Nazi rule. On January 20, the Wannsee Conference, which brought together Hitler and his most trusted and high-ranking officials, resulted in the formalization of what was termed "the Final Solution to the Jewish Question." Beginning in February and March 1942, Eastern European Jews who had been interned and suffered in ghettos and other concentration or labor camps were now sent to the newly built extermination centers, such as Belzec, Sobibor, or Treblinka, to be gassed. Little of this project was known to the world. Neither could Western European Jews predict that they would soon suffer the same fate as those in Poland and elsewhere in Eastern Europe, that is, deportation and death. The situation worsened in France, too, largely under the supervision and initiative of the Vichy government. On March 27, the first French convoy of Jews was sent to Auschwitz. Two months later, on May 29, an ordinance required that all foreign and French Jews wear a yellow star in the Occupied zone, as was the case in the rest of Nazi-occupied territories.

Beauvoir noted in her memoirs that, like others around her, she was "shocked and indignant" at this sight.[30] Even then, at the same time, she also remained somewhat indifferent to the increasing persecution of her fellow Jewish citizens. She certainly was not antisemitic and had fervently attacked any form of racism. Her Catholic upbringing and the banal prejudices of her bourgeois milieu may have shaped her inability to grasp fully the seriousness of what was happening.[31] Indeed, faced with the acute "anxiety" her former student and friend Bianca Bienenfeld who was Jewish experienced, Beauvoir said she "realized" their experiences were radically different.[32] Despite this realization, she failed to help Bianca, and in her memoir spends little time recounting Bianca's desperate decision to cross into the Unoccupied zone and go into hiding, as things tragically worsened not just for foreign but also for French Jews like Bianca.

Beauvoir's shock and horror failed to motivate her into action. She was not alone in the way she reacted. Many behaved and felt like her. The same month, French authorities decided to deport all foreign Jews who had been arrested and were interned at the camp of Drancy in the southeastern suburbs of Paris. The French government included children under the age of sixteen in the deportation convoys. Beauvoir did not write about the specifics of these events. She spoke only of the rumors that reached her and her friends. She still noted that, at the end of 1941 and the beginning of 1942, "antisemitic persecutions, police repression, shortages, rationing" were overwhelming. For her, as she found refuge in writing, "the atmosphere in Paris had become suffocating."[33]

The summer of 1942 proved the most fateful for Jews in France. On July 16 and 17, Vichy authorities carried out a massive roundup of every French and foreign Jew in Paris. What became known as the "Vél d'Hiv' roundup" had been a Nazi initiative, but it was organized and implemented by French police and authorities. Over the course of these days, they arrested almost thirteen thousand French and foreign Jewish men, women, and children living in Paris who were then taken to the Vélodrome d'Hiver, a sports stadium, where they had little access to food and water and were forced to live in terrible conditions.[34] Over four thousand of those interned at the Vél' d'Hiv' were children of all ages. This was not the end though, the following month arrests also took place in the Unoccupied zone. Foreign Jews, many of whom had been welcomed by the French government in the mid- and late 1930s as they escaped persecution and worsening living conditions in Eastern and Central Europe, were now considered "dregs" by the Vichy vice-president, Pierre Laval, who approved and authorized such measures. Beauvoir and Sartre did not witness these roundups. In order to escape their dreary and stifling environment, and catch a "change of air," they decided to spend the summer in the Unoccupied zone and set off for the South of France on their bikes.[35] Beauvoir wrote that, as they meandered around the Pyrenees, they came across "groups of refugees with a hunted look, most of whom were Jews," but neither she nor Sartre stopped to help.[36] When they returned to Paris, trains filled with Jewish men, women, and children had already departed for the east.

The question of Vichy's antisemitism and deportations may have haunted Beauvoir more than she was willing to admit. She recalled in her memoirs that, as deportations continued of both foreign and French Jews in 1943, "the horror of this fate obsessed" her and her friends. She confessed, though, that this "misery remained foreign to them, even as it poisoned the very air they breathed."[37] Those events took little space in her account of those years, at most several pages in a book of almost 500 pages. Beauvoir noted though that, faced with Bianca in the early years of the Occupation, she had experienced "an uneasiness that felt like remorse."[38] That uneasiness never overtook her indifference.

1943: WRITING, POLITICS, AND FRIENDS

The year 1943 proved a momentous one for Beauvoir. It was also a year where the tide of war finally seemed to be turning. The Allied forces had landed in North Africa in late 1942, which had prompted the Nazis to occupy the Unoccupied zone. For the first time, it seemed the Allies might be able to push the German army back. Heartening news came from the Eastern Front: the siege of Stalingrad by the Nazi forces, which had begun in the summer of 1942 and had proved incredibly devastating in terms of military and civilian casualties, finally came to an end in February 1943. The Soviet army was able to force the Nazi forces to retreat westward. The Nazi empire seemed fragile at last. News of this remarkable development trickled out, especially thanks to BBC radio that many now listened to, including Beauvoir and her friends. These early months of 1943 did not just signal a decisive shift in the military face-offs. Beauvoir and Sartre both became more directly involved in political activities. While Sartre was finally invited to join the National Committee of Writers, Beauvoir was inspired to write her first philosophical essay that reflected on the principles driving ethical action and the justification for violence. When she wrote it, she did not know about other instances of resistance, such as the Spring Uprising in the Warsaw ghetto, which began on April 19, where Polish Jewish men and women who had escaped deportation and death decided to battle the Nazis in a last-resort and unexpected revolt. In fact, as things outside France hastened, Beauvoir and Sartre found their lives changed for very different reasons.

For Beauvoir, the year meant personal success; though, at first, things seemed to have become more uncertain. Beauvoir had already been accused in late 1941 of lesbian relations with a former student and then cleared. In 1943, the Education Ministry decided to fire her. A report denounced the fact that, as an unmarried teacher, living in hotels, working in cafés, she hardly conformed to the codes of morality the Vichy government wanted to instill in its youth. Even worse, she assigned "dangerous" and "noxious" literature to her students, having them read "invert" (meaning homosexual) writers like Proust or Gide. For Vichy officials, Beauvoir represented the kinds of people who had brought down France and who must be purged if the "National Revolution" was to be carried out.[39] It mattered that Beauvoir was a woman. Sartre never faced the same scrutiny. He was actually able to have his first play performed, *The Flies* (*Les mouches*) in early July 1943. It was celebrated by those eager to denounce Vichy while the more conservative audience was either baffled or openly disliked it. Sartre became a public figure just as Beauvoir was suspended from her teaching post on June 17, 1943. This may have been a blow but, as she recounted, it proved a blessing. To find some sort of income, she found a job at Radio-Vichy where she penned rather "bland programs" on medieval France and folk culture.[40] More importantly, her dismissal meant she could devote herself entirely to her first calling and her only passion, literature.

Her Parisian life suddenly felt and tasted different. Her novel, *She Came to Stay* (*L'invitée*), was accepted by Gallimard director and National Committee of Writers founder, Jean Paulhan. It came out in the fall of 1943 to great acclaim. Even right-wing and collaborationist critics praised it.[41] Beauvoir was now a published author whose qualities had been recognized by her peers. Having finished her second novel *The Blood of Others* (*Le sang des autres*), she immediately set out on a third one, *All Men Are Mortal* (*Tous les hommes sont mortels).* The war also meant a life she had dreamt of finally realized. At the first performance of Sartre's play, *The Flies (les mouches),* they met Albert Camus, a writer and the editor of the Resistance newspaper *Struggle (Combat),* who, Beauvoir explained, had, like them "moved from individualism to involvement."[42] Literary success brought a renewed social life that Beauvoir enjoyed tremendously and saw as a form of "practical solidarity."[43] In cafés, bars, reading groups, and salons, she and Sartre made new friends. They met the psychoanalyst Jacques Lacan, the author Georges Bataille, and spent evenings with Camus, Michel Leiris, Raymond Queneau, and many others who became part of the Parisian cultural and literary intelligentsia after 1945. Their friends were their "family," and the many parties they attended were, for her, "first and foremost a celebration and a culmination of the present in the face of anguish at an uncertain future."[44] When they drank, talked, and danced at night, Beauvoir said they were a "sort of fraternity, hidden from the world, and unleashing its secret rituals."[45] An uneasy cohabitation characterized their life. In the cafés where they discussed their plans for political resistance or planned their next outings, they sat across from fascist journalists of collaborationist newspapers who openly discussed the "extermination of Jews."[46] In her memoirs, written almost twenty years later, Beauvoir does not hide that it was not the ongoing Nazi persecutions that occupied her daily thoughts but the "happiness" at having fulfilled her teenage dream of becoming an author.

CONCLUSION: 1944: THE PARADOXES OF THE LIBERATION

Terrible news suddenly fell upon Beauvoir and Sartre's circle of friends. A nineteen-year-old Algerian Jew named Bourla, who had become Sartre's student in 1941, was arrested in February, taken to Drancy, and deported.[47] The Nazi and Vichy authorities had not relented since the mass deportations of 1942. The month before Bourla's arrest, Jews had also been rounded up and deported in the thriving southwestern city of Bordeaux, which had previously been in the Unoccupied zone. Beauvoir did not note down these events, but Bourla's deportation haunted her. Until then, few of her immediate circle had been directly affected by Nazi and Vichy persecution.[48] Life carried on. What else was there to do? Beauvoir kept on enjoying dinners, parties, and outings, finding comfort in her small "family" of friends and like-minded intellectuals and artists.[49] She kept on writing, because writing, for her, was her way of "defining her relation to others." The failure of her play, *Useless Mouths* (*Les bouches inutiles*) in the spring, which had a run of only fifty performances, did nothing to deter her. She focused on completing her philosophical essay, which was published in the winter. This is how Beauvoir understood politics. She was neither activist nor fighter. Literature was where she channeled it all.

The Allied forces landed in Normandy on June 6, 1944, with battles erupting in the north and west of France. Could the Nazis finally be defeated? Uncertainty still prevailed, despite increased Resistance efforts. Bombings escalated. Beauvoir and others learned, to their horror, that, on June 10, the same day that Sartre's new play, *No Exit* (*Huis-clos*), was performed for the first time, the Nazis had again ruthlessly murdered. They had descended upon the small village of Oradour-sur-Glane, rounded up its 642 inhabitants and murdered all of them, sparing neither the elderly nor the children. If such violence had been common in Nazi-occupied Eastern Europe, it had not been the norm for Western European gentile civilians. The name "Oradour" became for her and all those in France hoping for an impending defeat of the Nazis the symbol of senseless violence exercised by a cruel enemy on a defenseless civilian population. Hopes for the end of the war did not mean fewer murders, less violence, and decreasing fears. The last convoy to Auschwitz departing from the Parisian suburban camp of Drancy left on June 31, three weeks after D-Day. In August, the Provisional Government led by Free France resistance military

A CARNIVAL OF FREEDOM. *Parisians celebrate the Liberation of Paris and the arrival of leader of the Free French Forces, Charles de Gaulle (Aug. 26, 1944).*

leader, General Charles de Gaulle, declared Vichy and any legislation it had issued "null and void."

The last summer months proved momentous and decisive. Paris was liberated in August by American and French forces. Fighting erupted in the streets between the Free French forces and Nazi occupiers. Parisians set up barricades using cobble stones, cut-down trees, benches, gates, and any material at hand. Others stormed the streets to welcome their "liberators." Sartre wrote about this for Camus's newspaper *Combat*. He described this day as a "provocative carnival" where "tanks and jeeps maneuver in a sea of humanity, carrying hundreds of improvised tourists."[50] As one historian has noted, the Liberation was a tremendously exhilarating moment where "the crucible of war and occupation had melded together to fight a common enemy for a common goal."[51] On that day, divisions, enmities, and suspicions seemed to have disappeared. Beauvoir chronicled these in her diary, though more as witness rather than active participant. But that moment was short-lived. The war was not yet over and, elsewhere in France, fighting continued. Few had statistics in hand. Still, the figures were daunting: Seven hundred fifty thousand French civilians had been sent to Germany as forced laborers to help support the German war industry. Thirty thousand French citizens had been shot as members of the resistance, hostages, or political opponents. Seventy-seven thousand Jews had been deported and perished in camps. Most had died in Auschwitz. A third of them had been French. Sixty thousand more French citizens had been deported to various labor and concentration camps. It took almost another year before the Nazis were finally defeated, and the war with Germany officially ended on May 8, 1945 (though World War II as a whole was not over until August 1945 when Japan officially surrendered). Those who had survived slowly began to return.

Beauvoir wrote that the French people woke up to a world that had been "destroyed."[52] In the aftermath of the Liberation, "they learned of the Gestapo's torture rooms" and of "mass graves." She added wistfully, "newspapers gave details of these massacres, of the executions of hostages, they published accounts of the annihilation of Warsaw," Poland's capital. Suddenly she felt the "horror" brought about by the abrupt and "brutal uncovering" of this history.[53] The dark years had ended. Returning to normality, or even prewar life, took awhile however. Material conditions did not immediately improve. The 1945 winter was especially harsh. Beauvoir wrote that, in fact, the situation worsened: "transports were disorganized," and coal, gas, and electricity were still scarce. Food was still difficult to get hold of. Cultural and intellectual life had not yet resumed, as the French were trying to rebuild a country from the disarray of the war and the political complications of the Occupation. French politicians who had actively worked for the Vichy regime, and intellectuals who had openly supported Nazism, were branded traitors to the

French nation. Collaborators were arrested and tried. Some were executed. These were uncertain times.

1945 was the year Beauvoir published her novel *The Blood of Others*. It signaled two major developments that changed Beauvoir's life: her commitment to literature, and her awakening to politics and the world that the war and the experience of Occupation had forced upon her. The novel focused on questions of complicity, resistance, and responsibility. These were the issues French people were wrestling with upon Liberation. Beauvoir had intended this book to tackle the issue of one's responsibility for and to others. She used different points of view to show how different people experienced the moral and political choices they had faced in those years. The male protagonist, Jean Blomart, had abandoned his comfortable bourgeois milieu to embrace politics and, ultimately, the Resistance movement. But it is Hélène, who is in love with him, whose story is the true focus of the novel. Hélène who, at first, is unconcerned by the cataclysmic events around her comes to realize that her life matters insofar as it is related to others. She witnesses the arrest of a Jewish friend of hers and has to make a choice: to stay indifferent to others' fate or join in events that have changed everyone's life. She joins her lover in the Resistance but is shot while carrying illegal documents. She dies but at least, the novel tells us, finally she felt one existed for someone, something. Like the characters in *The Blood of Others*, the war had a profound and complicated effect on Beauvoir. She could no longer ignore the world and politics. She explained that, with the war, she had renounced her individualism and "discovered solidarity" and her "responsibilities."[54] That was not quite accurate—and, in fact, something she came to truly practice only decades later. The war certainly did not immediately prompt her to change the course of her life and how she led it.

Still, the war had changed much in Beauvoir's life in other ways. She said that, as victory came upon them, all she could feel was the "shame she experienced for others," her fellow citizens, just as she "felt ashamed at [her]self."[55] Her joy was accompanied by weariness and the knowledge that she had been amongst those privileged and perhaps too indifferent to the plight of others like her friend Bianca Bienenfeld. Her dear friend, the jazz fanatic, prolific writer, and night owl, Boris Vian expressed similar feelings but in harsher terms: "I did not fight, I was not deported, I did not collaborate, I remained an under-nourished idiot for four years like so many others." Beauvoir did allude to her own complicity. She explained, without direct reference to her own case: "In this occupied France, one needed only to breathe to consent to oppression; even suicide would not have freed [her] from this oppression."[56] If the Occupation had been forced upon her, she had, nonetheless, realized she could not easily escape it. Beauvoir felt many different feelings during those four years. Writing in hindsight, she insisted that the war had been, maybe, the most important event to pull her out of her narcissism. It was only then, she explained, that she had understood her "fate was tied to the whole nation" and her "life ceased to be a game."[57] She failed some of her friends, like Bianca, who survived and remained friends with Beauvoir. She lost others, like Paul Nizan and Bourla. She also made her own world in the midst of deprivation and chaos in ways that brought her happiness and satisfaction. Once the war had broken out and engulfed their lives, she explained, all her relationships had changed.[58] At the same time, the war confirmed that "literature was as necessary to [her] as the air she breathed."[59]

| BECOMING AN AUTHOR: |
DESIRES, DIALOGUES, AND
ENGAGEMENT, 1945–1954

BY THE END OF THE WAR, Europe was in shambles. Nearly one hundred million people had been killed worldwide. More than ten million had been uprooted. Prisoners of war, displaced persons, concentration camp inmates, death camp survivors, civilians in occupied territories—all were exhausted, brutalized, and eager to return to a normal life. The Red Cross was given the daunting task of relocating six to seven million displaced people between 1946 and 1947. Images of concentration camps were broadcast for every European to witness the horrors of the Nazi regime. The world finally began realizing the true nature of the Nazi genocidal project. Europeans did not immediately take stock of this lesson, however: during the war many had been consumed by fear, hate, and suspicion of their neighbors, be they Jews, Poles, Soviets, Germans, or British. Neither did violence stop with the close of the war. Spontaneous purges of those considered collaborators took place in France, and there were pogroms against Jews returning to their homes in Poland. Violence had also consumed other parts of the world. Battles, occupation, forced labor, and internment camps had characterized Japan's attempt to annex most of Southeast Asia. Shockingly, the war there ended with a different form of violence: the American government dropped the atomic bomb on the Japanese cities of Hiroshima and Nagasaki on August 6 and 9 1945. Most Europeans probably did not see the images of the "nuclear mushroom" and its brutal devastation. Most heard about it. The news of two cities destroyed, along with the deaths of two hundred thousand civilians may have echoed their own experience, but they did not think beyond that as most focused on rebuilding their own cities, lives, and homes. They wanted to return to normal life. For writers and intellectuals, in France and elsewhere, the question remained: How to rebuild one's life and avoid the war, violence, and brutality that had taken over Europe for the last six years?

By 1945, "writing had become a demanding profession for" Beauvoir, because "it guaranteed her moral autonomy . . . and her freedom."[1] She explained that, unlike Sartre, she had chosen literature rather than philosophy. However, her explanations did not necessarily reflect reality, but rather the way she chose to talk about it. In fact, she did not abandon philosophy. Her novels attempted to craft a philosophical literature. For Beauvoir, literature was especially suited to such explorations since it allowed her the opportunity to develop a vision of how one encountered the world through a particular point of view. Literature, for her, did not mean only novels. Like Sartre, she wrote prolifically. Between 1943 and the early 1950s, she published almost constantly in a variety of genres. This diversity characterized her lifelong literary career: she penned a philosophical essay, *Pirrhus and Cinea* (*Pirrhus et Cinéa*) in 1944 and, the following year, a play entitled *Useless Mouths* (*Les bouches inutiles*), as well as a novel on freedom and responsibility, *The Blood of Others* (*Le sang des autres*), and another less successful one in 1946, *All Men are Mortal* (*Tous les hommes sont mortels*). Soon after that, Beauvoir published another philosophical essay, maybe her most assured: *For an Ethics of Ambiguity* (*Pour une morale de l'ambiguïté*) (1947), her travel narrative *America Day to Day* (*L'Amérique au jour le jour*) (1948) and the controversial book *The Second Sex* (*Le deuxième sexe*) (1949).

All these works mapped out her major preoccupations: What is the meaning of existence, of freedom? How does one become aware of oneself, free, and act in the world with others? What does it mean to be a subject, and how might one develop an ethics not grounded in religion in a secular world? These themes found their expression even in works that did not seem directly philosophical: in her articles, her travel diaries, and in her reflections on what the French called "the feminine condition," that is, the fate of women. If the war had changed her, it also influenced how she wrote and what she wrote about. After all, Beauvoir had begun her literary career in the midst of war and the Occupation. Her works examined the ways in which the world had been shaken up and how her life and others' lives had been affected. Becoming an author no longer meant just writing in isolation. It also meant engaging in the world. Writing was the means to explore the philosophical issues that preoccupied her and that, Beauvoir came to realize, had political consequences.

EXISTENTIALISM AND POLITICS

Like the character Jean Blomart in her 1945 novel, *The Blood of Others*, the war had a profound impact on Beauvoir, even if she did not immediately change the course of her life. It showed her that one must make choices and actively shape one's place in the world. As she explained in her memoirs, it "woke her up to the world around her." This world could no longer be ignored in the ways she and Sartre had done in the 1930s and the 1940s. Against this backdrop of devastation, ruins, and death, issues of "engagement," "responsibility," and "freedom" became urgent concerns for both her and Sartre. To be engaged in the world required imagining a different politics. From their Paris offices, Sartre, Beauvoir, and their friends attempted to map this new world and make their mark on it. They created a monthly magazine named *Modern Times* (*Les Temps Modernes*) after Charlie Chaplin's 1936 comedy, which had satirized the effects of the modern industrial world.[2] It was a literary, intellectual, and political magazine whose purpose was to chart a new space in the literary and political world. Its editorial committee included friends and political allies. The magazine was both wide-ranging and prestigious and boasted impeccable political credentials. Because of Sartre's

WORDS HAVE MEANING. *In the wake of war, at her desk, Simone de Beauvoir is now an author and editor (1945).*

newfound fame, some announced the publication of *Modern Times* as a momentous event, claiming it was the much needed "third voice" between the Marxist and the Christian "camp."[3] Its goal was "engagement"—that is, to be deeply and immediately engaged in the world. As the preface explained: "We are aligned alongside those who want to change both man's social condition and his self-perception. In order to do so, the magazine will take sides on every issue raised by political developments. But it won't take a political side, that is, it will not follow a party."[4]

Modern Times was both an instrument and a symbol of what it meant to be an engaged intellectual, focused (sometimes almost exclusively) on contemporary times, its injustices and possibilities. Its special issues tackled some of the pressing issues of the day, publishing in 1950, for instance, one of the first exposés of the gulags, Stalin's slave labor camps. They did so at a time when few were willing to criticize the Soviet Union, which, for most leftists, seemed to be the only nation committed to realizing socialist principles and bringing to life revolutionary hopes for a more just society. The magazine attempted to craft a new left, critical of political leaders and right-wing policy while remaining distinct from communism.

As they announced the birth of *Modern Times*, Beauvoir and Sartre joined many others who, across the political spectrum, also created magazines and newspapers designed to act upon, influence, and inform the public citizenry. Words had influence, and debate was deemed central to the emergence of an informed and critical public opinion. In France, a law promulgated on September 30, 1944, forbade the publication of newspapers that had been published in the Occupied zone during the Vichy years. Almost nine hundred publications were affected. Only those Resistance underground newspapers (such as *Combat* and *Libération*) and the Unoccupied zone mainstream press (such as the right-wing *Le Figaro*, the socialist *Le Populaire*, or the communist *L'Humanité*) survived. Amidst this postwar sweeping renewal of the press, other magazines appeared with a similar format to

Sartre and Beauvoir's, such as a magazine devoted to Pan Africanism and "the Black World" entitled *African Presence* (*Présence Africaine*). It was founded in 1947 by the Senegalese philosopher Alioune Diop, and Sartre and Michel Leiris supported it. In most of these new magazines, philosophy, politics, and literature were intimately mingled, attempting to craft a different leftist politics, some focused on the question of colonialism, others on that of a noncommunist left, or on a nonaligned Christian left. Leftist humanism was at the heart of Beauvoir and Sartre's project, as Sartre explained in a conference he gave in 1945 called "Existentialism Is Humanism."

What was this "existentialism" that Sartre promoted and that both he and Beauvoir had embraced? To many observers, it seemed "existentialism" had become the buzzword of the day: at once a politics, a youth movement, and a lifestyle. Existentialism was, first and foremost, a philosophy that provided a roadmap for the kind of politics Beauvoir and Sartre imagined. It was also, perhaps most importantly, the philosophically rooted atheist and humanist vision of the world that guided their lives. The term was not new. It had first been coined by Catholic philosopher, Gabriel Marcel, who had led weekly seminars with aspiring philosophers in the 1930s. Neither were its ideas completely novel. It had its roots in the 1930s when many French writers and intellectuals discovered the philosophy of Edmund Husserl and Martin Heidegger. The thinker Husserl had defined phenomenology as a mode of philosophy interested in analyzing and explaining how the world is known by one's self. It focused on the ways that perceptions (of the world, of oneself) were necessarily understood subjectively. Phenomenology argued there were no abstract universals separate from individual subjectivity. Those who, in the interwar, had been interested in phenomenology were also struck by the writings of German philosopher Heidegger, a student of Husserl's, whose work tackled the question of "being." In his mid-1920s texts, he broke rank with his teacher and explained that "being-in-the-world" was an anguished state whereby existence was experienced before any particular human nature. An individual experienced his being as always out of his grasp, since he was subject to language, to the vagaries of his situation, and the inevitable fact of his mortality. Heidegger was a major inspiration for Sartre and his 1943 philosophical text, *Being and Nothingness*, just as he was for Beauvoir, though to a much lesser extent. Phenomenology, nonetheless, had a profound influence on her. Although she often claimed she was not a philosopher, she turned to philosophical texts when life demanded it; for example, she had tried to escape the bleak mood of the Occupation by reading Hegel's monumental *Phenomenology of the Mind*. These works shaped Beauvoir and Sartre as they developed their own thinking regarding the meaning of human existence and of freedom, choice, and responsibility.

Several questions haunted them. What did individual choice and freedom mean in a world where God does not exist and religion cannot provide the roadmap to morality and politics? What, then, gives meaning to human life? How does one feel and experience one's sense of self and one's relation to others? How does one achieve freedom not just selfishly but in relation to a society made up of other individuals? The war had made these questions urgent, and the Occupation had showed them the difficulties of making such choices. Another preoccupation emerged in 1945: how to devise a way of thinking that did not blindly follow Marxist materialism (that is, society is first and foremost dictated by its material conditions) or a Christian vision of the world (where all life had been decided by a supreme being and morality was dictated by universal principles). Only the individual mattered, they thought, and could give meaning to his own life.[5] As Sartre explained to his audience in a talk he gave in October 1945, "existence comes before essence." There is no given human nature that exists before the moment the individual comes into being. He added, "Man is nothing more than what he does."

Here, Sartre and Beauvoir showed slight but important differences: while Sartre emphasized the "anxiety" that characterized human life, Beauvoir was more interested in the fact that individuals were always already tied to others and came into being with and through other beings. One's existence is necessarily bound up with the other—an abstract principle—and another conscience—that is, the conscience of other individuals experiencing the world. This is why "ambiguity" characterized human life. Every individual was caught between competing forces: the desire to realize one's freedom against the pressure that society and the world imposed upon oneself. She had pondered over this in her 1947 philosophical essay, *The Ethics of Ambiguity*: if childhood was a state of delusion because children did not realize they were not free, becoming an individual meant facing one's "situated freedom," or how one's freedom depended on the conditions surrounding one's life. How does one choose to act if so much is beyond one's control? Freedom therefore required abandoning "bad faith," namely remaining willfully ignorant of the (external) limitations upon one's freedom. Beauvoir and Sartre ultimately posed the same question: How does one become free, and does one choose freedom? Freedom could be an ambiguous condition because it was not a natural state but required struggle to attain it. It also demanded individuals realize they have a responsibility toward others.

For Beauvoir, existentialism "defined man through his or her actions."[6] Religion and blind hope were, for her, nothing more than a "lazy reliance on something other than the individual."[7] Life was made up of individuals first and foremost. (Christian) faith and (Marxist) ideology provided only inadequate solutions. In fact, she explained, "only the individual's will mattered."[8] Some found Beauvoir and Sartre's ideas pessimistic. They responded to that criticism in one voice. If we accept that only human action matters, they argued, then we can actually begin to imagine how we might not just act but also choose how to be in the world. Existentialism, for them, posited freedom (for oneself) and responsibility (to others) as guiding principles of human life. It suggested that politics must be grounded in action. It refused what they called "quietism" (waiting for others to do things) and "nihilism" (thinking nothing could ever be done).[9] Intellectuals and ordinary citizens who wanted a different world after the cataclysm of World War II found their vision appealing. Catholics, however, were outraged by Beauvoir and Sartre's atheist thoughts. Communists believed they were misguided by their supposed pessimistic view of human nature. Right-wing thinkers attacked this new brand of leftist politics. Beauvoir did not care about these criticisms, and these questions kept on driving her writings.

THE AMBIVALENT MEANINGS
OF POSTWAR FREEDOM AND JUSTICE

The questions of freedom, of an individual's relation and accountability to others, and of the legitimacy of violence were hardly abstract issues in postwar France. The Normandy landings by the Allied forces in June 1944 brought the end of war in Europe. Victory did not just bring about cries of joy. The liberation of France witnessed spontaneous acts of retribution. Accounts were settled often in ugly ways. In villages, former collaborators were summarily executed; in provincial cities, women accused of "horizontal collaboration," that is, of having slept with Germans, were dragged to the city square, their heads shaved, a swastika drawn on their foreheads, and then paraded in front of the whole town. In fact, very few of the women accused were guilty of this "sexual collaboration." More often than not, they were singled out for other reasons. But the accusation was a powerful one. In the two years following France's liberation, an alleged ten thousand collaborators died, while almost twenty-four thousand women were shorn. Vigilante justice took hold of the country, so much so that the new Provisional Government led by Free France hero, General Charles de Gaulle, passed a law forbidding any extralegal retributive justice. Eager to repair the taint of Vichy, de Gaulle's government set up trials designed to bring collaborators to court. Those who had "betrayed the nation" would answer for their action through the legal system. The French government's decision echoed the efforts undertaken by the Allied forces. The world was captivated by the Nuremberg trials, which began on November 20, 1945. The International Military Tribunal tried twenty-three high-ranking political, military, and economic leaders of Nazi Germany for war crimes and "crimes against humanity"—a legal concept that first came about in 1938 in the Kellogg-Briand Pact "for The Renunciation of War as an Instrument of National Policy" and which Germany had signed. The Nuremberg Tribunal inaugurated its use.

In France, too, justice was under way. Thousands of trials took place from October 1944 to the beginning of 1951, taking on the ominous name of "purges." They involved political leaders such as Vichy's president, the aging World War I hero Marshal Pétain, head of government Pierre Laval who had signed the papers authorizing the deportation of seventy-six thousand Jews, and Joseph Darnand, the founder of Vichy's militia. The courts also tried media personalities, journalists, broadcasters, antisemitic writers, as well as low-level collaborators, criminals who had flourished during the Occupation, and other noted Nazi sympathizers and Vichy officials. Almost fifty thousand individuals were tried (though historians have shown that a "total of 311,263 alleged cases of collaboration were sent for consideration to the courts").[10] Penalties ranged from the death penalty to forced labor, prison, and "national degradation."

One of the 6,763 individuals ultimately sentenced to death (though far fewer were executed) was the writer, intellectual, and newspaper editor Robert Brasillach.[11] His trial had begun on January 19, 1945. Beauvoir and her friend Merleau-Ponty attended the trial, which was a national affair, and she called it a "dramatic performance."[12] This was the first time an intellectual was taken to task for the words he had penned. The purges had targeted other journalists and editors but none was as infamous as Brasillach. Journalists, writers, and intellectuals who had celebrated Vichy or called for a fascist France, in short who had put their minds and words in the service of a reviled regime, now had to answer for their actions. Already in the 1930s, Brasillach had overseen the far-right and openly antisemitic newspaper *I Am Everywhere* (*Je Suis Partout*), which called for a fascist France modeled on Italy, Belgium, and Germany. He had become a prominent personality under Vichy, friends with high-ranking Nazi officials, and eager to promote close relations with Nazi Germany, sometimes to the displeasure of Vichy officials. During the Occupation, his newspaper became even more violent, often printing the names and addresses of French and foreign Jews it accused of "profiting" from the war, some of whom were indeed arrested, deported, or assassinated by the French Milice, the Vichy government's paramilitary force created in 1943 to eradicate any form of resistance to the regime and those it considered undesirable such as Jews. By the Liberation, the Milice was almost everywhere reviled since its actions relied on denunciations, torture, roundups, summary assassinations; and it actively cooperated with the Gestapo, even replacing the ordinary police in some instances. *I Am Everywhere*, which never relented in its antisemitism, publicly supported the Milice. Neither did Brasillach's call for a fascist Europe where France would proudly sit side by side with Nazi Germany wane during the Occupation. Brasillach was found guilty of treason. Like 1,500 others during this period, he was executed by firing squad, three weeks later, on February 6.

Brasillach's trial raised questions of the distinction between vengeance and justice, the legitimacy of violence, and the responsibility one has to others. This was a deeply personal and emotionally laden issue for Beauvoir. Brasillach was her contemporary, an ENS alumnus, who was supposed to belong to the "best minds" the country produced. One of his novels had been nominated for the prestigious Goncourt literary prize. Yet, he had become a fascist intellectual devoted to the cause of antisemitism. Beauvoir set out to write about these issues in an essay she published in the fifth issue of *Modern Times* in 1946, titled "An Eye for an Eye." Beauvoir recognized that "since June 1940, we have learned both rage and hate" and "we've wished for the humiliation and death of our enemies."[13] What did this mean now that the war had ended? "Private vengeance" would not do.[14] It was impulsive, personal, and did not necessarily right wrongs. Ultimately, she argued, punishment was still necessary. But it should be the punishment of an impersonal, abstract authority exercising justice in the name of the community. Beauvoir rejected individual violence but concluded the death penalty could, in cases like these, be justified because "to punish is to recognize man's freedom to do good and evil" and "to will what is good."[15] When the news of Brasillach's death sentence came down, however, some writers thought justice had gone too far and circulated a petition asking for his pardon. They argued he had never committed any acts: condemning an intellectual for his printed word now appeared too strong a judgment. François Mauriac, the centrist Catholic writer and Resistance figure, called for forgiveness. As a founding member of the National Committee of Writers, he had been involved in drafting a blacklist of collaborationist intellectuals, which included Brasillach. Yet, in 1945, Mauriac decided charity mattered more than retribution.

French intellectuals were divided on the issue. Camus, who at first opposed Mauriac, spent the night agonizing before signing the petition. Many prominent authors and artists joined him. Beauvoir and Sartre, however, refused to sign it. Though she later wrote on the issue of punishment and vengeance, Beauvoir never fully explained her decision, saying only in her memoirs that she "never regretted" her decision not to sign.[16] She explained that writers who had collaborated during the war "disgusted" her the most. Their collaboration was a "personal betrayal."[17] For her, there was nothing worse than a writer who had betrayed the ideals he or she embodied, namely fighting for something greater than oneself. In fact, she claimed (somewhat irresponsibly) in her memoir: "There are words as murderous as gas chambers."[18] Their refusal baffled many contemporaries because neither she nor Sartre had been actively involved in the Resistance during the

Occupation years, unlike some of those who had signed the petition. Still, they had emerged from the war convinced that the only desirable ethics was one of "engagement" in the world. Brasillach's trial had posed the thorny question of the meaning of action, resistance, and the weight of words.

In part, like other French intellectuals, Beauvoir and Sartre understood that these ethical concerns challenged their notion of politics. In the immediate postwar years, they attempted to define a leftist position that refused preexisting parties and positions. The question of the left's relation to communism was central to this attempt. Europe no longer dominated the world order. Its cities had been bombed, infrastructures were in disarray, and inflation was rampant. Food shortages were still common in 1946 (and, in fact, lasted well through 1949). Thanks to its military and political resistance and because it had suffered an incredible human toll during the war, Soviet communism had emerged out of the Second World War as a "symbol of resistance to Nazism." At the same time, the Americans were Europe's "liberators." The early signs of the face-off between the American-led "free world" and the Soviet Eastern Bloc soon put pressure on such alliances. The decision to embrace communism or not mattered just as much in France. The French Communist Party, which had been expelled from the government in 1947, was an important political player. It was the only party with a substantial working-class membership. By the mid-1950s, communists were elected mayor of twenty-seven municipalities in Paris and its suburbs. However, news of Soviet labor camps and of Stalin's authoritarian regime soon divided leftist intellectuals: How could one side with communism without siding with totalitarianism? Were not these labor camps as much an injustice as deportation camps had been during the war? Would denouncing this situation mean siding with the anticommunist right? These questions obsessed intellectuals like Sartre, Camus, and Beauvoir.

Sartre, who by 1945 had become a "symbol of intellectual resistance" despite his checkered Occupation years, entered politics more directly than Beauvoir did.[19] Sartre claimed intellectuals must be "engaged" in the world. Being an "engaged" intellectual for Sartre meant doing more than writing essays on politics but acting more directly in the world. Because Sartre believed that words can have power, he saw it as intellectual's duty to become involved in the messy world of politics. This engagement meant a range of public actions, from attending political meetings, giving speeches or conferences, writing political editorials, or actively militating in and outside political parties and using one's notoriety in the service of a political cause or organization. Beauvoir agreed but did none of these things. If politics mattered, so did other things for Beauvoir. In public (that is, in her writings, especially her memoirs, written almost twenty years later) she said there was no need for her to duplicate Sartre's position in the public world of political action and engagement.[20] The difference in their choices actually reflected Beauvoir's own complicated relationship to being an "intellectual."

Beauvoir's relation to politics was ambivalent. She had renounced her "selfish" indifference to the world. Still, writing remained her first interest. To her, literature was just as much an existential act as politics. It required ignoring bourgeois conventions that demanded restraint, challenging society's rules of propriety and morality. That deeply held belief was one of Beauvoir's guiding principles. Being an intellectual was Sartre's affair. In 1945, Beauvoir was not only a recognized author. She had come to occupy an important place in the literary world—even if, for some, she was merely Sartre's companion. Beauvoir devoted herself tirelessly to *Modern Times* and took very seriously her role as editor, reading manuscripts, reviewing articles, and deciding what was to be published in forthcoming issues. In addition to politics, the thick monthly volume showcased young and unknown writers. Beauvoir was passionately committed to bringing literature that she thought mattered into existence. For her, "literature emerges when something in life has become unhinged. . . . The first condition is to realize that reality is not a self-evident

A RECOGNIZABLE FIGURE. *Simone de Beauvoir at a public event (Aug. 1, 1947).*

and transparent thing, only then are we able to perceive it and bring it to life for others to see."[21]

Existentialist philosophy held that only the subjective point of view mattered. In literature too, a particular and unique point of view could yield a different way of looking at the world. Beauvoir felt exactly that when she first read the manuscript a friend had given her in February 1945 from an obscure woman, Violette Leduc. Leduc was a striking figure and, in many ways, Beauvoir's radical opposite. She was the illegitimate daughter of a small-town aristocrat and his maid—a situation that was, at the time, considered especially shameful. Raised by her single mother who felt ambivalent toward her daughter, she grew up acutely aware of being on the margins of the world. She failed her high school diploma in 1926 and took on various jobs that never suited her eccentric and intellectually voracious personality: first as book reviewer at a publishing house, then scriptwriter and receptionist at a film script company. During the war, Leduc became adept at black market dealings, which enabled her to survive. Her meeting with a gay writer, Maurice Sachs, with whom she fell in love, proved decisive because he encouraged her to write.[22]

In 1945, she mustered the courage to share her manuscript with Beauvoir, whom she idolized. Upon reading the manuscript—a fictionalized transposition of Leduc's life—Beauvoir wrote she discovered a "temperament" and a "style" that struck her as novel and daring. She met Leduc in her favorite café and took on the role of the mentor and editor, a role she kept throughout the rest of her life, meeting twice a week with Leduc to discuss her writing, and supporting her financially. After publishing her in *Modern Times*, she gave the manuscript to her friend Albert Camus, then editor at Gallimard, who published it in 1946. The novel, ominously titled *Suffocation* (*L'asphyxie*), was celebrated by critics but little read. Leduc's novels were shocking to a postwar audience: they unabashedly focused on female sexuality and offered a bleak portrayal of motherhood. Her 1948 novel *The Famished* (*L'affamée*) was nothing less than a passionate love letter addressed to Beauvoir. (Even Beauvoir asked her to rewrite passages that could be considered too obscene, and some of her prose describing graphic lesbian sex was censored by her publisher.) With Beauvoir's encouragement, Violette continued writing until the overwhelming success of her 1964 work, *La bâtarde*, which, accompanied by Beauvoir's long and laudatory preface, was recognized a great and unique novel. Leduc managed to do in her novels what Beauvoir never did: fictionalize herself unvarnished and unconcerned by the social moral conventions her characters transgressed. This was the "power of literature" according to Beauvoir. To write was to act in the world.[23]

AMERICAN INFLUENCES AND DIALOGUES

Sartre had been Beauvoir's first companion, her "double." He remained the first reader of her drafts, evaluating, commenting, just as she did for him. He was also her political ally, just as she was his. This was not a closed and insular intellectual and emotional companionship. Beauvoir was also involved, then and during her entire life, in other meaningful intellectual and influential relationships. Friendship and dialogue were essential to her. In fact, she once wrote, "they were the most important in her life."[24] Beauvoir was a devoted and loyal friend just as she was a demanding and supportive editor and reader. Her writing bore the traces of her many friendships and dialogues. Being related to others was not an abstract principle for her. It fed her writing, her perception of the world, and her life. Her life was bound up with others, influenced by others, and she crafted her place in the world in dialogue with others.

Dialogue also meant crossing borders and experiencing unfamiliar things and people. As the war came to an end, Beauvoir turned her eyes to other places and people outside her immediate Parisian world. That experience shaped her philosophical and political views. America figured large in these influences in the immediate postwar years. Her meeting and subsequent friendship with the African-American writer, Richard Wright, her four-month trip to the United States in 1947, and her love affair with American novelist Nelson Algren profoundly influenced not only the course of her life but also the kinds of writing she produced in these years.

Beauvoir and Sartre met Wright when he was first invited to give talks in Paris in 1946—an encounter that drew them to the

United States and radically challenged them as individuals and as a couple. Richard Wright was exemplary of the African-American intellectuals who had come to France seeking escape from the racism and segregation of American society. He was not the first one to cross the Atlantic Ocean when he moved to Paris in 1947 with his wife, Ellen, and his daughter, choosing to become French. Many before him had undertaken the same trip. Many African-American soldiers discovered France when they fought in Europe during World War I. The noted intellectual and activist W. E. B. Du Bois had traveled to France in 1919, on the occasion of the first Pan-African Congress, to present his study of the experience of black soldiers, which became an indictment of the American army's institutionalized racism. During the 1920s and early 1930s, others had crossed the ocean to come to Paris, which appeared to outsiders a haven of color-blind freedom. Jazz especially was celebrated in Paris. Josephine Baker became the queen of Parisian nights. The young Antillean students and writers who became active in the emergence of the *négritude* movement were inspired by the Harlem Renaissance. Like others before the war, Wright found a welcoming and eager audience in Paris.

Wright's writings had come to Beauvoir and Sartre's notice before his emigration to Paris. The grandchild of slaves, Wright had achieved recognition with the 1940 publication of his pessimistic and scathing story of an African-American man's experience of racism and segregation, *Native Son*. It was an immediate bestseller and was followed by the autobiographical account of his childhood, *Black Boy* in 1945. The lived experience of class and race infused his literary vision of the world. His works were situated at the crossroads of Pan-Africanism, a Marxist-inspired class politics, and a focus on embodied and subjective experience that appealed to French proponents of existentialist philosophy. Wright had joined the American Communist Party in 1933 but was soon disillusioned with it. Because of his involvement, American authorities considered him subversive and dangerous. Wright decided to move to Paris to escape the McCarthyist persecutions that dominated US life and the racism that pervaded American society. In typical fashion, Sartre and Beauvoir decided to publish extracts of Wright's works in the second issue of *Modern Times* in November 1945. Wright and Violette Leduc were the only novelists featured in this early issue. When they moved to Paris, Richard and Ellen Wright became close friends of Beauvoir and Sartre.

Wright's novels had a profound influence on Beauvoir. She found them both lucid and moving, and they influenced her thinking on otherness. Beauvoir's intellectual debt to Wright also embodies a particular paradox: Beauvoir's intellectual curiosity and openness to the world were displayed in her eagerness to learn about the experience of injustice, discrimination, and oppression from others—in this case from African-Americans who had suffered from slavery and still had to contend with Jim Crow segregation. Turning elsewhere for inspiration meant she could also be blind to what was happening in France closer to her. She began thinking about racism with the American-born Wright and not with the French Caribbean and African authors who had been writing about their own experiences of colonial racism since the 1930s and, like Wright, who had also been involved in communist or leftist politics, for example the Martinican poet Aimé Césaire or Senegalese writer Léopold Sédar Senghor. Beauvoir remained unaware, and disinterested even, of these thinkers' writings about the meaning of race, the experience of French colonialism (they were all colonial subjects), and the racism at the heart of French society. Beauvoir's first encounter with American society was framed through Wright's eyes, and her attention to and analysis of American racism and segregation owed much to him.

When Beauvoir boarded her plane for New York in late January 1947, she was following in others' footsteps: Sartre had gone there in January 1945 as an American correspondent for Camus's Resistance newspaper *Combat* and wrote dozens of articles on the topic of "America." Jacques-Laurent Bost also crossed the ocean in June, reporting for *Combat*, as did Camus the following year. Beauvoir was invited to give lectures. She had a complicated relationship to

America. In the 1930s, she had felt that "America offered a more fascinating spectacle on screen than on the printed page."[25] She loved "its jazz, literature, cinema" that had "nourished [her] youth."[26] The new world had long been an object of fascination for French novelists who wrote about the fearful spectacle of what modernity in America offered Europeans. As a young woman, Beauvoir had been entranced by American literature, especially the works of Herman Melville, William Faulkner, and Ernest Hemingway.

In the wake of World War II, the United States stood out as modern and vibrant compared with a devastated Europe. When Beauvoir arrived in New York, she said she felt America represented the future. But was this a future of soulless modernity? Or something better that Europe should try and follow? Many French intellectuals and writers like Beauvoir felt ambivalent toward America, especially its political dominance. The United States had welcomed many exiled French intellectuals during the war, from anthropologist Claude Lévi-Strauss to surrealist André Breton. It had helped save Europe. It was an immigrant nation. At the same time, for leftist Europeans, the United States now represented an aggressive and imperialist political power that sought to undermine the promise of Soviet communism. It was the land of unfettered capitalism, segregation, and enduring inequalities.

Beauvoir's trip fit in with her long-standing passion for learning about the world. Beauvoir and Sartre were avid travelers. They were passionate tourists throughout their entire life, visiting many countries for pleasure as well as politics. Her attentiveness to the world expressed itself in her insatiable thirst for travel. She consistently shared the experience of discovery of foreign places with her readers: her memoirs (and some of her novels), usually included long descriptions of places she visited, people she met, and her feelings and thoughts on both. Traveling was also an existentialist act: when Beauvoir traveled, she experienced a "personal adventure, a change in [her] relation to the world, to space, to time."[27] She confronted her own consciousness to matters and others radically different from her.

Beauvoir spent four months traveling back and forth across the continent. She began her visit in New York on January 25, 1947. After a series of conferences she gave at Vassar College, Mills College, Oberlin College, and other universities, she set off to discover the rest of the nation. She traveled to Cleveland and Chicago before heading to California in February. After a road trip that had begun in Los Angeles, she stopped in San Francisco before heading to Las Vegas. Of course, Beauvoir, who was a passionate hiker, did not just visit cities. She discovered the imposing scenery of the Grand Canyon, the New Mexico deserts, and endured twelve hours of bus travel to reach Texas where she stopped in San Antonio and Houston. The last leg of her trip was taken up by her discovery of the South: she spent most of March in Mississippi and Louisiana, reveling at the joys of New Orleans and seeing firsthand the lingering effects of slavery and the enduring impact of segregation in Jacksonville and Savannah.

Beauvoir explained that coming to the United States was an especially exciting enterprise as it required her to "get out of her own life."[28] As she walked through the streets of New York, it became obvious that "Paris no longer towered." This foreign country was "another world, that was autonomous and separate."[29] She added, "Her conscience was charmed by this sovereign Object that was revealing itself" to her.[30] She was especially struck by American women's lives and experiences. She was baffled by what she deemed their performance of ultrafemininity and felt American woman were less "free" than French women. She was also struck by the pervasive racism she observed, even more so as she traveled to the South. Beauvoir was dazzled, surprised, perplexed, and skeptical; and her travel diaries offered America as the mirror to the French society she belonged to. She published her impressions in the *New York Times* on May 24, 1947, under the title of "An Existentialist Looks at America." She then published her own travel diary in 1948, dedicating it to her friends Richard and Ellen Wright.

If America surprised her, it was also because of an unexpected meeting. When she traveled to Chicago, she got in touch with the novelist Nelson Algren, whose 1942 novel Wright had prefaced. Born and raised in the working-class South Side neighborhood of Chicago in an immigrant European Jewish family, Algren had begun his career as an aspiring journalist but soon turned to short stories and novels, and he was quickly recognized as a unique literary voice. His work charted the conditions of the downtrodden, the working classes, and those on the margins of society. His leftist politics and uncompromising character meant he had stayed far from the celebrity of the literary world, even after he was awarded the National Book Award for his 1949 work, *The Man with the Golden Arm*. Beauvoir and Algren became lovers, and she spent the rest of her time with him as he became her guide to American society. He insisted she witness the "reality" of American life, its economic equalities and profound racism. After Wright, he encouraged her to think of oppression and exploitation in different ways.

Theirs was an intense relationship. It also took place at a time when Beauvoir and Sartre's "necessary" companionship was being tested by their "contingent relations." Sartre had met the French-born journalist and actress Dolorès Vanetti during his 1945 American travels and was enjoying a passionate love affair with her, even contemplating marrying her (which Beauvoir deliberately never mentioned in her memoir although she confessed her "unease" at their intense relationship).[31] In direct echo, Beauvoir's relationship to Algren also tested the limits of her "contract" with Sartre. When she returned to France, she began a long and passionate correspondence with Algren (in English, as he never learned French), exchanging almost three hundred letters until 1964.[32] Theirs was a relationship characterized by equality and affinities as both were novelists, committed to social justice and political equality, and eager to change the world. She read the draft of his prize-winning novel, advising him on revisions. She wrote to him about a novel she had started drafting and shared the news of her life, her readings, and her travels.

It was not to last though, despite Beauvoir's repeated returns to the United States in 1948 and 1949 and their trips together. Algren came to visit her in Paris in 1949, and they traveled together. But their long-distance relationship came to an end with her last American visit in the fall of 1950. Algren wanted

AN UNEXPECTED LOVE. *Nelson Algren, Simone de Beauvoir (right), and a friend (left) on holiday in Cabres, Spain (Dec. 31, 1949).*

Beauvoir to marry him and move to Chicago with him. Faced with this proposition, which proved agonizing, Beauvoir realized she could not leave her Parisian life and, she claimed, she could not "selfishly" abandon Sartre who "needed" her.[33] Her engagement in the world needed an anchor: Paris was her home. The life of an immigrant or exiled writer did not appeal to her. Beauvoir could not uproot herself. Neither could Algren. She also valued her autonomy and freedom above all, principles that had guided her since her teenage years. Moving to the United States for Algren would have meant giving that up. Instead, in the ways she had done in her previous novels, she fictionalized the desires, dialogues, and temptations she experienced in the novel she began writing in 1949. That novel, *The Mandarins* (*Les mandarins*), ultimately garnered her literary fame and recognition but, though it was dedicated to Algren, also changed her relationship to him.

THE MANDARINS AND LITERARY CELEBRITY

On the surface, almost ten years after the end of World War II, Beauvoir's life seemed to have changed little. She still wrote and met friends and aspiring authors in her favorite café. She still lived in hotels. Her evenings were consumed by outings to music clubs, the theater, and, sometimes, the cinema. She shared her time between her editorial work at *Modern Times* and her own writing. Unlike the interwar decades, she was now a recognized novelist in her own right and a controversial figure thanks to her many writings and her association with Sartre. Writing, by then, was her life. As Beauvoir explained, "A day without writing tasted like ashes." But 1954 was in fact, a momentous and paradoxical year, which signaled the end of a time in her life, the hopes that had carried her and Sartre at the end of World War II, and the beginnings that brought both joy and horror.

Beauvoir had begun writing *The Mandarins* in 1949 and kept at it through the early 1950s. Its topic was the hopes, actions, and disillusionments of intellectuals in Paris in the years following the French Liberation, from 1945 to 1948. Like her 1943 novel, *She Came to Stay*, Beauvoir dramatized those in her life, their relationships, her own life, and the issues that had consumed them in this novel, so much so, that upon its publication in October 1954, readers and critics tried to identify the "real persons" behind her fictional characters. They were indeed transpositions: Robert Dubreuilh was Sartre, his wife Anne was Beauvoir, Henri Perron was Camus, his companion Paule was Violette Leduc. Readers' assumption that this was a barely veiled autobiography fueled interest in the novel and its author.

By focusing on the lives, anguishes, and hopes of postwar intellectuals, Beauvoir told the story of a particular moment in French Parisian life: the novel focused on well-known intellectual Dubreuilh, his decision to enter the political fray and failed attempt to create an independent left-wing organization alongside the communists who dominated the political scene. His wife Anne, a psychoanalyst, pondered over the meaning of this postwar life in the wake of deaths, deportation, and the Occupation. To her surprise, she found love and a renewed interest in life when she started having an affair with American novelist Lewis Brogan, a fictional transposition of Nelson Algren. (Algren never forgave her for making their relationship public; the novel was translated into English in 1956 and its publication angered him.) Henri Perron (who evoked the real-life Albert Camus) was torn between his desire to shape politics and his desire to write literature that influenced the world. Paule, a woman consumed by her desperate desire to keep her companion who no longer loved her, descended into paranoid madness. In the novel, Anne and Robert's daughter, Nathalie, stood out as a truly fictional character since, in real life, neither Beauvoir nor Sartre had any children. She was an especially tragic figure because she exemplified how so many young people had emerged from the war, troubled, disillusioned, and vulnerable to the uncertainties around them.

What captivated readers was the blend of individual lives and the historical world around them. The novel offered a window into individual subjective lives and the struggle all characters faced when they tried to relate to others and their sometimes futile attempts to be free and true to themselves. They faced the ambiguity of human existence. As Anne mused, "What will they do with this weighty past and this unshaped future?"[34] At the same time, the novel was like a mirror. The struggle to shape a noncommunist leftist politics was dramatized in the story of the novel's characters' involvement: their backroom dealings, sincere efforts, and passionate political ideals that drove them; their sincere efforts to create a different political world; and the compromises that had to be made for their cause to succeed. The war still hovered over the characters' lives. Anne often wondered what life meant when one lived in the shadows of those dead in concentration camps. The issues that Beauvoir had written about in her previous text reemerged here: the question of collaboration, purges, and whether to forget the past. A few characters took it upon themselves to murder suspected collaborators who had not been punished by the law. Anne and Henri had to contend with unsavory figures who had more than shady attitudes during the war and yet were thriving in the postwar era. Nathalie, Anne's daughter, was haunted by the arrest, deportation, and murder of her young lover, a Jewish Spaniard, Diego. Beauvoir wrote an existentialist novel that fictionalized the philosophical and political themes that had preoccupied her and Sartre since the mid-1940s. Though conventional in style and format, the novel resonated powerfully in postwar France.

CONCLUSION: THE WEIGHT OF THE WORLD AND THE BURDEN OF FAME

The novel came out at a time when, both domestically and internationally, the world was changing and seemed to finally emerge from World War II. By the 1950s, Paris looked different. It had finally recovered from the war. Young Parisians dressed in black gathered in cafés to debate what they believed was the absurdity of life. They danced in smoky Left Bank basement bars to American be-bop jazz, listening to some of the new performers that entranced the postwar world. Boys and girls flaunted social conventions, seemingly rejecting bourgeois norms of behavior. They were derisively nicknamed "existentialist youth," and Sartre and Beauvoir were held responsible for this new culture. After the wave of strikes that had seized the country in 1947, plans for renovating society were in the air. While a young priest, the Abbé Pierre called for a national campaign against homelessness in the wake of the terrifying 1954 winter, modernization efforts (in the shape of new construction and more cars on the streets of Paris) heralded a new age for France. While young middle-class existentialists gathered in the exciting bustle of St-Germain-des-Prés basement bars, working-class neighborhoods endured increased police crackdowns, as authorities kept an eye on the Algerian workers and other immigrants from France's colonies.[35]

But the wider world meant bleak politics. The Berlin blockade of 1948 vividly reminded one that the Cold War was well underway. The Korean War ended. France's postwar Fourth Republic was mired in instability with endless changes in governments. In 1954, two events reminded Parisian left intellectuals of new challenges. The French were defeated at Dien Bien Phu in the spring. This was a devastating and humiliating defeat for the French army at the hands of the Viet Minh, communist nationalists led by Ho Chi Minh calling for their independence and the end of French colonial rule. France lost its southeastern colony of Indochina (which included Vietnam, Laos, and Cambodia). At the same time, something else shocked France and, again, changed the course of Beauvoir's life. The Algerian War of Independence broke out. It would shape the culture and politics of metropolitan France for the next eight years.

1954 was indeed a momentous year. While French intellectuals like Beauvoir and Sartre had to deal with the political ramifications of the Algerian War, the most brutal war of decolonization, a new phase in their life had begun, especially for Beauvoir. *Modern Times* had become an important political and literary voice. After the bitter and devastating end of her relationship with Algren in 1951, she had begun another relationship just when she thought middle age meant the end of her romantic and sexual life. Claude Lanzmann was seventeen years younger than her. He was a journalist, and his commitment to politics had been forged during the war, as he escaped antisemitic persecution and joined the Resistance. She had met him through her work at *Modern Times* to which he participated. He moved in with her (for the first time in her life, she lived with her lover), and he became her writing and traveling companion.

Even more striking, and to her great surprise, in late fall 1954, Beauvoir's novel about postwar intellectuals won France's most prestigious literary prize, the Goncourt prize. She was only the third woman to receive it since its creation in 1903 (after Elsa Triolet in 1944 and Beatrix Beck in 1952). The prize changed her life. With the prize money, she finally bought a small flat for herself. She gave only one interview in the wake of the news of the Goncourt prize to the communist newspaper *L'Humanité*. Still, she became a literary celebrity. Paradoxically, it was this novel and the prize that legitimated Beauvoir's place in the literary and intellectual world, even though she had already published a lot. As her friend Colette Audry explained in the communist cultural magazine *Les Lettres Françaises* a month after the Goncourt prize, Beauvoir "had chosen for herself the life of an intellectual." Her 1954 novel, *The Mandarins*, was important because it showed the "wounds of individual maturing and the seriousness of collective experience." Beauvoir, she said, "asks readers to reflect on themselves and their own situation."[36] Audry insisted Beauvoir had always cared about this issue. In fact, the first book that had showed her interest in asking people to reflect on their place in the world, had been on the topic of women's situation. In *The Second Sex*, published five years earlier, she had "accomplished the difficult task of thinking about women's situation through the prism of history and social structures."[37] For Audry, both books came from the same intellectual and political concerns. It is true both works expressed Beauvoir's interests in existentialism, phenomenology, and politics. What Audry failed to explain, however, was that if *The Mandarins* had brought fame to Beauvoir as a novelist, this was not quite new for Beauvoir. In 1949, *The Second Sex* had already made her into a scandalous figure.

CHAPTER 4

| BEING A WOMAN: THE MAKING | OF A FEMINIST PHILOSOPHY, 1949 AND AFTER

ON APRIL 21, 1944, the French government in exile issued an ordinance granting women the right to vote. In contrast to most other European countries (except for Italy), French women had until then remained second-class citizens without political rights. The right to vote was now enshrined in the preamble of the new constitution of October 1946 and had been exercised seven times by women in the previous year.[1] Beauvoir did not pay much attention to these events. In fact, although, like other French women, she now had the right to vote, she only rarely exercised that right (neither did Sartre). This was not her focus. Despite finally being recognized as full political subjects, French women were nonetheless still subject to a series of cultural expectations and social restraints. While higher education was now open to them and many worked outside the home, women were still expected to be mothers and housewives first. Even the constitution of the new Fourth Republic reminded them of this fact and stated that "the nation guarantees woman the exercise of its role of citizen and worker, as long as these do not interfere with her role of mother and her social mission."[2] The new president and Free France hero, General Charles de Gaulle, had also reminded citizens in a 1945 speech that, in order to rebuild itself, France needed "twelve million beautiful babies."[3] Even as women were now legitimate political actors, to many, including de Gaulle, it was their role as mothers that mattered most.

Beauvoir, of course, did not fit the model promoted by de Gaulle. She was unmarried. Worse, she had an unconventional romantic life. She did not have any children and did not aspire to motherhood. She was an economically independent professional woman. Worse, she was an intellectual. As her friend Colette Audry wrote in an article about Beauvoir, it might "bother many to think of a woman intellectual."[4] To be a female novelist and female intellectual was still considered an anomaly or an exception. In fact, while many, including de Gaulle, spoke about women's place in society, they did not seem ready to move beyond "traditional" visions of femininity. That issue also preoccupied Beauvoir. After the end of the war, in the midst of these momentous changes and debates, Beauvoir turned to that question. The book she ended publishing on the issue, five years after women were granted the vote, would cause a scandal and propel her onto the public stage.

By the late 1940s, Beauvoir had become a recognized novelist of some fame, though not yet the kind of fame that came in the following decade. She was still mostly associated with Sartre. She was often photographed in her regular Left Bank haunts. Though Beauvoir insisted she cared little about how she dressed, she had always struck a striking and rather elegant figure.[5] In the 1930s, Beauvoir had never embraced the masculine clothing and "flapper" style that some fashionable Parisian middle-class young women had adopted to show their newfound independence. Neither had she cropped her hair, as New Women then were prone to do to some contemporaries' horror. However, during the Occupation years, she began wearing cloth turbans. She later explained that, since there was little access to hairdressers, turbans were easier. Simplicity was necessary since they were busy trying to survive the harsh and bleak winter months and focused on food rationing and more important daily necessities.[6] That hairdo

A SCANDALOUS AUTHOR. *Simone de Beauvoir working at her desk (Jan. 2, 1953).*

(a turban or turban-style) would define her public image for the rest of her life. In the aftermath of the Occupation, turbans also occasionally popped up through the country. That choice had less to do with fashion or practicality, as in Beauvoir's case, and more with the events of the Liberation. Fashion could also be political, and women's bodies and self-presentation had cultural meaning that some tried to subvert (as Beauvoir did, and feminists later claimed) or others tried to negotiate out of necessity (in the face of norms and constraints).

FRENCH WOMEN'S BODIES IN POLITICS AND MOTHERHOOD

Beginning in the summer of 1943, head shavings erupted everywhere in France. In villages and towns all around the country, women of all ages, origins, and professions were accused of "horizontal collaboration," that is, sleeping with the Nazi occupier. Neighbors, ordinary citizens, members of the Resistance and later of the Free French forces initiated and participated in these public shaming spectacles.[7] These women were "shorn women" (*tondues*). To most observers, shorn women represented the shame of a humiliated nation. (That word never applied to women who had been deported and had also had their head shaved.) Their shorn heads became the symbol and synonym of their "collaboration" with the enemy, often understood to mean sexual collaboration. The specter of prostitution, immorality, and unregulated sexuality hovered in these accusations. In reality, these women were often singled out for very different reasons even if accusations always pointed to their sexuality.[8] Women's bodies and sexuality represented the nation and became the focus of a community eager to find unity and redemption. The violence unleashed against these women allowed their symbolic "exclusion from the nation, as a French person and as a woman."[9] To hide their humiliating ordeals, some of these women also started wearing turbans until their hair grew back. They had little in common with Beauvoir but, in both cases, fashion, bodies, and the performance of femininity had political meaning. What it meant to be a woman had always been on the minds of politicians, thinkers, and critics.

Historically, motherhood and reproduction had been assumed to be women's first and ultimate destiny. The Civil Code, which had been established under Napoléon in 1804, laid out these principles. It solidified the power and authority of men—as husbands and fathers—over women. This extensive legal code was still in full effect by the twentieth century and was not amended until the 1960s. But women's situation was not solely the result of this set of laws. Over the course of Beauvoir's lifetime, legislators and politicians made it their task to regulate women's sexuality and reproduction. Procuring or seeking an abortion had been illegal since 1810. After World War I, most French lawmakers were especially concerned with what they perceived to be France's lagging birth rates, especially now that millions of men had died on the battlefront. To them, the family was not a private matter but a question of national interest, and it was the role of public policy to encourage population growth. In 1920, a law instituted "penalties for anyone who recommended abortions, sold instruments that could induce abortion, sold or distributed contraceptives, or discussed birth control."[10] The law now targeted contraception as well and limited women's abilities to manage their sexuality and reproductive decisions. Female bodies were of utmost importance to the future of the nation.

The return of a conservative and authoritarian political regime during the Occupation years intensified this situation. Vichy's head of government, the aging Marshal Pétain, had explained his vision once he was granted full powers: France had suffered from the disorder and chaos of the interwar years. The New Woman was a symbol of this decadence, and France's military defeat had been the price to pay for such cultural disorder. Now, Pétain reminded French people, France must return to the values that had been jettisoned: Work, Family, and Fatherland—the new regime's slogan. According to these conservative, Catholic, and right-wing leaders and critics, family was the foundation of the nation. The Vichy regime asked legislators to enact this particular vision: in 1941, it "prohibited divorce in the first three years of marriage, discouraged abortion, and gave financial incentives to encourage couples to have large families."[11] Married women were discouraged from working outside their home, and those who had been civil servants were fired. Beauvoir, of course, did not fit into these categories because she was unmarried. She remained a high school philosophy professor. The regime's celebration of motherhood was the foundation of its overarching authoritarian, xenophobic, and antisemitic program. In her memoir of this period, Beauvoir wrote of her hatred for the new regime's conservative values and reactionary measures. Even more so since, according to this ideology, France's decadence was the result of women like her, who had remained unmarried, childless, and had independent careers. (Pétain's ideology echoed her own family's that she had fought against growing up.) In 1943, she was fired from her teaching position by the Education Ministry for "immorality." Motherhood was certainly one of the "myths" that Beauvoir attacked most boldly in what became her two-volume study of the situation of women. In 1945, Beauvoir was not so much interested in the meaning of women's new political rights, although these caused incredible anxieties as well as hopes among her contemporaries. She focused on something else altogether.

When Beauvoir decided she might attempt a more openly autobiographical form of writing, she thought that first, "in order to speak of myself, I needed to describe" what it "meant to be a woman." Beauvoir often explained that she realized at this moment she had "failed" in her philosophical logic because she had, until then, remained "too abstract" in her concerns and had not "seen there was something specific" and concrete to the experiences and lives of women.[12] As she made women's lived experiences her subject matter, she was "surprised" by what she turned her eye to: she found it "strange but also stimulating to suddenly discover at the age of forty, an aspect of the world that was so glaring and yet so invisible to all."[13] She spoke of this moment as a revelation: there was something particular about the social, cultural, and economic situation of women that she felt needed to be addressed.

The first sentence of *The Second Sex* stated that Beauvoir had "long hesitated to write a book about women" because the topic was both "irritating" and "old-fashioned."[14] This was both true and untrue. Her turn to this topic certainly surprised her readers. When the first book was published in 1949, three years after she began working on it, most assumed this was a novel and unusual venture for her that departed from her previous works. In fact, despite Beauvoir's portrayal (which was slightly disingenuous), the project was not as radical a turn as most assumed. It actually made sense in light of what she had written about up to then. Already, in the mid-1930s, the first collection of short stories she had written (and that publishers had rejected) focused on five female characters whose fates illustrated the constraints, limitations, and opportunities afforded women. Inspired by her own life and that of her now-deceased best friend Zaza, she charted the lives of young women constrained by bourgeois Catholic morality. Few of her characters escaped the double standards of a society that allowed few opportunities for women. She had wanted, then, to "rebel against the religiosity that had long oppressed" her and express her "disgust towards it through the stories of young women" she knew and who "had been its sometimes complicit victims."[15] This first collection already exhibited some of the existentialist concerns that characterized Beauvoir's later writing: the question of an individual's choice within the context of his or her life.

The Second Sex was therefore the logical continuation of the philosophical issues concerning alienation, ambiguity, and freedom that had absorbed Beauvoir in her literary and nonfictional writings. Her study of the condition of women expanded the themes that had structured her acclaimed 1943 novel *She Came to Stay* (*L'invitée*), though few contemporaries noticed this: individuals do not live alone. For Beauvoir, individuals become aware of their own existence through their relation with others. In that case, if one's own life is limited by external constraints, how does one attain freedom for oneself? And what might personal freedom mean when one was also accountable to others? This had been the theme of Beauvoir's 1945 war novel, *The Blood of Others* (*Le sang des autres*), which was organized around the vagaries, hopes, and ultimate sacrifice of one of its main characters, Hélène. In a similar fashion, her study of the condition of women explored images and expectations as well as women's lived experience. That approach was also clearly shaped by her philosophical training: for Beauvoir, who had read much phenomenology (from Husserl to her friend Maurice Merleau-Ponty), consciousness emerges in the crucible of one's sensory, physical, and emotional experience of the world. When Beauvoir sat down to read about the topic of women, she was actually carrying on her long-standing philosophical interests and literary ventures. She also had on her mind more recent readings that had influenced her view of freedom, oppression, and justice.

THE MAKING OF A PHILOSOPHICAL OBJECT AND A POLITICAL QUESTION

To her surprise, as soon as Beauvoir started her study barely a year after the end of the war, it took on a life of its own. It was remarkably ambitious, bringing material from a variety of disciplines to bear on the topic, from biology to history, philosophy, and literary analysis. Beauvoir sat for weeks reading all kinds of works on the subject. When Beauvoir began working on *The Second Sex*, Sartre had already published in 1946 a short, almost polemical, but powerful essay on the nature of antisemitism, identity, and politics, titled *Anti-Semite and Jew (Réflexions sur la question juive)*. In the immediate aftermath of the war, Beauvoir and Sartre felt especially concerned with the question of oppression and persecution. Sartre penned *Anti-Semite and Jew* without doing any research or outside reading. In contrast, Beauvoir spent much time reading history, philosophy, and literature in the ancient and revered Bibliothèque Nationale. She had already spent the early years of the war reading Hegel there while waiting for Sartre to return from the POW camp. Beauvoir's and Sartre's books were conceived rather differently, even if their aims were rather similar: to diagnose the ways in which otherness is imposed on certain beings and naturalized to appear evident and impossible to contest. Beauvoir set out to explore how society refused to recognize the ways being a woman meant embracing— and sometimes refusing—a series of gendered expectations imposed on female beings. Recently published political and philosophical writings influenced how she framed the question of women as a legitimate and serious political and philosophical issue. She turned not only to the topic of antisemitism, as Sartre had analyzed it, but also specifically to racism that her friend, African-American novelist Richard Wright, had so vividly dissected and passionately denounced in his fiction.

Beauvoir was struck by the ways in which racism and antisemitism were sets of beliefs that became ideologies—that is, organized systems of thought. These ideologies identified certain beings as radically different and inferior both in mind and in body. Wright's novels had shown her how these ideas structured a system of racial oppression. Beauvoir had first read Wright's novel in the 1940s, and *Modern Times* published one of his stories, "Fire and Cloud" in its late 1945 inaugural issue. She first met him when he visited Paris in 1946. Wright and his wife were Beauvoir's hosts in New York and guides to American society when she stayed in the United States for several months in 1947. Perhaps most important, Wright introduced her to what was at the time the most prominent "scientific" study on the question of race and racism in contemporary America. In his 1944 thousand-page work, *American Dilemma: The Negro Problem and Modern Democracy*, Swedish sociologist Gunnar Myrdal argued that race was a human invention rather than a biological fact. Myrdal showed how the political ideals of equality, meritocracy, and opportunity faltered when it came to social, economic, and political life. Not only did he trace how whites remained willfully ignorant of African-Americans' situation, but he explained that African-Americans did not "do well" in American society because their lives and experiences had been conditioned by a historic system of oppression, prejudice, segregation, and exclusion. As Beauvoir explained to her lover, Chicago-based novelist Nelson Algren, she hoped to do for women what Myrdal had done for African-Americans. But she also took her cue from Wright, suggesting analogies between the ways racism and sexism shaped people's lives. She wanted to both reveal and demonstrate how culture and history, not biology, created and shaped gender identity. Hers was a more wide-ranging project than Myrdal's, which would go beyond describing and analyzing the present.

Reflecting on racism echoed Beauvoir's belief that "social relations and recognition" from others and from society at large
were crucial in the "formation of the self."[16] In her introduction to
The Second Sex, Beauvoir clearly drew analogies between the situation of women and that of "Jews" and especially "Blacks." She
explained that "refusing the notions," that is, the myths and stereotypes of "an eternal feminine, of a black soul, and a Jewish
character, did not mean denying that there were Jews, blacks, and
women," but rather recognizing there was a system that identified
them as different, inferior, and a minority.[17] The logic was the
same: one group of people thought themselves as the subject, and
they did so in contrast and opposition to another identified as
"other." But there was an important difference between these
similarly oppressed groups and one that warranted her study of
the topic: unlike "American blacks, or Jews," women were not a
(numerical) minority. In fact, she added, "there were as many
women as there were men on earth."[18] Even more striking, what
had made the exclusion of women so invisible to most was that
they were never identified as a separate group, with its own "past,
history, religion," unlike "American blacks, ghetto Jews, workers"
and "proletarians."[19] So while women had been forged by these
ideas, like other oppressed groups, there was also something particular and unique about women's oppression.

Beauvoir was not the first thinker to make such analogies.
They had been made as early as the eighteenth century. Long
before anything resembling the French Revolution, the English
feminist writer, Mary Astell, had asked: "If all men are free, why
are all women born slaves?" Referring to the injustice of slavery
that was seen as an immoral, un-Christian, and a barbaric practice by some abolitionists (who were still a minority then), she
pointed to the paradox of freedom. Freedom was a right only
granted to (white) men. Slaves and women were deprived of it
and therefore similar. In her 1700 *Reflections on Marriage,* Astell
argued in favor of women's education in order to undo the unequal foundations of marriage. Education for women had also

been a concern for the English thinker Mary Wollstonecraft, who argued in her 1792 *A Vindication for the Rights of Women* that women were, like men, endowed with reason and they should not be considered inferior to men. Two centuries later, Beauvoir took on the task of broadening the topic. To denounce the second-class status women held, it was urgent, she argued, to recognize first that women were defined as secondary, auxiliary, and inferior, the same way other groups had been throughout the world and in history. It was Beauvoir's task to make this situation visible, point to the similar logic that connected sexism and misogyny to other forms of racism and to demonstrate how there was something specific to the situation of women. If "man" was a "Subject," abstract and absolute, "woman" was first and foremost the "Other."[20] Examining the "woman question" was at once a political and philosophical issue.

MAKING A TEXT

If essence did not come before existence, as existentialist philosophy explained, what did it mean to say being a woman was something that was made, not something that was natural? It took Beauvoir almost a thousand pages to examine this question. She began *The Second Sex* by explaining that "woman" was always "the other" and asking how this has become such an enduring fact in human history.[21] Taking on this question required her to examine the issue from all points of view (biology, history, and literature) and to show how current theories were inadequate in dealing with the issue. Her first volume opened with a section on biology. Even though the body was sexed, this did not mean that "society's customs and habits" follow "from biology."[22] As required by rigorous philosophical practice, Beauvoir began from the ground up. She first described the workings of cells, then turned to the function and role of eggs and sperm in the reproduction of life. She then asked readers to ponder why one would "conclude from such an observation that woman belongs in the home?"[23] Comparing the animal world to the human world allowed her to insist that humans were involved in a more complex system of existence and relations. She pointed out that, if "in nature, nothing is ever completely clear-cut," why should the workings of the human body be trapped in a set of rigid and unchanging meanings?[24] She explained that, after all, the human "body is not a thing but a situation."[25] The body is not just a collection of cells, hormones, and drives, it is "a body subjected to taboos, laws" and exists when "the subject" (meaning the individual) "realizes his or her consciousness."[26] For her, the body does not exist outside the society in which it was born. It is never just a biological entity but is always given meaning by individuals.

Once she had laid out these grounding principles, Beauvoir turned her attention to two of the main theories that attracted the most attention in her time: psychoanalysis and historical materialism. Both emerged in the nineteenth century and addressed the conditions of the individual's bodily and material existence. Beauvoir did not dismiss psychoanalyst Sigmund Freud's ideas. She explained that he had, rightly, demonstrated that "sexuality plays a considerable role in human life" because "sexed bodies" are involved "in relation with other sexed bodies," which meant that "sexuality"—the realm of one's own sexual desires, fantasies, and practices—was involved in almost every aspect of an individual's life.[27] Neither did she contest Freud's major insights, including that children realized their own sense of self in relation to others and that they possessed sexuality. However, she explained, "psychoanalysis takes for granted facts that remain unexplained."[28] For her, despite interesting insights, psychoanalysis failed because it took for given rather than interrogated and analyzed the way things were. It did not take women's consciousness, experience, and life seriously because it defined female sexuality as a mere copy of male sexuality. Ultimately, it could not explain why women were the "Other."[29] Beauvoir's critique of psychoanalysis was provocative because, by the 1940s, this previously little known set of theories had been widely embraced and developed further by thinkers, artists, and writers to policymakers trying to map out a new society.[30]

Equally daring was her critique of "historical materialism," that is, the theory of history and change that structured Marxist ideas and had become the theoretical foundation or cornerstone of a number of communist thinkers and leftist sympathizers in postwar France. Beauvoir agreed with historical materialism's insight that "humanity was not just an animal species, but a historical reality" created by human actions.[31] The sum of human actions made up what became historical change. She explained nineteenth-century thinkers had failed to properly explain women's condition because they had focused too narrowly on economic developments, such as the establishment of private property.[32] For Beauvoir, it was not enough to think of women only as workers: women were involved in both the means of production and in reproduction, or the production of children.[33] Reproduction had an economic and social function as well as an individual one. Marxist and communist thinkers had realized this but had failed to consider how, even with the eradication of class relations, alienating labor conditions, and the oppressive system of private property, women were still involved in a particular relation dictated by sexuality, namely their childbearing abilities. If psychoanalysis had narrowly focused on the sexual at the expense of the social, then historical materialism narrowly focused on the social at the expense of the sexual.

Beauvoir's opening analysis allowed her to stress her guiding principle, which had been a long-standing philosophical conviction. For her, "a life is a relation to the world. The individual defined him- or herself by choosing his or her path in the world."[34] This is why, she insisted, "we must turn to the world itself in order to find some answers to our questions" regarding the enduring and invisible status of women as inferior and other in societies.[35] Turning to the world involved examining human history and the ways in which women's situation had been shaped and had evolved through time. In the second part of the first volume,

Beauvoir mapped out the situation and history of women from ancient times all the way to the twentieth century. She had been inspired, in this, by the method used by anthropologist Claude Lévi-Strauss whose study, *The Elementary Structures of Kinship*, she had read before it was published in 1949.[36] Just as anthropology looked to other societies to understand the makings of human society and to show how laws and beliefs were not "natural" but man-made, Beauvoir turned to history to emphasize how women's situation was the result of a long and uneven history. She pointed to legal, social, and economic factors that determined women's lives. She also emphasized how, despite restrictions and constraints, women had nonetheless managed to write or make important changes. Such an overview was not completely new; she borrowed from the late medieval author, Christine de Pizan, and her 1405 *Book of the City of Ladies*. Pizan had created a compendium of "great women" to disprove the notion that women were unimportant and to dismantle her contemporaries' belief that women had nothing to provide. Like Pizan, Beauvoir set out in the last part of the first volume to dismantle the "Myths" that helped create and sustain the inferior condition of women.

Beauvoir stated that "history had shown that men had always held concrete power" and had organized "women's dependency."[37] This historically constituted hierarchical relationship between men (subject) and women (other) had been justified through stories that had become naturalized into culture. Because they had no basis in reality and were repeated over and over through centuries, they had become "myths." Women had been portrayed throughout history as mysterious, dangerous, or unattainable, as either whores or virgins, as all-knowing or incapable of reason, as devoted and motherly or indifferent and narcissistic. Women could be any of these images because, as Beauvoir reminded her readers, they were portrayed by men in a society that privileged men's point of view. In these myths, women did not and could not have an independent existence aside from masculine fears, passions, and assumptions. As evidence, Beauvoir offered an analysis of the some of the great writers of her age: Henry de Montherlant, André Breton, and D. H. Lawrence among others. She then explained that such cultural myths were not just the stuff of literature but in fact permeated everyday life and every individual's relation to the world. "Today," however, Beauvoir claimed, "women are unseating the myths of femininity."[38]

LIVED EXPERIENCE, SEX, AND EQUALITY

If some of Beauvoir's analyses in her first volume were disturbing to some readers, the follow-up volume proved more controversial. It was conceived in phenomenological and existential fashion (that is, concerned with the ways consciousness processed and mediated the experience of the world) and focused on women's "lived experience"—the title of the second volume. Beauvoir traced what would constitute a woman's life: from childhood to old age. Throughout, she emphasized the ambivalence of living as a woman, where disgust and shame shaped desire and pleasure. She first detailed how little girls were taught to "learn" femininity and see it as defining feature of their lives. Girls were made ashamed of their own bodies from a young age (because they had to hide in order to pee), were encouraged to become as passive as the dolls they played with, and to rate themselves according to their physical beauty rather than their actions and intellect.[39] A hierarchy was thus established between boys and girls. The family was the first place where such beliefs were taught. Having explained how even the most private and seemingly "natural" areas of human life were involved in gendered individuals, Beauvoir then argued that culture at large further encouraged girls to be narcissistic and accustomed them to less freedom than boys. While "there are lesbian tendencies in every young girl," teenage girls learned how to think of themselves as "objects of [male] desire."[40] Menstruating bodies caused shame, and the prospect of sexual intercourse caused anxiety among teenage girls. Yet, both were experienced as inevitable if one was to become a woman.

Beauvoir did not shy away from topics that would have been considered unseemly outside the realm of medicine, psychoanalysis, or even sociology. She tackled women's sexuality in all its facets. She discussed female physical pleasure and orgasms in order to stress how these had been transformed into the four categories of "a sin, a fall, a defeat, a weakness."[41] It is not that women did not enjoy sex, but that "while men have a right to satisfy their sexual desire, women were confined" either to chastity or to sex within marriage.[42] Female sexual pleasure was systematically devalued or dangerous because, for women, it meant the risk of pregnancy.[43] Only lesbians (to whom she devoted a chapter) escaped that fear. But, as Beauvoir detailed, to be a lesbian did not necessarily mean a "perversion" of proper female desire. One's erotic partner was a matter of "choice."[44] Female sexuality was determined by history, culture, and myth.

Female sexuality was also used (and misused) as the origin of the two main destinies that were prescribed to women by society: marriage and motherhood. Marriage, according to Beauvoir, was first and foremost a man-made institution that established unequal relations between husband and wife. Though society promised conjugal happiness, sexual harmony, and a blissful family life, marriage was nothing more than a contract that offered women only one fate: rather than independence and autonomy, women entered into a life of domesticity characterized by childrearing, cooking, cleaning, and other chores.[45] Even if women took pride in their abilities to be housewives, Beauvoir insisted this was essentially a form of labor that was never recognized as such but instead considered "natural" and a woman's destiny. The laws that established the authority of husband over wife and deprived married women of rights only strengthened this institution over time.

Beauvoir spent the most time on what she considered the greatest "hypocrisy of bourgeois society," that is, the myth of motherhood. She stressed that pregnancy could be a complicated and ambivalent experience in which women felt both "enriched" and "mutilated."[46] She insisted that motherhood was not an instinct but something that was learned. In fact, she considered motherhood to be a "choice" and an "engagement that one made towards another human being," a "child."[47] Her most scathing critique concerned the ways in which women's bodies were controlled and regulated and, again, the hypocrisy with which male legislators and decision-makers dealt with the matter of abortion and contraception. She insisted on society's "hypocrisy" as it portrayed abortion as a "disgusting crime that no one should mention" when, in fact, it was an unavoidable feature of women's lives.[48] The fact that abortion was illegal made it unsafe and dangerous for women since it could result in infection, hemorrhaging, and even death. She again noted the irony in society's double standards: "the society that is so eager to defend the rights of a foetus is completely uninterested in children once they are born."[49] The remedy was simple. Beauvoir argued that free and legal birth control and abortion would actually allow women to "freely choose pregnancy" and motherhood.[50] She spent a large portion of her second volume on sex and its effects because she believed that by eliminating cultural, social, and legal constraints on sexuality would allow freedom and self-realization for women, as well as men. In order to do so, fear and oppression had to disappear. Only then would every individual enjoy freedom and autonomy.

Women, however, had been complicit in their own oppression because they had readily accepted the myths, constraints, and restrictions that were imposed on them by society. Beauvoir singled out "the mystic," the "narcissist," and the woman hopelessly in love as particular examples of women willing to believe and participate in myths of femininity.[51] These types had appeared in her novels as negative portrayals of women. In the end, Beauvoir did not offer a strategy or a program. Her analysis was the solution. She demonstrated that the subjection and inferiority of women must be eradicated because only then would true freedom, equality, and reciprocity emerge for both men and women.

It was not just a political ideal but also a philosophical principle. This was what *The Second Sex* attempted to show.

A SCANDAL AND A REVELATION

The Second Sex did not spontaneously become a bestseller. Rather, its publication was carefully prepared. Beauvoir, along with Sartre, had learned that one needed to tease the public and attract its attention. From May to July 1948, *Modern Times* published extracts of what the magazine called "a soon-to-be published work on the situation of women." Beauvoir had long been in the habit of publishing some portions of her manuscript while she was still composing it. Just as Sartre had done (he first published extracts of *Anti-Semite and Jew* in the magazine's December 1945 issue), Beauvoir released some carefully chosen selections from her ambitious 972 pages. The first extract concerned "woman and myths" (which became the third section of her first volume). It examined and criticized the ways some near-canonical and well-respected novelists, conservative Henry de Montherlant, Catholic Paul Claudel, and surrealist André Breton, had written about women in their novels. Beauvoir knew, however, that her book would surprise, even shock her readers—an idea she enjoyed, even relished. As she wrote to her lover, Nelson Algren, on August 3, 1948, this "is a big and long piece of work that will probably require another year or month to be really good." She added that, "to [her] delight," she "had heard that the portion published in *Modern Times*, has enraged some men. It's a chapter devoted to the aberrant myths about women that men cherish and the ridiculous and kitschy poetry they produce from it. [These men] seem to have been affected at their most sensitive point."[52] She finished the first volume soon after, in the fall of 1948.

In May 1949, *Modern Times* published three more extracts that included some of the more controversial material of her second volume, focusing on "the sexual initiation of women," "the lesbian," and "motherhood."[53] Even more so than the first extracts, these shocked and enraged some readers. The reaction, again, pleased her. The first volume appeared in June 1949. If Beauvoir meant to be daring, the publicity was less so: the book featured a banner with a photo of Beauvoir with Sartre and the less forward but more sensationalist title: "woman—the unknown."[54] On August 6 and 13 of the same year, Beauvoir released more extracts, this time not in the serious political and literary magazine she edited, Modern Times, but in the glossy photo-heavy popular weekly magazine, Paris-Match, that usually featured celebrities, fashion, and other news. The headline was, this time, more explicit and announced that "a woman calls upon other women to embrace freedom."[55] It was a huge success, and twenty thousand issues were sold in the first week. The rest followed very quickly.

The second volume was published in November 1949. The volume opened with two epigraphs by philosophers Soren Kierkegaard and her first reader, Jean-Paul Sartre. The famous sentence, which has since defined Beauvoir's study, came from the introduction to the second volume. As Beauvoir summed it up, more simply and forcefully, than she had done in the introduction to the first volume: "One is not born a woman. One becomes a woman."[56] Beauvoir had become a recognized author in 1943 with She Came to Stay. In 1945, she had become a recognized literary figure: the author of novels and philosophical essays, one of the editors of Modern Times, but also unfairly dubbed an "existentialist queen" who had been anointed "Our-Lady-of-Sartre" by the press. In 1949, with The Second Sex, she became a controversial celebrity in her own right, whose work challenged the very foundations of society and culture.

Reactions were, of course, mixed. The well-known Catholic writer and Resistance figure, François Mauriac, was horrified by Beauvoir's text. He was outraged when the chapters on female sexuality were published in Modern Times in the spring of 1949. In the conservative newspaper Le Figaro, he tried to dismiss the text as the unfortunate and derivative expression of misguided existentialist and surrealist philosophers who embodied, for him, the decadent state of cultural affairs in postwar France. For Mauriac, such decadence was the result of the Occupation years. Overall, unsurprisingly, Catholic circles did not welcome Beauvoir's analysis. (Even Beauvoir's friend, the leftist writer and Resistance editor Albert Camus was baffled and shocked by the book, a response that disappointed her.) Some leftist Catholic commentators praised its modern tone, but most others were shocked by the graphic descriptive style and the violation of privacy that, they felt, Beauvoir's discussion of sexuality involved.[57] The papacy included *The Second Sex* on its index of forbidden literature.

Despite their commitment to progress and emancipation, communists were also scathing. The Communist Party remained rather conservative when it came to matters of morality, sexuality, and marriage; and its newspapers attacked Beauvoir's study. She was accused of both ignoring and misunderstanding working-class women's concerns. She was also accused of being "too American." Her focus on female sexuality was nothing more than an expression of American vulgarity and individualism, and her book nothing more than the product of American mass culture's influence.[58] Some even compared her book to the Kinsey *Report on Human Sexuality,* which had been translated into French in 1948 almost immediately after its American release (and which Beauvoir had read).[59] Communists also especially dismissed Beauvoir's book because she was a known representative of the nonaligned left and associated with Sartre. As one historian noted, these attacks reflected the weight of Cold War politics on the French political and literary world.[60] In an unexpected turn of events, *The Second Sex* actually united Catholics and communists in their rage against the book.

Although *The Second Sex* generated much controversy and discussion among the French world of intellectuals, it had little political influence. Few critics directly addressed her lengthy discussion of abortion or of female sexual pleasure. A few journalists joined the debates, praising the book. Another journalist called it "revolutionary." Friends, colleagues, and *Modern Times* contributors defended her and set out to explain the book's purpose, as did Beauvoir's longtime friend and former communist, the leftist writer and activist Colette Audry.[61] Many ordinary readers were grateful for Beauvoir's graphic and bold descriptions, and her analyses of conventionally taboo topics. The book sold extremely well. Beauvoir received thousands of letters following its publication. Readers never stopped writing to her after that.

It would be easy to assume that Beauvoir had been a visionary when she sat down to write *The Second Sex*. In fact, her work was part of a larger social and cultural movement. Books by women who wrote about their own experience in the first person proliferated in the immediate postwar period. There were accounts by women who had been deported or been members of the Resistance. Recently created women's magazines, such as *Elle*, regularly featured testimonies by and articles on women's experiences.[62] There was also an increasing number of women who, like Beauvoir, wrote fiction and journalism. Many of them had also been involved in the Resistance during the war. This was the case of Beauvoir's friend, Colette Audry. Historian, author, and archivist Edith Thomas pioneered the genre of the history of women. Others like Françoise d'Eaubonne or Dominique Aury had won prizes for their works. Some were already writing novels but had not yet found success, like Marguerite Duras, Nathalie Sarraute, and Violette Leduc, whose autobiographical novels had inspired Beauvoir on the question of lesbian sexuality. Many of them wrote about female heroines or from a woman's point of view and on topics usually considered unseemly and that often included sexuality—just like Beauvoir had done in *The Second Sex*.

Beauvoir was not alone. Like her, many of these women (though not all) had been educated at elite institutions and had experienced the war and the Occupation as a life-changing experience. *The Second Sex* was therefore not an oddity but more a symptom of the times changing. Beauvoir was aware of this, which is why, as one historian noted, she "emphatically positioned herself in a new generation of women," which, unlike its "elders," sought the conditions for a different and more equal society.[63] This is also why it resonated so powerfully with readers across France and around the world.

CONCLUSION: AFTERLIVES

Theoretically, *The Second Sex* blended all of Beauvoir's intellectual and philosophical influences: phenomenology, Marxism, existentialism, and psychoanalysis. Its ultimate aim was to denounce the oppression of women and put forward the principles that she had always believed in: choice, freedom, autonomy, and equality. While it created intense discussions in France, these were short-lived. *The Second Sex* was more widely read outside France. It was very quickly translated into dozens of other languages. It was released in 1953 in the United States and immediately became a bestseller. Her American readers did not know that the translator had cut many portions of the text and, more troublingly, had erased or mistranslated many of the philosophical concepts and ideas that were central to its argument. This did not deter readers. The book's attraction lay in the fact that it covered almost every aspect of women's lives and experiences, including those that few dared to discuss but that were becoming a topic of discussion in the postwar era.

Very few of Beauvoir's French readers were feminists, and no feminist organization had supported the book. In the United States, however, *The Second Sex* shaped a generation of female readers, many of whom embraced feminism and helped create what is now referred to as "second-wave feminism." Betty Friedan took direct inspiration from it to begin writing her 1963 critique of the myth of the housewife, *The Feminine Mystique*. She was not alone, and the book made its way to many throughout the 1960s. For Kathie Sarachild, who became the leader of the group Feminist Revolution, Beauvoir was "the French woman who exposed male supremacy . . . and gave us our feminism." For her, reading

Beauvoir as a teenager was a revelation. She "felt physically, as if my eyes were being opened. . . . It seared me with a consciousness so strong" she could no longer ignore it.[64] Radical feminists found much to think about in *The Second Sex*. Women's Liberation founder, Ti-Grace Atkinson decided to write to Beauvoir in 1962 rather than contact Betty Friedan as she had been advised. She went to France several times to visit Beauvoir and explained that she "became a feminist because of her" and "went into philosophy because of her."[65] The Canadian activist Shulamith Firestone, who moved to New York in 1967 where she helped found the New York Radical Group and later the Redstockings, dedicated her 1970 study, *The Dialectic of Sex*, to Beauvoir. Her book attacked the oppression that reproduction represented for women and advocated reproductive technologies as a tool to end gender inequalities. She always said her best ideas had come from *The Second Sex*.[66] Kate Millett's now canonical 1970 *Sexual Politics* owed much to *The Second Sex*, so much so, in fact, that Beauvoir once commented that "while a very good book," Millett had taken "it all, the form, the idea, everything" from her.[67]

In 1949, Beauvoir did not call herself a feminist. Neither did she think of herself as one. She was not an activist. Neither did she call, then, for the reform of laws on divorce, abortion, contraception, and the other topics that *The Second Sex* analyzed and criticized. In the next decades, a different set of political battles engulfed her, before she finally joined French feminists. But many of the readers who fell in love with the book found it inspiring and often spoke of the ways it determined them to participate, support, or associate with the many incarnations of the second-wave feminisms that swept through Western societies in the late 1960s and 1970s. Her book had many lives and shaped Beauvoir's life in unexpected ways.

CHAPTER 5

BEING FREE IN THE WORLD: | ETHICS AND ENGAGEMENT, 1954–1964

AS SHE ACHIEVED LITERARY recognition in France and elsewhere in the world, Beauvoir found herself involved in seemingly contradictory projects. At the same moment that the world came rushing into her life, in the form of a conflict that soon consumed her, she decided to begin writing about herself. Beauvoir's novels had certainly always found their origin in her life—though she insisted they were not autobiographical. This time she embarked on a new form of writing, the memoir. It was as if the more the world was weighing on her and at the very moment she became a well-known celebrity, featured in magazines and even TV programs on the Left Bank, she decided to write about herself in different ways. This fit with her existentialist commitment that held individuals only realized their sense of self through their actions. Now, Beauvoir acted as an individual by writing about the world and about herself. At the same time that she became a presence on the world stage, she wrestled with what it meant to be an individual accountable to others.

She was joined on the literary scene by other and younger female authors, some of whom she had mentored, who proved as controversial as she was. In the year that Beauvoir received the prestigious Goncourt prize, another novelist garnered as much if not more attention than she did: a young woman, barely eighteen, Françoise Sagan, published a surprising short novel, *Hello Sadness* (*Bonjour tristesse*). Sagan, who had read all of Sartre's work and had been fascinated by Beauvoir's *The Second Sex* as a teenager, wrote about an indifferent and disenchanted girl in a world seemingly devoid of morality. To French commentators, the novelist and her heroine were the scandalous embodiment of a new postwar generation. Her novel became an even greater international bestseller than Beauvoir's work. That same year, another book caused a scandal, *The Story of O* (*Histoire d'O*), a quasi-pornographic text, published under the pseudonym Pauline Réage. Critics wondered whether a man had in fact written this: After all, was it possible for a woman to talk about sex in this way? Authorities charged the publisher with obscenity, and publicity was forbidden for several years. Several other female novelists fictionalized ambiguous and troubling female heroines. Four years earlier, Marguerite Duras, had become known to the public with *Sea Wall* (*Barrage contre le Pacifique*), a story of her childhood in France's colony Indochina. The novel showed a young poor white French girl whose mother was slowly going mad after a series of failing business ventures. Left to her own devices, the young girl began a relationship with a wealthy Chinese man—a transgression of colonial society's racism that shocked French readers.

The topic of sex may have been a welcome distraction and a novelty for some, even for those who read *The Second Sex* five years earlier. For others, the emphasis on sex and especially on young women's sexuality was the symptom of a French society in the throes of decadence because it was unable to maintain its glory and greatness. After World War II, France's empire, which had always been perceived as one of the foundations of its greatness, was very much on people's minds. Indochina, which comprises modern-day Vietnam, Laos, and Cambodia, had been a French colony since 1886. France had been able to recover Indochina after its occupation by the Japanese army during the war. However, communist forces led by Ho Chi Minh, who had spent his student days in Paris where he had met budding Caribbean and African intellectuals, now demanded independence from French colonial rule. The war officially began at the end of 1946. It pitted nationalist communist forces against the French and the Emperor Bao Dai. Rather than recruits from France, the French government used colonial troops from Morocco, Tunisia, Algeria, Laos, and Cambodia to fight the insurgent nationalist forces. The war quickly became known as "the dirty war," and leftist intellectuals, as well as the editor of the Catholic magazine *Spirit* (*Esprit*), argued for the end of colonialism and supported Ho Chi Minh. The writer and jazz performer Boris Vian penned a song in February 1954 that denounced the war, called *the Deserter* (*Le déserteur*). It was sung by Marcel Mouloudji, an up-and-coming singer that Beauvoir loved, who explained he would evade conscription because his job was not to kill other people like him. The song was immediately banned.

This war was not just a French affair. It was the theater of Cold War face-off, as the United States and the Soviet Union provided resources to each side. *Modern Times* took sides and charted this face-off between Western capitalism and Eastern communism. European empires were being challenged from within by their colonized populations seeking independence but also from outside by these new political forces seeking to control power relations on the international scene. The war ended with the overwhelming defeat of the French army at Dien Bien Phu in the spring of 1954. Beauvoir looked from afar as Vian's antimilitarist song was considered an outrage in the face of the war's outcome. This was the pressing issue weighing upon French intellectuals. In the wake of World War II, colonialism was now the greatest injustice to fight against. Beauvoir thought a victory by Vietnamese nationalists against the French empire was a good thing and "made her happy."[1] But, unlike Sartre, she did not write about this conflict or the end of the French empire. Neither was she involved in anticolonial activism, aside from her editorial work at *Modern Times*, as it seemed somewhat remote from her Parisian world.

It was not Vietnam but Algeria that soon "consumed her thoughts, her sleep, her moods."[2]

THE ALGERIAN WAR: A REVOLUTION

By the early 1950s, Paris had returned to its role as one of Europe's intellectual and cultural centers. To young people listening to Elvis Presley's rock-and-roll on vinyl or queuing to attend a concert by African-American virtuoso jazz performer Miles Davis in Left Bank clubs, there was no better place to be. Paris was again a bustling and cosmopolitan metropolis. Beauvoir enjoyed this tremendously, as it reminded her of her carefree interwar years. With Sartre, she could be seen and was often photographed in Left Bank cafés, bars, and clubs. It was also an attractive refuge for many anticolonial intellectuals, writers, and activists, thanks to its long history as a destination and refuge for black expatriates.[3] Caribbean, African, and African-American thinkers gathered together for meetings, events, and other activities, blending the political and the intellectual. The magazine *African Presence* (*Présence Africaine*) had been created in Paris in 1947. Sartre had been involved, as had Camus, but Beauvoir did not pay much attention. The magazine's editors organized the first "International Conference of Black Writers and Artists" on September 19, 1956, at the prestigious Sorbonne. Many of its delegates were prominent writers. Beauvoir's friend the African-American novelist Richard Wright participated. So did the Martinican poet Aimé Césaire who had compared colonialism to European Nazism in a 1950 text, *Discourse on Colonialism* (*Discours sur le colonialisme*), explaining they were part of the same desire to control and dominate. There was also George Lamming from Barbados, Léopold Sédar Senghor from Senegal, and a young Martinican psychiatrist, Frantz Fanon, who had published *Black Skin, White Masks* (*Peau noire, masques blancs*) in 1952. Inspired by phenomenology and Sartre's study of antisemitism, it was a powerful examination of the effects of colonial racism on the colonized. At the conference, Fanon gave a talk on the links between racism and culture.

Others who, like the Vietnamese nationalist leader Ho Chi Minh, had been educated in France in the 1930s, called for an end to all colonial domination throughout the world. Anticolonialism was gaining ground and was very much in the news. India had won its independence from the British in 1947. In France, though, many people refused to believe in such a fate for the French empire as, to them, World War II had demonstrated the importance of the empire to the French nation-state. For these people, the loss of Indochina only strengthened their desire to preserve French colonies. For opponents of empire, it was now time to recognize colonized people's rights to self-determination and to correct a historical injustice. It is within this context that Algerian nationalists called for their independence.

POSTWAR EXISTENTIALISTS. *Simone de Beauvoir and Jean-Paul Sartre in a Left Bank café (1959).*

Trouble had been brewing for a while, but few people in France had noticed. Beauvoir had taken a trip to Tunisia and Algeria before and after the war.[4] She had marveled over the beautiful scenery but talked little of the dire conditions in which colonized Algerian Muslims lived. In fact, she said nothing of the violence that shook Algeria in 1945.[5] On May 8, the day Europeans celebrated their victory over Hitler, Algerian Muslims gathered to demand political rights at Sétif and elsewhere. Demonstrators clashed with the police and the army. A hundred European bystanders were killed. In retaliation, the French went on a week-long campaign to "squash" those they deemed dangerous. Thousands of Algerians were killed. This massacre prompted some Algerians to call for the independence of Algeria and more specifically for armed revolutionary struggle. Nationalist movements had been gaining ground since the 1930s. Algerians' experience of fighting for France in wars had further radicalized many of them. Algerian nationalists' claims were not new, but their choice of methods was. In the late 1940s, Beauvoir did not write about this nor did she seem to notice. Many at *Modern Times* argued for prompt and swift decolonization, but the urgency of anticolonialism had not yet made its mark on her. Her prize-winning 1954 novel, *The Mandarins*, which showed how Parisian leftist intellectuals were obsessed with politics, had not mentioned the topic. It was the events that erupted in 1954 that changed her mind. Slowly, she began seeing her role in politics differently. As she wrote less than ten years later, she came to realize that, this time, she "wanted to be on the right side of history."[6]

The Algerian War of Independence officially began on November 1, 1954, when Algerian nationalists launched coordinated bomb attacks throughout Algeria against French military and police targets, leaving eight dead and four wounded. At the outbreak of the war, multiple nationalist movements organized into the National Liberation Front, or FLN (*Front de Libération Nationale*). The FLN declared they wanted the "restoration of the Algerian nation." Algeria had been colonized in 1830 through a series of brutal military conquests. Since then, a deeply divided and racialized society had emerged. Multiethnic European settlers were a minority, approximately one million. There were almost nine million Algerian Muslims who, though citizens, had no political rights (or restricted ones for a minority) and whose lives were shaped by this unequal racist system. There was also a substantial Algerian presence of mostly men in metropolitan France because the French government had needed workers and confined them to poor working-class neighborhoods and shantytowns outside Paris and other big cities. Unlike Indochina, Morocco, Tunisia, or other West African colonies, Algeria was legally and administratively part of France and so not exactly a colony. This contradiction was a deeply held universal truth by ordinary citizens and political leaders alike. Prime minister Pierre Mendès-France's response to the FLN demands in 1954 was simple: Algeria "is France, not a foreign country."[7] It was and would remain French, Mendès-France insisted.

The conflict quickly escalated. As French police and military forces expanded the use of torture to gain information on the Algerian "terrorists," the FLN set out on a campaign aimed at furthering the cause of Algerian independence, using targeted violence such as bombs and assassinations against those who lived in "colonist centers" and that included both "Europeans" and "Muslims."[8] To ruthlessly squash the "rebellion," the French government called up millions of reserve soldiers in a draft. Even as it was raging, the government refused to acknowledge the conflict or recognize it was involved in a war. Although TV newsreels showed images of young conscripts boarding ships to cross the Mediterranean, the French government still referred to "events in Algeria." It was a war without name. But it was given a name by those who denounced the injustice of colonialism and supported the FLN's claim for independence, including Sartre and the *Modern Times* team. They were joined by a right-leaning intellectual, Raymond Aron, who argued in a book he published in 1957, *The Algerian Tragedy*, that there was neither economic nor political advantage to the French presence in Algeria. However, Sartre, Aron, and others remained a minority. Most of the left, including the communists, maintained Algeria should remain French. From 1954 to 1958, left-wing governments followed this policy. The conflict revealed profound divisions within French society: Beauvoir was shocked to witness the "chauvinism" and "racism" of her fellow citizens, who thought it normal that Algerian workers in Paris be subjected to "searches, police raids, and roundups."[9]

Beauvoir found the silence and indifference of most of the country maddening. She was also horrified to witness that few understood colonialism as a "system" organized through a racist vision of the world. France seemed indifferent to the wave of decolonization taking place around the globe. The Bandung Conference had just ended. In April 1955, twenty-five newly independent countries, including India, Burma, and Pakistan, had met in Indonesia, which had become independent ten years earlier, in the city of Bandung to draft a statement condemning Western colonialism and calling for unity against colonizing forces. Richard Wright attended the meeting and relayed its content to the "International Conference of Black Writers and Artists" that took place in Paris less than a year later. The silence was deafening. Most French people did not want to listen. When the newspaper *Le Monde* carried a series of "front page articles in September 1956 on the Montgomery bus boycott and race relations in general all over the deep South," very few commentators saw an echo between American developments and the headlines in Algeria. Beauvoir, who had visited the United States, understood these connections.

French communists were instead obsessed with Soviet leader Nikita Khrushchev's denunciation, in February 1956, of Stalin's totalitarian policies and mass terror, only three years after Stalin's death. The official revelation of the use of arbitrary arrests, executions, and even torture, as well as the charge of a misguided foreign policy, stunned and divided French leftists, especially those who had faithfully supported Soviet communism. This division of the left strangely echoed some of Beauvoir's scenes in her novel *The Mandarins*, which was, that year, put on the papacy's forbidden list, next to her 1949 *The Second Sex*. Meanwhile, Tunisia gained its independence on March 20, 1956, one year after Morocco. This news was soon overshadowed by the French government's decision to extend special powers in Algeria. The Prime Minister Guy Mollet, who was a socialist and had previously supported negotiations, authorized the use of special military tribunals, broadened the army's responsibilities, legalized the use of internment camps in France and Algeria, extended military service to twenty-seven months, and doubled the number of conscripts. At the same time, he ordered an inquiry into rumors and accusations of torture and violence against Algerians.

Beauvoir and Sartre had heard about "broken bones, burnt faces, burnt sexual organs, ripped nails, screams, convulsions."[10] She noted this in her diary, as Sartre wrote articles denouncing the war. It was becoming evident no Algerian was spared and the most horrifying violence defined this war. Again, this was not just a French affair. The Algerian War shaped France's involvement in the 1956 Suez crisis. Eager to undermine Egypt's support for FLN rebels, France joined the British in a military confrontation with Egypt, now led by nationalist leader Gamal Abdel Nasser. But, within the context of the Cold War, the United States and the Soviet Union got involved and forced France to retreat. Meanwhile, most French people were happy to ignore these developments and forget about politics and global affairs. Instead, they watched the young actress Brigitte Bardot who entranced and shocked viewers with her unrepentant sexuality in her husband's film, *And God Created Woman* (*Et dieu créa la Femme*). The "new Lolita," as Beauvoir called her, became front-page news.[11] For most, Algeria was forgotten in favor of Bardot's alluring presence at the 1956 Cannes film festival. For Beauvoir, Sartre, and their friends, however, "Algeria blocked their horizon."[12] She could not think of anything else.

BEING AN INTELLECTUAL IN THE WAR: 1955–1958

Beauvoir had seen the demanding work of political activism as Sartre's affair. She had often declined invitations to meetings, opportunities to speak at rallies, or membership in organizations. It was not that she did not care. The experience of World War II and the Occupation had shown her the world could not be ignored. Still, she felt she would merely replicate Sartre's positions.[13] She did, however, hope for a political regime that would implement socialist ideals. Despite her reluctance to echo Sartre, she traveled with him to China in 1955 for several weeks. They had been invited by Mao Zedong to review the glories of the Chinese communist revolution and witness firsthand a concrete revolution's outcome. Beauvoir was impressed by the "profound and authentic revolution China [was] undergoing."[14] She had never encountered a country "so foreign" where poverty and hunger seemed to have been eradicated, and the "working class" now made this "new order" that was entirely "oriented toward the future."[15] She set out to write about it because, in part, she explained, "well-fed Westerners are incapable of imagining themselves outside of their own skin."[16] But writings like these, which she published two years later in 1957, echoed her own hopes rather than any active engagement on her part. She wrote it because, disappointed by the US involvement in the Korean War a few years earlier, Beauvoir felt the West was too wedded to imperialism and corrupted by capitalism to offer its citizens anything meaningful. Writings, like *The Long Journey* (*La longue marche: essai sur la Chine*), her text on China, were composed over time, in the peace of her small Paris apartment. At the time, she certainly did not see her political involvement extending beyond her writing.

That changed with the Algerian War. As the conflict raged, she was shocked to read reports and testimonies, many of them sent to *Modern Times*, on "entire army battalions that pillaged, burned down, raped, and massacred" and to discover the extent to which "torture was employed as a normal and essential means of obtaining information" from Algerian men and women even when they were not involved with the FLN.[17] At the same time, she became more and more incapable of tolerating her fellow citizens' racism and indifference to what was happening in Algeria.[18] Every time she went out at night, she was reminded of this. There seemed to be no escape and she felt like an "exile" in her own country: she wrote that "going out for a café, or a drink, even walking into a bakery" or going to a restaurant or the cinema meant she was reminded of her own "complicity" in this conflict and of others' shameful indifference.[19] How to face this? How could she act? Traveling to Italy for summer holidays to escape the charged political atmosphere, as she kept doing, was not enough.[20] She had written about choice and responsibility in 1945. This time, things were different. As she explained, "After years against the tide, I felt again swept by history and I wanted to be more involved in it. The example of men and women around me was inspiring. For three years, I had focused on my private life . . . Now I wanted to be useful."[21]

Beauvoir knew she had to become involved. The Algerian War obsessed her. Even literature felt "insignificant."[22] Her involvement took different shapes, in part necessitated by events. Often, she intervened to help others she thought had shown more bravery and boldness than she did. She testified at trials, for instance, for one of her former students, Jacqueline Guerroudj, a philosophy teacher in Algeria who had helped carry bombs for the FLN. Jacqueline was saved from the death penalty but her accomplice, who had placed the bomb, was not.[23] Beauvoir also worked tirelessly at *Modern Times* with Sartre who stayed up entire nights to finish articles or speeches. Along with the American-style weekly *Express* (*L'Express*), *Modern Times* published soldiers' and brutalized Algerians' testimonies.

Strikingly, the years that involved Beauvoir in the world of politics were also the years when she began a massive autobiographical project. Beauvoir explained that "she was struck by her own aging in the years 1954 to 1962." Because she "was disgusted by the crimes taking place in the name of France" she decided to "nostalgically turn to her past."[24] But her memoirs were more than a retreat and a refuge from the messy and disturbing outside world. They embodied her philosophical ambition: to show how one's self is always shaped by others and related to others. At the same time, for Beauvoir, who had always kept a diary since her teenage days, the literary genre of the memoir was one she had never tried up to then. She had written novels, novellas, philosophical essays, and political articles. Writing a memoir was a new challenge for a now-accomplished novelist. An autobiography was more than a chronicle or a diary for her: it was truly a "literary creation" because it "required imagination and self-reflection as much as memory."[25]

Two years after the beginning of the Algerian War, and her Goncourt prize, she began her first memoir. It focused on her childhood and teenage years—years that Beauvoir had argued in *The Second Sex* were the most formative for a woman and where, she had explained in *The Ethics of Ambiguity*, one still had the illusion of freedom. *Memoirs of a Dutiful Daughter* (*Mémoires d'une jeune fille rangée*) was a coming-of-age story telling the tale of how a once "dutiful" young girl had lost her faith, discovered literature, experienced freedom, and decided she must craft her own life. It was her best friend Zaza's death—the teenager who could not free herself—which had "been the price of her freedom."[26]

Beauvoir was also becoming an intellectual, using her words in the service of political causes. She was not alone. In 1957, Catholic intellectual Pierre-Henri Simon published a pamphlet *Against Torture*. The following year, *Express* editor, Jean-Jacques Servan-Schreiber, wrote of his own experience as a soldier in what was a scathing indictment of the army. In the face of torture, massacres, roundups, and camps, the FLN argued only terrorism would force the French government to back down. Indeed, the question of the use of violence was a difficult topic for the French left and divided many. Beauvoir and Sartre had first been skeptical of FLN tactics. But Francis Jeanson, a former student, journalist, and *Modern Times* contributor, who was part of an underground network helping the FLN, convinced them only violence worked against state violence. That issue caused an insurmountable rift between Sartre and Beauvoir and their friend Albert Camus. Camus was an Algerian-born European and believed in reform and compromise rather than revolution and violence. He argued for a "truce," but few, by 1958, either in Algeria or in metropolitan France, listened to him. The war bitterly divided even those who had been allies and friends during the Occupation.

In 1958, nothing seemed to improve. Beauvoir later noted, "The rest of the world seemed less bleak" than France.[27] She felt anxious. Sartre drank too much and took amphetamines to keep working through the night. They both kept working on their own writing. Meanwhile, various governments' inability to find a solution to the war was undermining the foundations of the Fourth Republic. The army staged a coup in order to pressure the return and appointment of World War II hero, the conservative Charles de Gaulle. The prospect of de Gaulle's return was welcomed by most French people. The parliament approved it. Beauvoir, however, could not bear the idea and lost sleep and the ability to write.[28] A referendum was organized on September 28, 1958, which asked French voters to approve the constitutional changes de Gaulle asked. Despite demonstrations and fierce opposition from parts of the left, most voters agreed. The Fifth Republic was born. The new constitution included expanded executive powers for the newly elected President de Gaulle. Algeria was still French, but all Algerians were granted the political rights they had been promised for over a century. At the same time, a curfew was declared for all Algerian workers. For Beauvoir, Sartre, and their friends, this was a "treason" that meant only one thing: the return of "fascism."[29] Beauvoir wrote that de Gaulle's return was like the "resurrection" of Vichy's leader, Marshal Pétain (though they had been bitter opponents during World War II). But what felt like a "bitter defeat" galvanized her and Sartre to further action.[30]

As soon as *Memoirs of a Dutiful Daughter* was published in 1958, Beauvoir sat down to continue the tale of her own life. What was happening around her provided the perfect counterpoint. Now that, after 1954, she had "discovered" politics and felt compelled to engage in the world, she decided to reflect on her apolitical years between 1929 and 1944. It may be "arbitrary to slice up one's life," as Beauvoir once admitted, but she nonetheless gave meaning to these two decades by identifying two events that she felt defined her life: her meeting with Sartre in 1929 and the end of the war in 1944.[31] Here, she charted her hopes and frustrations, her friendships and relationships, as well as her life during the Occupation. She insisted upon her youthful political indifference—a point she made now long after the fact. She was writing in the midst of the Algerian War, at the very moment when the horrifying facts of torture were becoming public. Indeed, as she told a journalist, "it is very difficult to look back to one's past without modifying it somewhat."[32] Still, in many ways, this memoir told the story of how she had become an adult in the midst of war. *The Prime of Life* (*La force de l'âge*) was written twenty years after the fact. Beauvoir did not hide her ambivalence, nor did she try to embellish her role during the war. She talked of her inability to understand her young Jewish friend, Bianca. Still, to a careful reader, there was much that Beauvoir had been blind and indifferent to, especially when it came to French and foreign Jews' plight. But, at the time, no one commented on her ambivalent memories. Forty thousand copies were preordered even before its publication in 1960.[33] Some thought she had written her "best book," and Beauvoir assumed that readers who liked this memoir shared her political opinions.[34]

THE SHAME OF TORTURE: 1958–1962

The following years became especially difficult. Torture took center stage in the denunciation of the war, thanks to the publication of a short book in late February 1958, entitled *The Question*

(*La question*)—a play on "la question," the medieval juridical term referring to inquisitors' use of torture, that also pointed to the moral questions raised by the Algerian War. The communist anticolonial activist and editor Henri Alleg published the account of his imprisonment and torture in Algeria. Sartre wrote a preface on March 6, 1958, in *L'Express*. Both Alleg's and Sartre's writings were seized and censored. Almost sixty thousand copies of Alleg's book were sold before being banned by the government. *The Question* was important because, for the first time, someone published "as a victim rather than as a bystander or perpetrator of torture."[35] It had little influence though on the outcome of the 1958 referendum a few months later and de Gaulle's return to power. In the meantime, Beauvoir handed in to her editor the final draft of her first memoir, *Memoirs of a Dutiful Daughter*. To her surprise, it was an immediate bestseller. Readers felt, as one wrote her, they had "been swept off their feet" by it.[36] But that success did little to alleviate Beauvoir's anxieties and her unshakeable feeling that she could no longer bear her own homeland.

The government did not relent. Revelations kept mounting despite government censorship. Internment camps still held over six thousand Algerians in metropolitan France and thousands more in Algeria. There were insistent rumors of "disappearances" of suspected FLN fighters and supporters, and the refusal by the authorities to investigate. Now reports and testimonies confirmed the army regularly turned to torture and rape. Violence and death seemed everywhere. Beauvoir felt more depressed: she was saddened by the news of her friend Boris Vian's unexpected heart attack in June 1959, several months after her relationship with Claude Lanzmann had ended. She felt France had become "fascist," the army acted like the "Gestapo," and its soldiers like the "SS," when, for her, "the life of Muslims mattered no less than that of my fellow citizens."[37] The Algerian War seemed to bring back the ghosts of World War II. She noted, "Ten thousand Algerians are boxed at the Vel' D'Hiv, like Jews, in the past used to be at Drancy."[38] The difficulty, as Beauvoir added, was that "people would rather be moved by a natural disaster than by a crime to which they are complicit."[39] In 1959, Alleg's editor published *The Gangrene* (*La gangrène*) documenting the torture of five Algerian students in Paris by the French police. The Algerian War was no longer something that happened across the Mediterranean. It happened in the French countryside and in Parisian working-class neighborhoods.

Another tragedy struck at the beginning of 1960: Camus died in a car crash in the South of France. Despite their bitter falling-out over the fate of Algeria, Beauvoir and Sartre were profoundly moved by the death of the one who had been "their companion during those hopeful years" and who "smiled so well."[40] With Sartre, she found hope and distraction elsewhere. They were invited to visit Cuba by one of its revolutionary leaders Che Guevara, who had read both Camus's and Sartre's works in his youth (but not Beauvoir's). After several years of armed struggle, the Cuban Revolution had overthrown the anticommunist dictatorial regime led by President Batista in January 1959. Five years after China, and the disillusionment with Soviet Russia, Cuba embodied the utopian dream of socialism come to life, against the force of what Beauvoir called "American imperialism." It showed Beauvoir and Sartre that armed struggle could bring people's socialist ideals to life. Even then, trips like these could not completely distract them from the suffocating hold of the Algerian War and its injustices.

In May 1960, a Tunisian-born lawyer, Gisèle Halimi, who had been involved in trials of FLN fighters, asked to meet Beauvoir. She told her the story of Djamila Boupacha, a young Algerian woman who had been arrested in February, along with her father and brother-in-law. She was suspected of having planted a bomb in a restaurant in central Algiers. Boupacha was indeed a FLN supporter. She was not alone. Like other Algerian women, she had joined the cause of independence. And, like others before her, she had helped underground FLN networks by playing on French assumptions about the supposed "passivity" and "traditional habits"

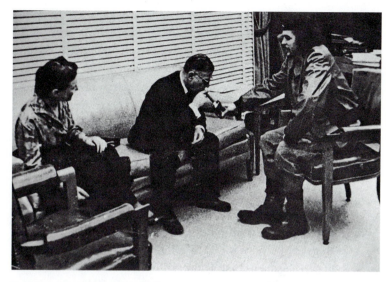

THE PROMISE OF SOCIALIST REVOLUTIONS. *Simone de Beauvoir and Jean-Paul Sartre meet Cuban Revolution leader Che Guevara (1960).*

of North African women who were assumed apolitical. Neither was Boupacha the first Algerian woman to be tried. In November 1956 and January 1957, Djamila Bouhired had planted bombs in Algiers. Bouhired was arrested, tortured, and tried. With her lawyer, Jacques Vergès, she contested the legitimacy of the court. In the face of illegal and immoral authorities, the Algerian revolutionaries who stood accused and their committed defenders called for justice and revolution for Algeria.

Boupacha had been raped and tortured, like Bouhired and many other Algerians before her. What made her situation different was that Boupacha had agreed to testify about her ordeal and Halimi had convinced her to sue French authorities for the torture she had endured. This was a daring move but, Halimi believed, a necessary one. Beauvoir agreed. These were grave matters. Boupacha could be sentenced to the death penalty, just as Bouhired had been. Beauvoir immediately agreed to help. She did so in the way that most suited her temperament, by lending her name and writing in defense of Boupacha. They set up the Committee for the Defense of Djamila Boupacha, which included names as diverse as Caribbean intellectuals Aimé Césaire and Edouard Glissant, Algerian writer Jean Amrouche, and the former Resistance figure and ethnologist Germaine Tillion, who had been deported to Ravensbrück, had worked in Algeria and later denounced the French state's systematic use of torture.[41] Their strategy was simple: publicize the case so that it would throw light on the shameful horror of the war.

Beauvoir published her article in June 1960 in the pages of *Le Monde*. It was titled "For Djamila Boupacha," echoing Vergès's own 1957 text, "For Djamila Bouhired."[42] Beauvoir's article was powerful: it made multiple points all at once blending Beauvoir's feelings about the war, her politics, and her philosophical outlook. She began by pointing out: "What is most scandalous about the scandal of torture, is that one gets used to it."[43] It was no longer enough to unveil what she had called "the unbearable truth of torture."[44] She suggested the French public had become accustomed to hearing about these acts, and what was most shocking, as Beauvoir had noted in her diary many times before, was the indifference in the face of such scandalous practices. How to shake this indifference? Beauvoir focused first on the details of Boupacha's ordeal: she described rather graphically how she had been tortured and raped. She did not want to "spare" readers. Her emphasis on Boupacha's body, and on the specifics of torture would not have surprised her long-time readers. Already in *The Second Sex*, Beauvoir had not hesitated to detail the brutal ordeal of illegal abortions that women had to endure. Beauvoir also understood female bodies had cultural and political meaning. The violation Boupacha experienced mattered even more because she was a "virgin."[45] Beauvoir emphasized "Djamila's status as a virginal 'young girl.'"[46] So did the usually apolitical Françoise Sagan in her defense of Boupacha in *L'Express* that same month. Just as Bouhired had become the "face of the [Algerian] revolution," Boupacha became the icon of the immorality of the war.[47]

Beauvoir's article shocked readers. It also resonated power-fully since Beauvoir made sure to explain that Boupacha's viola-tion was only one in a long list of unbearable acts against the Algerian population to which every French person was complicit: "men, women, old people, children have been gunned down during raids, burnt down in their villages, shot down, their throats cut, disemboweled, martyrized to death; in internment camps, entire tribes have been left to suffer from hunger, the cold, beat-ings, epidemics."[48] Beauvoir continued listing the many ways Algerians had suffered. In this manner, she showed how torture was both an ethical and a political issue. In 1946, she had argued justice was needed to punish the collaborator Robert Brasillach who had betrayed the ideals of the French republic. In 1960, it was justice that now betrayed the principles of the French republic.

Beauvoir and Halimi succeeded in making Djamila Boupa-cha an "affair," but the tide did not yet turn. Francis Jeanson's re-sistance network was also being tried for treason. New Wave filmmaker Jean-Luc Godard saw his film, *The Little Soldier*, cen-sored because its story of a deserter in the Algerian War featured torture (it would only be released three years later). Beauvoir and other intellectuals kept on writing. In the August 1960 issue of *Modern Times*, readers found two blank pages followed by a long list of signatories. Names included Beauvoir and Sartre, of course, as well as others associated with the magazine. There were film-makers, artists, writers, actors and many others: novelist Mar-guerite Duras and Caribbean writer Edouard Glissant were listed alongside filmmaker Alain Resnais whose 1955 documentary *Night and Fog* had denounced the inhumanity of "concentra-tionary systems" and whose 1959 fictional film *Hiroshima My Love* denounced how "inequality of races" caused wars and violence, from Vichy France to Hiroshima. New Wave filmmaker François Truffaut and novelists Michel Butor, Alain Robbe-Grillet, and Nathalie Sarraute were also listed. Celebrity novelist Françoise Sagan had signed as had renowned actress Simone Signoret. All these people had agreed to a manifesto: the *Declaration of the*

Right to Insurgency in the Algerian War. It had been drafted by two leftist intellectuals, Maurice Blanchot and Dionys Mascolo, who explained that the signatories supported anyone who refused to fight in the war and stood behind anyone who helped the FLN. It concluded, "The Algerian people's cause which decisively contributes to the ruin of the colonial system is the cause of every free person." The blank pages in *Modern Times* were followed by the testimony from a young student, Zohra Drif, who had been sentenced to twenty years of forced labor, and a text entitled "Genocide in Algeria" documenting the murders of Algerians by the French army. The pages were blank because the declaration had been censored. It appeared in full a month later in another newspaper. By the end of November, there were 255 signatories. The communists did not support it. What became known as the *Manifesto of the 121* (for the original number of signatures) signaled a turn in the public face of the war. Meanwhile, Beauvoir kept on writing. She published her second memoir, *The Prime of Life* (*La force de l'âge*) while Sartre published his *Critique of Dialectical Reason* (*Critique de la raison dialectique*).[49] Both were, again, huge popular successes. However, the year ended as sadly as it began: On November 28, 1960, Beauvoir's long-time friend Richard Wright died of a heart attack.[50] Mourning mingled with her anger.

While Halimi managed to organize Djamila Boupacha's transfer to a metropolitan prison for her trial, press censorship increased. Sensing the beginning of a shift in public opinion, President de Gaulle organized a referendum in January 1961, asking the French people if they were in favor of Algerians' "right to self-determination." 71 percent answered yes. De Gaulle began contemplating negotiations: France might lose Algeria after all. This change in opinion did not, however, mean the end of the war. The referendum galvanized "European" settlers to action, as well as the military officials and conservatives who wanted to keep Algeria French. In February 1961, a determined group of mostly army officers gathered into a semiclandestine guerilla-style organization called the OAS (Secret Armed Organization). Many of its members belonged to the far-right and were committed to fighting those who supported Algerian independence by whatever means necessary, including terrorism. Indeed, violence seemed to increase as the OAS joined the fray on both sides of the Mediterranean, intent on terrorizing and shaping public opinion. They attempted to topple the French government in April 1961. The coup failed but the OAS did not stop there.

Neither did Beauvoir and Sartre stop their own involvement. That summer, in Rome, they met the Martinican intellectual Frantz Fanon. Originally trained as a psychiatrist, he had been appointed to an Algerian psychiatric facility in the early 1950s where he had witnessed the psychological ravages of colonialism. Fanon had immediately joined the FLN cause of "national liberation." Because of his close involvement and writings in support of independence, he had to go into exile to Tunisia in 1957. By 1961, when he met Sartre and Beauvoir in Rome, he was gravely sick with leukemia. Beauvoir found him fascinating. She said that when she "shook his feverish hand, [she] felt as if she could touch the [revolutionary] passion that consumed him."[51] She added, "Next to him," one felt that "life was a tragic adventure that often turned horrifying but that nonetheless had an infinite price."[52] She identified with his anguish at the effects of violence and admired his unshakeable determination and commitment to the cause of the Algerian revolution. Beauvoir was rarely dazzled by those she met, but she felt Fanon was an "exceptional" and rare person.[53] At this meeting, Fanon asked Sartre to write an introduction to the powerful political pamphlet he had just completed, *The Wretched of the Earth* (*Les damnés de la terre*) that explained the necessity of violent armed struggle in the face of colonial state violence. After this meeting Beauvoir felt calmer for a little while. Anger and exhaustion returned quickly, however, when Boupacha was condemned to death on June 28, 1961.

Despite the energy provided by their meeting with Fanon, there seemed to be little hope. While the OAS launched a series of bomb attacks and assassinated those identified as opponents, the government did not ease up on its repression of Algerians. On the evening of October 17, 1961, several hundred Algerian workers tried to demonstrate peacefully in Paris to protest the curfew imposed on them. The police reaction was brutal. Hundreds were wounded, many were taken to internment camps, and unnamed bodies were found the next morning in the river Seine. To this day, the exact number of dead remains unknown. *Modern Times*, *L'Express*, and other leftist and Catholic newspapers denounced what had just happened. Beauvoir agreed with a friend who lamented that, "The French were truly like the Nazis."[54] Communists had finally rallied the anticolonial left against "fascism" in

THE SHAME OF TORTURE. *Simone de Beauvoir, lawyer Gisèle Halimi (left), and legal scholar Professor André Hauriou hold a news conference in support of Djamila Boupacha (Nov. 27, 1961).*

France and were demonstrating against the war and the OAS. Beauvoir sat down to write the introduction to the book defending Djamila Boupacha who still languished in prison while awaiting her execution.[55] There was still no clear and certain sense of the outcome of the war.

However, things accelerated at the beginning of the new year. Suddenly, President de Gaulle, now convinced that it was France's "historical" mission to grant Algeria its independence, started negotiations for a decolonization settlement.[56] The situation was still tense but the tide seemed to be turning at last. The OAS, now desperate to preserve "French Algeria," embarked on another series of "terrorist attacks." On January 4, 1962, they bombed the Paris headquarters of the Communist Party. Between January and February, they set off another 180 bombs. At the end of January, Beauvoir and Halimi published their book on Djamila Boupacha. The cover displayed a striking portrait of Boupacha by Pablo Picasso. Beauvoir and Sartre became OAS targets, alongside other prominent politicians and newspapers. They were targeted because they had, in part, become some of the most famous faces of the anticolonial left. (Sartre's home had been subjected to an unsuccessful bomb during the summer of 1961.) Sartre's apartment was bombed and threats were made against Beauvoir. They moved into hotels, just as they had in the 1930s, but this time, to find refuge rather than freedom. (The OAS even attempted to blackmail famed "Lolita" icon, the actress Brigitte Bardot.) On February 7, the failed bombing of Minister of Culture André Malraux's apartment led to the disfiguration of a five-year old girl. Those events horrified most French people. An innocent French child had been harmed, and public opinion turned against the OAS for good. European settlers in Algeria started crossing the Mediterranean into France. As Beauvoir noted, it was when the war was unraveling and decolonization was becoming certain, that the conflict revealed its "ugliest" side: "Never was the Algerian War the most odious than in the final weeks in which it agonized, it showed its true face."[57] The public in France was, at last, ready to leave Algeria.

In the end, the Evian accords declaring Algeria was no longer a colony were signed on March 18, 1962. Only three days before, the OAS had murdered francophone Algerian writer Mouloud Feraoun. The agreement was ratified by a referendum on April 8: this time, 91 percent of voters agreed that Algeria should be independent. Again, Algerians were not asked to vote. As far as official authorities were concerned, this was a French affair, and Algerians had no say in the matter. For Beauvoir, the end of the war "was taking place under the worst conditions."[58] People had voted not out of conviction but because they had been scared by the OAS's use of violence on metropolitan soil. Djamila Boupacha was liberated the following month. Beauvoir felt relief but little joy. The last four years had been exhausting. She had not suffered directly, but she had lost friends, witnessed unjust violence, and seen the worst of her fellow citizens. At the end of her memoir, Beauvoir wrote, "After she returned from holidays, she moved back into her apartment. The blue and cold Fall poured into her studio. For the first time in years, [she] crossed Algerian workers in the streets who were smiling."[59] Beauvoir did not offer any comment. She added, "The sky felt less heavy. Now she could begin looking back."[60] The war that had no name had ended at last.

CONCLUSION: WRITING THE SELF AND A LIFE ENMESHED

The Algerian War ended abruptly, but its effects lingered for a long time. As soon as the war ended, Beauvoir forged ahead with *The Force of Circumstance* (*La force des choses*), which ended up being a lengthy two-volume autobiography on the period from 1945 until 1962. Again, Beauvoir provided stories of the intellectual milieu in which she lived, reflections on her writing and on Sartre's work, and long accounts of her travels throughout the world. But it was the Algerian War and its emotional and political effects on her life that made up most of the memoir. Beauvoir talked at length of the ways she had become an engaged intellectual with the Algerian

War. Her emphasis on her own "lived experience" of the war resonated with many of her readers who wrote to her as soon as it was
published in 1963, barely a year after Algerian independence.
Many had felt as ashamed and as alienated as she had.[61] But Beauvoir also felt deeply misunderstood by the public who seemed not
to have grasped the historical weight of this conflict. It was the
epilogue that struck her readers and the critics. It seemed strangely
melancholic. Meditating on time and age, Beauvoir concluded,
"she had been swindled."[62] That last statement suggested not joy
but bitterness. The end of the memoir in July 1962, only four
months after Algerian independence, further emphasized that
this war had been all consuming, an obsession, and a turning
point. Beauvoir's tale of a life enmeshed in the world suggested
lost innocence that was never to be recovered. All she could say
was that she "had aged."[63]

Beauvoir continued devoting herself to the world of politics
and literature. They could no longer be separated. In 1964 she
wrote a long preface for Violette Leduc's novel, *The Illegitimate
Child* (*La bâtarde*). She praised the novel because it showed "a
woman turning to her self's innermost secret and telling her story
with the most daring honesty as if there was no one around to
listen."[64] This kind of literature embodied the "victory of freedom
over fate."[65] Beauvoir's comments on the novel revealed much
about her own vision of the world in the wake of the previous ten
years. Her unwavering faith in misunderstood but talented writer
Violette Leduc (whom she had long supported financially), her
analysis of the cultural phenomena that the actress Brigitte
Bardot embodied, her involvement at Gisèle Halimi's side in the
defense of young Algerian fighter, Djamila Boupacha, and her
own autobiographical writing slowly crystallized what Beauvoir
had long thought about but never really directly addressed: "The
problem [of women's situation] was still not solved." She did not,
however, fully join feminist battles. As the 1960s unfolded, politics
seized her, and Beauvoir was compelled to act as the politically
engaged intellectual she had become.[66]

CHAPTER 6

ACTING IN THE WORLD: POLITICS, PARADOXES, AND DISILLUSIONS, 1961–1970

BY THE EARLY 1960s, Beauvoir had become one of the preeminent literary voices in France. The world around her was changing rapidly, sometimes in unexpected ways. Beauvoir did not pay much attention to any of this. For her, in 1961, only the Algerian War mattered. The last words of her 1963 memoir simply read that, after these exhausting and difficult eight years, she had "aged."[1] She was fifty-four years old. The three memoirs she had written so far had provided her the opportunity to reflect on the time that had passed. Now, she had to reflect on an event that proved more upsetting than she had anticipated: the death of her mother. Beauvoir did what she had always done, she told the story of her mother's illness and her death in a short novel she published the following year, in 1964. She spoke about the indignity of illness and the loneliness of death, as well as the hypocrisy of the medical profession that infantilized those in its care. Beauvoir had never been close to her mother who "knew very little about her life," "was shocked by her books," and yet "flattered" by her daughter's success.[2] She did not hide the ambivalence of her feelings toward her mother as well as her own failings, noting that, too often, they had "paralyzed one another."[3] She gave her book the sardonic title of *A Very Easy Death* (*Une mort très douce*). This moving account of age and death again offered a meditation on the ways consciousness was always embodied.

This new decade did not just involve loss and sadness for Beauvoir. After 1962, it also involved contradictory emotions. This was the paradox of her life after the Algerian War ended. Success, celebrity, and politics demanded her attention. However, at the same time as Beauvoir delved in the world, she sometimes felt disenchanted. In 1964, she prefaced her long-time protégée's Violette Leduc's novel, which came out to great acclaim. Finally, French readers saw what Beauvoir had always known: Leduc was a rare and powerful literary voice which deserved attention. *Modern Times* now enjoyed over twenty thousand subscribers. Sartre and Beauvoir had become world-renowned postwar intellectuals. People listened and their opinions mattered—on all topics from the Civil Rights movement that shook America, to the nuclear threat, to the decolonization movements sweeping through the world. It is true the specters of the past were not yet buried: several controversies resurrected them and, this time, Beauvoir, intervened directly. The 1960s, in fact, inaugurated her most politically involved period as writer and public figure. She and Sartre traveled everywhere, thanks to their status as politically engaged intellectuals though, often, Beauvoir felt ambivalent about this intellectual tourism. They were asked to intervene in debates and lend their names to causes. Still, she stayed away from activism. Even as they were becoming more involved, Sartre and Beauvoir felt disillusioned in the face of what they saw as failed attempts at justice, equality, and progress especially in socialist countries. Beauvoir often felt out of touch with her contemporaries, especially as the world changed around her.

The economic recovery that had begun in the 1950s had engulfed most of Europe. Unemployment declined drastically and prosperity became available to large numbers as more and more people now had the income to purchase cars, televisions, fridges, and move into new modern-looking housing blocks built in most cities across Europe. Better lives, however, did not necessarily mean the end of political conflicts and tensions. In August 1961, the East German communist government built a wall separating West and East Berlin. The wall, the East German authorities claimed, was designed to "protect against fascism." The wall did more than protect. It also prevented East Germans from crossing over into West Germany, as more than two million had done since 1945. The wall was an extensive cement construction that involved barbed wires, tower guards, alarms, and more than ten thousand soldiers who did not hesitate to shoot those attempting to cross. The wall divided families and neighborhoods. Western European powers did not react but people feared another world war might erupt. On October 22, 1961, American tanks faced off against Soviet tanks at Checkpoint Charlie. They did ultimately stand down. A war had been avoided. This was the new face of the Cold War.

That same year, in France, ethnographer Jean Rouch and sociologist Edgar Morin decided to film an experimental documentary about Parisians' everyday life, *Chronicle of a Summer* (*Chronique d'un été*). A small camera crew meandered through the streets of Paris and asked random individuals whether there were happy. What did happiness mean to a Parisian in 1961? The Algerian War was never directly mentioned but hovered in the background. A young Congolese student shared his experience of colonialism with an Italian immigrant and car factory worker, Angelo. Micheline, a young professional woman, unveiled she was a survivor of Auschwitz and her father had died there. Life was exciting, freer, some argued. Others did not know how to answer. Beauvoir's response would have talked of disenchantment and mourning.

SPECTERS OF WAR IN THE WORLD

In the early 1960s, Beauvoir and Sartre were literary and political celebrities. They towered in the French world of politics and letters. They were still controversial, admired by many and reviled by others. They were no longer a couple in the conventional sense, and had not been for a while. Sartre enjoyed a number of relationships and affairs. Among these, a relationship with a nineteen-year-old Algerian-born philosophy student, Arlette Elkaïm, which had begun in the late 1950s, proved the most enduring. After the end of her relationship with Claude Lanzmann, Beauvoir had met a young philosophy student in 1960 named Sylvie Le Bon, who became her most trusted and cherished companion until her death. Though Sartre and Beauvoir saw one another every day, as they had done for the last thirty years, and understood their involvement in the world to be a common enterprise, their emotional and sexual lives lay elsewhere. To the world, however, Sartre and Beauvoir were still a mythical couple. Their celebrity spilled over in their lives: they traveled even more widely than before, always together. Often, these invitations came because they were seen as the most important Western left-wing intellectuals, still committed to socialism, and whose analyses (as in the case of Sartre in those years) attempted to bring Marxist theory to life. They had already visited China in 1955, and Cuba and Brazil in 1960. In 1962, they were invited by the Union of Soviet writers to spend a month in Russia. Beauvoir wrote that Moscow "dazzled" her in contrast to China.[4] They were then invited to give a series of conferences in Japan in September 1966, where more than one hundred photographers awaited them.[5] Everywhere they went, photos of them appeared in magazines and newspapers.

Beauvoir confessed later that, despite her long-lasting passion for travel, these trips held little joy for her.[6] She was still reeling from the exhaustion of the Algerian War. But exhaustion never stopped her. Being an intellectual required that she ignore these personal feelings. Being a left-wing intellectual also meant she and Sartre had to face the disillusions they experienced when they saw communist regimes had not always brought freedom and happiness to their citizens but could be as authoritarian and brutal as right-wing dictatorships. When they returned to Moscow in 1966, they felt much had changed. After the forced resignation of Nikita Khrushchev, censorship returned with force and political repression tightened. The Soviet regime imprisoned writers, and communist dissidents were divided over how best to influence the course of politics.[7] Sartre and Beauvoir refused to attend the Soviet Writer's Congress the following year.[8] The Chinese Cultural Revolution initiated by Mao Zedong mobilized Chinese youth who were charged by their leader with "purging" society of its bourgeois and ideologically suspect members. The issue divided the *Modern Times* editorial committee and confused Beauvoir.

It was not just the communist East that worried and disappointed them. The West seemed not to have learned the lessons of decolonization. After the atrocities of the Algerian War that Beauvoir and others had denounced, the Vietnam War looked

POLITICAL TRAVELS AND DISILLUSIONS. *Simone de Beauvoir and Jean-Paul Sartre* (left) *visit Moscow and talk to Russian artist Gleb Sainchuk, who has drawn them (May 1, 1966).*

to be a repetition of the horrors of Western imperialism refusing to face the tide of history. Beauvoir was "outraged."[9] When the Vietnam War escalated in 1965, after ten years of conflict, many around the world publicly decried American involvement in this "imperialist war." Mass protests had not yet engulfed the United States, though Civil Rights movement activists and students on college campuses mounted campaigns against it. Whereas the Algerian War had divided French people and only a minority opposed it at first, this time, the opposition to the war was widespread: intellectuals, the media, young students, workers, and political elites criticized American involvement. Beauvoir and Sartre were, of course, among them. Polls taken in the fall of 1966 and 1967 indicated that 68 percent and 72 percent of French people supported an American withdrawal from Vietnam.[10] After all, to outside observers, the United States appeared to be the theater of political violence and fierce conflicts: Europeans had watched television broadcasts about the assassination of President John F. Kennedy in 1962 and that of the African-American antiracist activist Malcolm X three years later. It seemed Fanon's writings on the violence of decolonization born out of the violence of (colonial) racism had predicted more than the Algerian War of Independence.

In an effort to initiate a worldwide public denunciation of the Vietnam War, Sartre and Beauvoir became involved in a novel initiative. In the fall of 1967, they took part in the recently founded International Tribunal on War Crimes, otherwise known as the Russell Tribunal. The tribunal had been set up in the wake of the 1966 publication of Nobel Prize–winning British philosopher Bertrand Russell's *War Crimes in Vietnam*. Because Russell could not preside over the proceedings, it was Sartre (who had refused the Nobel Prize three years earlier), who was asked to take his place. Since President Charles de Gaulle refused to allow the tribunal to meet in France, its meetings took place in Stockholm. This was not a tribunal in the traditional sense. There was no official court, nor any government overseeing it. Inspired by the

1945 Nuremberg trials and the 1948 Universal Declaration of Human Rights, it was to judge whether the United States was guilty of war crimes in Vietnam.[11] International in focus, it involved many prominent intellectuals and writers such as the African-American novelist James Baldwin (who could not attend), the student activist Stokely Carmichael, Yugoslav historian Vladimir Dedijer as well as pacifist activists, dissidents, and lawyers such as Gisèle Halimi.

Beauvoir was one of the participants.[12] Her presence had been sought at the same time as Sartre's. Tribunal members read and listened to reports drawn up by independent investigators on the American use of chemical weapons (which had been prohibited since World War I) and whether the United States was involved in genocide. Beauvoir was, yet again, horrified by photos

WAR CRIMES ON TRIAL. *Jean-Paul Sartre (center), Simone de Beauvoir, and Yugoslav historian, Vladimir Dedijer hold a press conference to report on the Russell Tribunal in the People's House, Stockholm (Apr. 10, 1967).*

and films of "burned, mutilated" and wounded civilians, and of "children whose arms had been torn, faces deformed, and bodies eaten away by napalm." She commented, "The bodies burnt from the napalm of phosphorus reminded them of the photos [they] had seen in the Hiroshima museum."[13] While she took the ambitions and purpose of the tribunal seriously and found the work fascinating, she said she was often bored during the deliberations.[14] Even though she approved of the efforts to mobilize against the Vietnam War, she explained acting like a lawyer or prosecutor did not suit her.

War crimes were not just an issue for other nations elsewhere in the world. France was beginning to face its own past. It was not the torture, internment, and violence of the Algerian War that fueled debates. In fact, as Beauvoir noted, most French citizens and politicians alike were only too eager to forget this brutal conflict. In France, and elsewhere, people began reflecting on the nature of Nazi crimes. World War II still haunted Europe, especially as the world was becoming more aware of the specificity of Nazi crimes against European Jews. In France, many authors and Jewish survivors had written about the Holocaust immediately after the war (which was not referred to in these terms then). At the time, however, the French government had not distinguished between those deported for their political opinions and activism, and those who had been persecuted and deported because they were Jewish. Instead, the emphasis had been on the unity of the French nation. Recovery and reconstruction had meant forgetting the complexities of Nazi oppression and French complicity. In 1955, Alain Resnais's short and moving documentary, *Night and Fog*, had spoken eloquently about the "concentration world" the Nazis had created; yet, it had said nothing of the ghettos and death camps where Jews from all over Europe had been sent to die. Those questions were reignited with what became known as the "Treblinka affair."[15] This controversy involved Beauvoir, who tackled the difficult task of addressing France's recent past.

Unlike most other French intellectuals, Beauvoir realized the importance of tackling the nature of the Nazi genocidal project since she had paid attention to the Eichmann trial, which had taken place in Israel in 1961. Eichmann had been a high-ranking Nazi officer and bureaucrat who had authorized the deportation and murder of many Jews across Europe. His trial had been televised for the world to watch. Another philosopher, the New York–based German Jewish exile Hannah Arendt had attended the trial and published her analysis in 1963 in a book entitled *Eichmann in Jerusalem: A Report on the Banality of Evil.* Although Arendt's book caused a scandal in the English-speaking world, few in France had read it. In 1966, it had not yet been translated into French.[16] Despite some coverage by the mainstream media (including an article by Claude Lanzmann in *France-Soir,* and a piece by *Modern Times* contributor, the philosopher Robert Misrahi), the trial had not featured heavily in the French news. It was, at the time, overshadowed by the Algerian War and the escalation of metropolitan violence.[17] Beauvoir took her cue from this controversy and, in keeping with her participation in initiatives like the Russell Tribunal, took an active part in the "Treblinka affair."

In 1966, a young twenty-eight-year-old Frenchman, Jean-François Steiner, published what he claimed to be a historical account of the fate of Jews in the Treblinka extermination camp. As Beauvoir explained in her preface to the book, Steiner, "like many young Jews of his generation who have not experienced Nazism, are now asking questions."[18] (Steiner's father had been deported to Auschwitz.) In an interview, Steiner explained he had been motivated by his desire to address his "embarrassment at being a child of this people of whom six million allowed themselves to be led to slaughter like lambs."[19] In the book, he focused specifically on the uprising organized by an underground Jewish resistance group that took place in Treblinka on August 2, 1943, and that nearly succeeded in derailing the camp machinery that murdered almost a million Jewish men, women, and children. Steiner's narrative took the counterpoint of explanations that prevailed then which had usually emphasized the universalism of the Nazi murder machine. He sought instead to reveal its intentional antisemitic mass murder project. However, Steiner's insistent focus on the "heroic" figures of those who rebelled meant that, in contrast, the majority of Treblinka's Jewish victims were portrayed as "passive," as if most "victims of the genocide" had been complicit "in their own death."[20]

Five years after Arendt's study, Steiner's book was a bestseller. *Modern Times* had already published extracts in February 1966, preparing the ground for the book's publication in March.[21] It sold one hundred thousand copies in the first year. Beauvoir's preface helped tremendously. She had first met Steiner when he published an article on his time as a soldier in Algeria in *Modern Times*. She was enthralled by the book and said as much in her preface. It was, however, a scandal for many intellectuals. While she warned that his efforts were "courageous," that he might even be "accused of antisemitism," her own analysis hardly helped Steiner's cause.[22] She defended his controversial use of fictional dialogue and "staging." Rather than engaging other scholars on the matter of the nature of the genocidal project and on antisemitism, Beauvoir borrowed from Sartre's 1960 *Critique of Dialectical Reason* and analysis of "voluntary servitude." She insisted on the fact that the Nazis had "divided" their victims "in order to conquer," ignoring the ways Nazis had ruthlessly targeted a population, Jews, and implemented their genocidal project. Instead, borrowing from a Marxist framework, she problematically compared Jewish victims to "workers under capitalism" who had been "serialized" by an oppressive system.[23] Beauvoir failed to grasp the foundational elements of the Nazi project and attend to its Jewish victims' experience. In this, she echoed her own inability twenty years earlier to fully grasp what her young friend Bianca Bienenfeld had experienced as she hid from the Vichy regime.

Still, she defended Steiner against accusations that he had portrayed "Jews as cowards."[24] Beauvoir did not shy away from the debate, giving interviews in the *Nouvel Observateur*, and insisting Steiner must be read and his insights discussed. Here, Beauvoir showed her intellectual loyalty and convictions: she never went back on her support of those she wholeheartedly approved. She had done as much seven years earlier, in 1959, when she had defended literary newcomer André Schwarz-Bart's Goncourt-winning Holocaust novel, *The Last of the Just* (*Le dernier des justes*), which had been accused of plagiarism, just as she had always defended Violette Leduc against accusations of obscenity. More than ever before, Beauvoir felt words mattered and understood her celebrity, name, and prestige should be put to use for particular causes.

WOMEN'S LIVES AND A CHANGING SOCIETY

Beauvoir's name did matter. In the early 1960s, for the first time, a number of studies on her work were published, their titles pointing to her thought on "freedom," "the refusal of indifference," or "the failure of Christianity."[25] A 1964 poll asking French women which female figure they most admired had ranked Beauvoir second.[26] She was not just famous: a new generation of readers was rediscovering her earlier works. Many younger people were reading *The Second Sex* for the first time. Some of these readers asked her to contribute and support their efforts on behalf of women. In the 1930s, Beauvoir had not been a feminist, and feminism had little meaning for her. Neither had she claimed that mantle when she published *The Second Sex* in 1949. In fact, she had asserted that what mattered most was, first, analyzing the conditions of women's oppression before considering acting. Still, her novels continued fictionalizing these same preoccupations.

In 1966, Beauvoir published *Beautiful Images* (*Les belles images*), the title of which evoked the myths that, too often, as she had explained in *The Second Sex*, women succumbed to. The novel charted a moment in the life of a middle-aged woman, Laurence. She could have been a "modern reader" of women's magazines, such as *Elle* created in 1945, after World War II—a woman of her time. Laurence was an accomplished professional, working in publicity, and who worried about the fate of her two teenage daughters. Laurence sought comfort from her boring marriage with a lover. Beauvoir describes a woman unsure of who she is or should be, who finds herself unable to answer her anguished teenage daughter's question: "Why do we exist?" Laurence embodied many of the female figures Beauvoir had portrayed in *The Second Sex*: forged by others, unable to craft their own sense of agency, and embroiled in the trappings of femininity, despite their apparent professional and personal successes. As Beauvoir explained several years later, she had wanted to portray "a problematic heroine" who "discovers the world she lives in."[27]

Beauvoir's character encapsulated what was happening around her. Women's lives had changed. More women entered universities, earned an income, and had professional careers. Consumerism and modernization had reshaped their living conditions. But too many of the legal restrictions weighing on their lives were still in place. Despite the political rights that they had been granted in 1946, there were still few women in politics. Women constituted less than 4 percent of parliamentary representatives in the 1951 and 1956 legislative elections. It was elsewhere that challenges were mounting. New groups had emerged, specifically focusing on and appealing to women, such as the protestant *Young Women's Movement* (*Mouvement de jeunes filles*). Many of these young women had experienced the war and had read *The Second Sex*, "claiming for themselves a philosophy of engagement" inspired by Sartre's and Beauvoir's existentialism.[28] At the same time, an older generation of women intellectuals and writers had come to prominence alongside Beauvoir, including her long-time friend, Colette Audry and the sociologist Evelyne Sullerot. Many of these women had resisted during the war (unlike Beauvoir), embraced communism, or been favorable to left-wing ideals. They were not only accomplished but also committed to changing the status quo they had inherited and were active publicly and even politically. Some attempted to take matters into their own hands.

One of the issues that rallied many of these movements was the issue of birth control and abortion. The 1920 law that made birth control and abortion illegal and that forbade any publicity or advocacy for birth control was still in effect. A doctor and gynecologist, Marie-Andrée Lagroua Weill-Hallé, decided to tackle the issue. She had read Beauvoir's works and, like her, did not consider herself a feminist. She was also an unlikely advocate because she was Catholic. However, her years as doctor had shown her the horrifying ordeal and effects of abortions performed without anesthesia by doctors who looked upon their patients with contempt.[29] That experience had convinced her that women must be able to have control over their own bodies. The newspaper France Observateur's provocative headline, "Are 600,000 Abortions Better Than Birth Control?" summed up her feelings.[30] In March 1956, she created an organization called "Happy Motherhood" designed to help women argue for the right to birth control, promote its use, and advocate for the sexual education of couples that Weill-Hallé deemed crucial for happy family life. Protestants overall supported Weill-Hallé's efforts. Catholics were predictably hostile to it. Communists also opposed it (just as they had attacked Beauvoir's The Second Sex in 1949), as they were overall more conservative when it came to matters of sexuality, and believed this distracted from questions of class and economics. Weill-Hallé asked Beauvoir, whose respectability had been enhanced by the overwhelming success of her 1958 Memoirs of a Dutiful Daughter, to lend her name and write a preface to the pamphlet she published in 1959, Family Planning.[31] Beauvoir readily agreed: she had long argued that motherhood could be a burden and too often imprisoned women. She was more circumspect when she saw the ways the book was received and wryly noted, "At the word abortion, faces turned away; as for sex, it was everywhere absent."[32]

In 1960, "Happy Motherhood" became the "French Move-ment for Family Planning." In addition to Beauvoir, its board in-cluded Colette Audry, Clara Malraux, the *Express* co-editor Francoise Giroud, *France Observateur*'s political editor Gilles Martinet, League of the Rights of Man director Daniel Mayer, and many other prominent personalities.[33] Catholics were still opposed to it, and older feminist organizations remained ambiv-alent. Still, a greater number of women under thirty and working women were able to attend its clinics where contraceptives, diaphragms, and spermicides could be prescribed, since it was a private club and therefore not officially a medical office.[34] That year, Weill-Hallé publicized the issue with another book again prefaced by Beauvoir, *Fearing Love* (*La Grand' peur d'aimer*) in which she chronicled her work with women and couples. *Family Planning*'s activities exploded after 1965, and leftist organizations and women's organizations began openly supporting its work.[35] As the details of Beauvoir's arguments gained a greater reader-ship, more and more people (and even some Catholics) became convinced of the need to reform the laws governing women's marital status, right to birth control, and equality in work.

By the time Beauvoir published *Beautiful Images* in 1966, clamors for political and legal change in women's status started emerging across the political spectrum. Once the Catholic hier-archy had renounced its staunch opposition and the Communist Party finally rallied the left's commitment to abolishing the 1920 law, reform seemed inevitable. A Gaullist deputy who was firmly convinced of the necessity of birth control, Lucien Neuwirth, in-troduced a bill in December 1967 calling for the legalization of birth control, especially the contraceptive pill. The law was de-bated, some of it amended, and passed on December 19, 1967. The Neuwirth law, as it became known, was promulgated less than ten days later, on December 28, 1967.

Despite this momentous legal victory, Beauvoir had not been involved beyond lending her name to prefaces she authored and board membership. It was not that she did not care about the fate of French women. Her collection of short stories, *The Woman Destroyed* (*La femme rompue*) published in 1967 proved her enduring interest in women's condition and lives. Again, the novel illustrated the analyses introduced in *The Second Sex*. It chronicled the lives of three women: an intellectual woman in her sixties (who strikingly resembled Beauvoir), a divorced housewife and mother, and the monologue of a woman rendered "hysterical" by the world around her. Its tone was rather bleak, in stark contrast to the hopes raised by recent legal changes.

However, as with *Beautiful Images*, Beauvoir felt her readers misunderstood her book and lamented that they did not see the critique of the myths of femininity embedded in her fiction. She complained that, instead, her female readers overly identified with her female characters. Though her novels fictionalized what was happening around her, Beauvoir no longer was in sync with her readership. She admitted later that "between 62 and 68, [she] did not pay much attention to what has happening in France."[36] She had worked tirelessly for the Russell Tribunal. She had defended Steiner's book. She agreed to be part of a Canadian documentary about herself and Sartre, yet she answered questions about her involvement in feminism with impatience. Instead, she continued traveling.[37]

POLITICAL TRAVELS AND DISILLUSIONS

Beauvoir traveled to Egypt and Israel in February and March 1967. She had always dreamt of visiting Egypt "ever since [she] was a child."[38] The opportunity came in the wake of *Modern Times* special issue on the Arab-Israeli conflict. She and Sartre were invited with Claude Lanzmann and exiled Egyptian journalist Ali el Saman by Mohamed Hassanein Heikal, a friend and spokesperson for the Egyptian president, Gamal Abdel Nasser.[39] Like many Europeans before her, Beauvoir was awed by the Nile as well as ancient Egyptian relics, sculptures, and mummies held in the museum.

But the sight of the pyramids "next to dusty neighborhoods and the number and agitation of tourists" did not fulfill her long-held fantasies of ancient Egypt. Pyramids looked to her nothing more than "stones piled up one upon another."[40] Beauvoir felt ambivalent about modern Egypt: if she found the old city full of life, she felt modern Cairo's "elegant streets and luxurious shops

INTELLECTUAL TOURISM. *Simone de Beauvoir with Claude Lanzmann (left) and Jean-Paul Sartre (right) visit the pyramids and the Sphinx of Giza (Feb. 1967).*

lacked charm."[41] Beauvoir's account resembled the travelogues of nineteenth-century colonial tourists entranced by ancient civilizations and uninterested in their present. She noted the poverty of villages they went through but said little else about them. She seemed oblivious to Nasser's project to modernize Egypt, preferring to admire its ancient past.

The only topic that captured her attention was the situation of Egyptian women. Every time she went to a new country, Beauvoir paid attention to the condition of women's lives, just as she had reflected on American women's lives in her 1947 travel diary. This time, though, her perception proved biased and partial. After meeting some Egyptian feminists, Beauvoir concluded and told her audience at a conference she gave in Cairo that Egyptians behaved toward women "like feudal lords, colonialists, and racists."[42] Though she was thanked after her speech by several women, Beauvoir's opinions did not necessarily reflect reality but repeated what she had already mapped out in *The Second Sex* almost twenty years earlier, namely her belief that Islam was a backward religion when it came to equality between men and women. Although Beauvoir had always criticized the oppressive tenets of European Christianity, she fell prey to the orientalist belief that Muslim nations were less civilized than Europe, revealing one of the blind spots that haunted many intellectuals in those years.

She said the strong feelings she experienced while visiting Egypt did not leave her as she visited Palestinian refugees in Gaza. She was moved by refugees' living conditions and the "seriousness of the situation," but found Palestinian leaders too "intransigent." She recounted a "tense" conversation where Sartre argued that the best course of action would be to find a way to "balance the right of Palestinians to return to their homeland and the recognition of Israel's right to exist," a position she also held.[43] After their foray into Gaza, they visited Israel. Beauvoir did not like Tel Aviv. She was fascinated by kibbutz life, however, where recent Jewish immigrants worked and lived together in socialist-inspired collective communities. Again, Beauvoir was especially keen to learn about women's and young people's lives.[44] She remained skeptical when her Israeli guests told her feminism was unnecessary in their country since, she observed that traditional gendered divisions of labor prevailed, even on the kibbutzim.[45] She and Sartre asked Israeli leaders what they thought of the "Arab question." Beauvoir concluded that she did not better understand Israeli culture and that Israel remained "foreign" to her.

Events soon challenged Beauvoir's attempt to balance Palestinian refugees' rights with that of Israel's right to exist. Beauvoir wrote, "After the Vietnam war, the political event that most affected her in these last few years, was the Six Day War" of 1967.[46] Until then, Beauvoir explained she had "approved of the creation of Israel" in 1948 "but never felt particularly attached to it." In 1947, she had joined the League for a Free Palestine, which supported the creation of the state of Israel with Sartre, and other French intellectuals Raymond Aron, Paul Claudel, Vladimir Jankélévitch, and Emmanuel Mounier.[47] She had not questioned that commitment, even after visiting Palestinian refugees. When the Six Day War erupted, Beauvoir found herself torn because she "had felt friendship for both nations."[48] Egyptian forces, backed by Syria and Jordan, initiated a blockade of the straits of Tiran in May 1967 that prevented Israeli naval forces from coming and going. (There had been a previous conflict there in 1956, following Nasser's nationalization of the Suez Canal. Egypt had lost militarily but triumphed politically.) Israel retaliated a month later on June 5, with sweeping air and ground attacks. Beauvoir said she was "especially scared for Israel," and the news of the war prevented her from returning to her work.[49] She noted, "In France, public opinion was so divided and impassioned that one could speak of another Dreyfus Affair. Families were torn apart, friendships ended." The right opposed Israel while the noncommunist left was far from united on the issue. Beauvoir said she did not see Israel as an "imperialist aggressor," although she empathized with Palestinians' plight and did not approve of Israeli policies toward Arab populations.[50]

When, to everyone's surprise, Israel won the war, European observers remained just as divided. Israel had swiftly defeated forces that had seemed more powerful. It had expanded its territory, gaining control of Jerusalem, Gaza, the West Bank, the Golan Heights, and the Sinai desert from Egypt and Jordan. Beauvoir found herself at odds with most of the French left that was outraged by Israeli policies and embraced the Palestinian cause. Even French Jewish families, she wrote, were torn over the issue.[51] Antiimperialist leftist activism was more divided than it had been about the Algerian War, and Beauvoir found herself no longer in tune with younger generations and others on the far-left regarding the conflict.

Just as events like the Six Day War caused her anguish, she felt mostly disappointment at the outcome of socialist revolutions of the previous decade. Beauvoir wrote she could no longer have "blind faith for revolutionary programs" as she had once done for the Soviet Union.[52] She was disappointed by Cuba and events in Latin America. Even Algeria seemed not to have fulfilled the hopes unleashed by independence. Beauvoir said she found Algerian domestic politics "nationalist and reactionary" and the condition of women "deplorable."[53] In the United States, racism still prevailed despite the Civil Rights movement, sit-ins, marches, and the legal gains of the mid-1960s that had ended segregation. On April 4, 1968, Martin Luther King Jr. was murdered and, soon, the revolutionary "Black Panthers were hunted, imprisoned, and assassinated." There seemed to be little hope for progress. Beauvoir wondered whether these disappointments would lead to a worldwide uprising, but added wistfully, that she was not sure she "would live long enough to witness" such uprisings.[54]

MAY '68: THE WORLD EXPLODES

Yet, "revolutionary impulses" did reemerge. When "May '68" erupted in Paris and throughout France, Beauvoir was sixty years old. She had just published the bleak and pessimistic collection of stories, *The Woman Destroyed*. (It had been published in install-ments in the popular *Elle* magazine.) Few would have predicted the events of "May '68" that engulfed not only France but most of the West, from Prague to San Francisco. It was an "explosion."[55] A generation of young people born after the war had come of age and eagerly demanded political, social, and economic reforms. State socialism and communism no longer held the same promise that they had thirty years ago. The Vietnam War and other decol-onization conflicts had convinced this younger generation of the need for more radical oppositional politics. In contrast to the self-deception, frustration, and rage that Beauvoir had fictional-ized in her short stories, the events of "May '68" brought her hope and energy. These revolts and demonstrations pointed to the cri-tique of consumerism and commodification that she had talked about in *Beautiful Images* and clamored for radical reinvention. She noted after the fact that, in contrast to "the defenders of estab-lished order [who] refused to see anything else but a youthful and pseudo-romantic explosion in the events of May, it was, in fact, a societal crisis; not only a generational crisis."[56] Beauvoir was right: "May '68" was a social, political, and cultural revolution.

What some have called France's "last revolution" when speak-ing of the events of May '68 began elsewhere.[57] In April 1968, the former oppositional leader of Czechoslovakia, Alexander Dubcek, gave a speech in which he called for a new form of socialism "with a human face" and announced reforms: the reaffirmation of the freedom of press, and the rights to gather and to express opinions. He called for a more democratic Czechoslovakia at the crossroads of the communist East and the capitalist West. This was the Prague Spring. The promise of a brighter, more peaceful, and more democratic future seemed more elusive in the United States: at the beginning of 1968, America was reeling from the news of the January Tet Offensive, which had revealed the determination of the Vietnamese forces and highlighted the short-sightedness of American forces. College campuses were bristling with mounting protests against the Vietnam War and demonstrations against the racism of American society. The Black Panthers, founded only a year earlier, pressed the limits of non-violent activism and engaged in community initiatives designed to reveal the profound inequities afflicting African-Americans. In February, they were joined by Student Non Violent Coordinating Committee leaders such as Stokely Carmichael, who had returned from the 1967 proceedings of the Russell Tribunal. The assassination of Martin Luther King Jr. on April 4, 1968, in Memphis, however, sent shock waves through the nation and the world.

In contrast, at first glance, little seemed to have changed in France. President de Gaulle was still in power. The young pop idol, Claude François, enchanted listeners with his catchy tunes on the weekly TV program aimed at young people *Hello Friends* (*Salut Les Copains*). Despite the apparent well-being of a French society gleaming with consumerist objects, discontent was brewing. Unemployment resurfaced, affecting first those entering the job market. Factory workers like *Chronicle of a Summer* participant, Angelo, or the Algerian immigrant workers living in shantytowns were not privy to the benefits of the "Glorious Years." Those joining university ranks (many of whom were women) were impatient for change. In 1968, because of the postwar baby boom and greater access to secondary education, the number of university students had grown tremendously. However, these students found derelict infrastructures unable to welcome them, antiquated courses, and professors that seemed out of touch and old-fashioned. Older commentators and journalists did not notice the discontent or the political and intellectual effervescence that had begun seeping from the universities to the streets. A journalist wrote in March 1968 in the widely read newspaper *Le Monde* that "France is bored."[58] Barely two months later, his headline proved foolish and short-sighted.

The demonstrations, riots, and strikes that erupted in May did not come out of nowhere. The intellectual world had been bristling with new ideas and concepts. Thinkers like ENS philosophy professor Louis Althusser and sociologist Edgar Morin (who had been expelled from the Communist Party in 1951) were reinventing Marxist thought. Other intellectuals developed different theoretical visions of the nature of society, culture, and individuals, a strand of thought that came to be known as "structuralism." Thinkers as diverse as the psychoanalyst Jacques Lacan, the anthropologist Claude-Lévi-Strauss, the literary theorist Roland Barthes, and the philosopher Michel Foucault each explained that human culture is best understood as the expression of larger structures that shape it. Individuals come into being through these existing structures. Many of these thinkers rejected existentialism with its focus on individual autonomy and freedom. They also refused Sartre's model of "engagement" and thought he and Beauvoir were politically outdated. While *Modern Times* published a special issue on structuralism, Beauvoir remained unconvinced (just as she had criticized the 1950s "New Novel," which had earlier swept through the literary scene). Few people outside intellectual circles read these new theories when they were published in 1966. Nonetheless, their emergence suggested a challenge to conventional thought and a desire for a different society. At the same time, discontent and frustration simmered in French society.

"The events" of '68, as they became known, took everyone by surprise. Beauvoir said she did not "realize the importance of the first troubles."[59] The first demonstrations took place on the university campus of Nanterre, just outside of Paris. This brand new university, built in 1964, was designed to welcome two thousand students and help relieve overcrowded Parisian institutions. In 1968, however, it was already over-enrolled with twelve thousand students. The very location of Nanterre seemed to embody the contradictions of postwar French society. The university was built in a working-class suburb next to shantytowns that housed almost ten thousand immigrant workers (most of them Algerian) who lived without running water or electricity. For many of the students, anti-imperialism, anti-militarism, criticism of consumerism and of the injustices of a bourgeois society that oppressed both workers and immigrants came together in pamphlets and manifestos they wrote and circulated throughout the spring of 1968. Mobilization against the Vietnam War radicalized many students and when the university was closed in response to a student protest, the situation exploded.

After the closing of Nanterre on May 3, the same day that talks between the North Vietnamese and the Americans began in Paris, students went to the center of the capital to demonstrate and were met by police forces.[60] In the face of an unexpected and ruthless police crackdown, student and teacher unions called for another demonstration three days later. More than twenty thousand marched on May 6, protesting the sealing of the Latin Quarter neighborhood and the closing of the Sorbonne by authorities. The police responded with tear gas and barricades were built. Tensions remained high as negotiations between students and authorities failed. The government refused to back down and, on May 10, police and students clashed in a confrontation that lasted all night. As Beauvoir noted, "on the night of May 10," the "barricades" on the Left bank, "burned cars" and the violence unleashed by the police showed "the riot had become an uprising."[61] Students took back the Sorbonne. A general strike mobilizing both students and workers was called for May 13.

When demonstrations erupted, Beauvoir did not go down to the streets to join those protesting as she had done during the Algerian War. She listened to the radio, which broadcast news of the events hour by hour.[62] Sartre, on the other hand, enthused by what he saw, declared his support for the students on radio Luxembourg on May 12.[63] The student demonstrations gained support from workers, intellectuals, artists, and others who were outraged by police brutality and critical of de Gaulle's policies as well as eager to challenge capitalism, imperialism, and consumerism. Almost one million marched on May 13. As one historian has noted, "there were more than 450 demonstrations on that day throughout the country especially in towns with working-class populations."[64] The prime minister, Georges Pompidou, tried to contain the situation and the Sorbonne was reopened. However, the following weeks did not bring a return to "normalcy." Indeed, Beauvoir wondered, "Whether repression could contain the new forces that had just been unleashed?"[65] Like her, others hoped revolution rather than repression would prevail.

Students continued occupying the lecture halls and corridors of the ancient and venerable Sorbonne university, plastering its walls with whimsical and witty slogans such as "Take your desires for reality," or "Under the cobblestones lies the beach." These were not empty demands. Informal groups met to decide how best to transform society, many demanded greater sexual, social, and political freedom. Others debated how to join forces with other student movements elsewhere in the world. Beauvoir never became an active participant but, like other intellectuals who were both fascinated and eager to support what was happening, she "went often with [her] friends prowling through the corridors and quads" of the Sorbonne. As they "meandered," they "talked and listened" to some of the discussions taking place: "many focused on the Israeli conflict and the Palestinian issue."[66] This movement was not led by intellectuals. It had erupted from below. As one slogan claimed, "Power is in the street."

What turned May '68 into "France's last revolution" and differentiated France from other '68 uprisings throughout Europe was the worker mobilization that followed and the ways it spread throughout the country. After the May 13 demonstrations, workers spontaneously went on strike and started occupying factories not just in Paris but eventually throughout the whole country. Nine million workers went on strike. A week later, there were almost twenty-three occupied factories. More than eighty thousand workers demanded radical changes in their working conditions.[67] They criticized the capitalist system that alienated them.[68] As Beauvoir noted, these demonstrations showed "the contradictions of "neo-capitalism," which is why an entire "system" had been challenged and workers had been as concerned as students."[69] As she and Sartre were in the habit of doing, Beauvoir lent her name to this mass popular opposition that seemed close to unseating established power: the newspaper *Le Monde* published a manifesto which explained to readers that Simone de Beauvoir, Colette Audry, Jean-Paul Sartre, Michel Leiris, and Daniel Guérin "call on all workers and intellectuals to support the struggle and movement initiated by students and professors both morally and intellectually." They were invited by students to talk at the Sorbonne on May 20.[70] Even then, Beauvoir and Sartre remained more witnesses than participants.

To most French people watching the events on their televisions, a revolution was underway. Almost half a million demonstrators marched in Paris on May 30 demanding President de Gaulle's resignation. In the face of this intractable situation, de Gaulle announced on that day he was dissolving parliament and calling for an election, accusing strikers and demonstrators of being "communist agitators." Strikes subsided. To the left's surprise, de Gaulle's party won the majority. But the government's authority had been shaken. When de Gaulle proposed a referendum less than a year later, on April 27, 1969 (just as he had done to end the Algerian War), his reform proposals were rejected by more than half the voters. He resigned, to the delight of young leftist activists and older intellectuals like Beauvoir.[71]

At the end of 1968, Beauvoir and Sartre went to Prague to support communist reformers in the face of the brutal Soviet crackdown, which left thousands dead. In her memoir, Beauvoir recounted the events but her tone suggested more distance than many of the previous struggles she had joined. That visit, though, brought about Sartre and Beauvoir's definite break with the Soviet Union. Back in France, they offered the use of *Modern Times* to some May '68 student leaders, but the project folded.[72] In the end, the May '68 revolution may have failed, but there was still the promise of radical changes as a new generation clamored for reforms. Though they had not been active participants, Beauvoir and Sartre understood political change was still possible and lent the weight of their celebrity and prestige to the collective struggles that emerged in the wake of May '68.

CONCLUSION: NEW GENERATIONS, NEW POLITICS, 1968–1970

Surprisingly, Beauvoir confessed that "unlike other intellectuals, May '68 had not shaken" her.[73] It is true the Algerian War had been a much greater shock that had consumed her entirely. For most of the 1960s, she was absorbed by events outside France. She did not belong to the younger generation of intellectuals who had come of age after the Second World War and who imagined a different world, unburdened by the weight of two world wars and the Cold War. While young people descended into the streets and built barricades, Beauvoir was involved in another project at odds with what was happening around her. She had begun a study of old age in 1967. She had already tackled the issue briefly in *The Second Sex* and at the end of *The Force of Circumstance*. This time, her interest emerged out of her experience and that of her mother's death.

Beauvoir imagined this study of old age as "symmetrical to *The Second Sex*."[74] She aimed to describe the experience of old age in its "totality."[75] But writing on this topic proved more challenging than writing on the condition of women because, as she explained, old age remained a "shameful secret," a "forbidden topic," and an invisible problem.[76] It was not considered a serious subject. When she went to the Bibliothèque Nationale, Beauvoir found little written on the topic. Undeterred, she continued, even "ordering three enormous [American] books" from Chicago.[77] She remained determined to break society's "conspiracy of silence" that marginalized, "ostracized," and forgot the elderly.[78]

Over six hundred pages, Beauvoir set out to show why old age was an urgent political and social issue, and denounced the "misery, loneliness, infirmities, and despair" that too often characterized older men and women's lives.[79] As in *The Second Sex*, the first part examined biology (concluding that, unlike sex and gender, with aging, biology could not be distinct from culture), anthropology, and history. She insisted aging was a "process" societies must understand rather than ignore.[80] It was not just a "biological fact, but a cultural one."[81] If the experience of aging depended on one's social and historical context, Beauvoir emphasized that the elderly were neither passive nor resigned to this state. Unlike *The Second Sex*, the second half of the book, titled "Being-in-the-World," was more "personal" and included "testimonies" she had sought and reflections on her own situation.[82] She argued that the elderly were oppressed and discarded by a society that feared age and death and created a second-class of citizens whose living conditions worsened as they became invisible.

The Coming of Age (*La vieillesse*) was published at the end of January 1970. Because she wished to "reach as many people as possible," Beauvoir uncharacteristically agreed to give radio interviews.[83] The book was an immediate success, which she enjoyed since she was especially proud of this book. She was now sixty-four years old. The paradox was that, as Beauvoir felt she had finally published "truly original work," a younger generation who had come of age with May '68 turned to her for her theories on the question of women, otherness, and oppression. They demanded radical change and action. Beauvoir had always enjoyed those younger than her and was now called upon by young women to act. In 1970, the newly founded Movement for Women's Liberation [Mouvement de Libération des Femmes] asked her to join them. Now, Beauvoir came to realize she needed to contribute more than words. This time, feminism seized her.

| REFLECTING ON THE WORLD: | FEMINISM, FAME, AND SCANDAL, 1970–1986

IN HER LAST MEMOIR, Beauvoir explained that while she had been intellectually engaged these last three decades, she "had never been an activist."[1] Instead, she continued, "since 1962, the world has evolved." She had "experienced new things, but" had not "changed."[2] Beauvoir may have claimed she had not changed, but her relation to the world and to others did, most notably her relation to political activism and the cause of women. Throughout the 1960s, Beauvoir did not join feminist coalitions, unlike her friend Colette Audry. At the time, she still hoped that "socialism might provide the best path for women's emancipation."[3] Neither had she directly participated in reform movements or campaigns. In fact, she had always expressed ambivalence toward that kind of political involvement, stating that she left that work to Sartre.

When interviewed in 1966 by Francis Jeanson on the meaning of feminism, Beauvoir had explained that "feminism is a way of living individually and of struggling collectively."[4] Beauvoir certainly felt she had crafted her life according to these principles. She had acted when she felt compelled to do so, first as writer, then as intellectual. She had been one of the intellectuals involved in calling for Algerian independence. She had testified at trials, marched with others in street demonstrations, and written powerful editorials and articles in support of Algerian FLN fighter Djamila Boupacha. But she had never felt she was an "activist." Indeed, despite her recognition that political ideas like feminism involved "collective struggle," she had never fully embraced any organized collective action, even during the Algerian War. Something had changed since then. She wrote that, now in 1970, she understood the need for collective struggle: for her, it meant "losing the childish illusion that [she] was at the center of the universe."[5]

Beauvoir may not have been swept off by the explosions of May '68 but her positions nonetheless shifted after these events, as did Sartre's, in large part because of the demands made by a younger generation. Ever since she had started teaching philosophy in high schools, Beauvoir had enjoyed socializing and meeting with young people. Now that she was in her sixties, Beauvoir "especially enjoyed living in the company of young people"; she felt energized by their "intransigence, radicalism, demands and the freshness of their gaze" upon the world.[6] May '68 in France and protests around the West had reminded her of that.

These young radical leftists called upon her and Sartre to join them. Sartre especially had been enchanted by the promises and possibilities opened up by May '68. For Sartre, being an intellectual now meant something different than it had before. Beauvoir explained he had decided that "the new intellectual . . . endeavors to become integrated with the masses so as to bring about the triumph of true universality."[7] When a group of young Maoists, named the Gauche Prolétarienne (known as GP), asked him to help further their cause, Sartre gladly accepted. Inspired by their former teacher, philosopher Louis Althusser, GP members were opposed to the policies of the established Communist Party. They agitated and called for a true revolution that would come from the working classes rather than intellectuals and political leaders. Unlike other far-left groups, they embraced violence as a means of action in the face of "fascist state violence."[8] They published a magazine, *The People's Cause* (*La Cause du Peuple*), that was "without owner, was written directly and indirectly by the workers, and was sold on the streets by the militants."[9] When two of the organization's newspaper editors were arrested, Sartre accepted taking over as the magazine's director. The first issue was released on May 1, 1970. When the newspaper was seized on June 25, 1970, quickly followed by a ban of the GP and arrests, he and Beauvoir founded a group "The Friends of *The People's Cause,*" dedicated to defending free speech and, with Lanzmann, filmmakers Louis Malle and François Truffaut among others, they went into the streets to sell the newspapers.[10] Lending the weight of one's name to this cause was a way of foiling state repression. Beauvoir reluctantly agreed to do the same with another far-left publication, *The International Idiot* (*L'Idiot International*). Still, unlike Sartre, leftist activism was not where most of her energies were devoted.

Engaged Intellectuals. *Journalists surround Simone de Beauvoir and Jean-Paul Sartre after their release from police custody for selling in the streets the far-left newspaper,* The People's Cause (La Cause du Peuple), *which was banned by the government (June 26, 1970).*

"I AM A FEMINIST," 1970–1972

Feminism became a major force and an important form of political mobilization and an urgent topic by the early 1970s. Public speech regarding women and sexuality had already begun loosening in the 1960s. Throughout the decade, people started talking more about issues that had been considered taboo or shameful. Topics such as sexual pleasure were covered in call-in radio and television shows.[11] Reforms such as the Neuwirth law had extended these discussions. May '68 had also unleashed a different form of speech. Students gathered to talk of sexual revolution; some argued "lesbians and queers" must defiantly "stop lurking in the shadows." The meaning of women's liberation was intensely debated.[12]

May '68 slogans had encouraged people to "make love not war." But that slogan did not necessarily reflect reality nor change it. Young women who had participated in the far-left groups that had sprung up during and after May '68 quickly found out that radical politics did not involve changing gender roles: they were expected to help and not lead, to be domestic auxiliaries and even sex objects rather than political leaders. This led many of them (even more so for those who rejected what they called "heterosexual domination") to break off and create their own separate groups devoted to women's lives and rights. These groups were diverse. Some focused on the question of housework and unequal pay; others on the issues of reproductive rights, healthcare, and childcare; or on traditional gender roles and the objectification of women and their bodies. On August 26, 1970, nine radical feminists created a stir when they left a wreath dedicated to the "Wife of the Unknown Soldier." The Tomb of the Unknown Soldier was one of the French Republic's most revered memorials, reminding the French nation of its fallen soldiers. The wreath reminded the public that women were forgotten and ignored in national histories. A politicized and radicalized generation had come of age.

Although Beauvoir felt her positions regarding women's situation had more or less stayed the same, something had changed. She decided her theoretical and political commitment must come with practical action.[13] In contrast to the 1960s, Beauvoir was now disillusioned with socialism and realized it would not bring about change for women. She was impressed by the energy and political commitment of the women involved in the Movement for Women's Liberation [Mouvement de Libération des Femmes]. The MLF (as it was known) had come about when many young and older feminists came together energized by the need for a distinct sustained political movement dedicated to women's rights. Radical and far-left publications had welcomed feminist writings, but many young feminists felt this was not enough. In October 1970, the far-left magazine *Partisans* published a piece entitled "Women's Liberation: Year Zero." The MLF proclaimed this year its founding year. Feminism, gender, and sexuality were now on the agenda.

According to Beauvoir, several MLF members came to see her in 1970 asking for her support in a campaign for the legalization of abortion, which was still a crime punishable with prison. They proposed publicizing the issue with a manifesto that would feature both famous and ordinary women. Beauvoir happily agreed, seeing here the manifestation of what she had called for in *The Second Sex*, namely to fight against the "tragic consequences" of the "repression of abortion."[14] But she did more than that. She joined feminist demonstrations and activism. On November 20, 1970, she marched alongside four thousand women in an international demonstration asking for reproductive rights.[15] Later, she also participated in the occupation of a school where young, pregnant, single girls were being forced to reside.[16] She published an article in *The People's Cause* where she "denounced" society's hypocrisy on the issue: what was one to make of a society where a fifteen-year-old girl could be "emancipated" through marriage yet a "seventeen-year-old single mother" was still under her parents' authority?[17]

On April 5, 1971, the *Manifesto of the 343* (*Manifeste des 343*) was published on the front page of the magazine *Nouvel Observateur* (*New Observer*). The manifesto featured Beauvoir's signature along with a long list of women who "declared they had had an abortion." Making such a declaration was a risky enterprise since it could have legal consequences. Like Beauvoir, many of the signatories had also been actively involved against the Algerian War. Colette Audry, Marguerite Duras, Violette Leduc, and Françoise Sagan had signed the *Manifesto of the 121* against the war ten years earlier. There were also film stars Jeanne Moreau and Catherine Deneuve. Radical feminists Christine Delphy, Emmanuelle de Lesseps, and Monique Wittig who had, a year earlier, commemorated the Wife of the Unknown Soldier, added their names to the long list of ordinary and unknown women. The manifesto caused a huge sensation. (Anyone confessing to having had an abortion risked prison at worst and criminal prosecution at best.) The text explained that every year "in France, one million women have an abortion." "Unlike other human beings," women, it added, "do not have the right to their own bodies." It called for legal and free access to abortion, so that women "are not ashamed of their own bodies" and "of being a woman." To be a feminist meant to fight for the legalization of abortion (although the manifesto emphasized, this was not the "ultimate goal of women's struggles, but the most basic demand, from which political action would derive"). The manifesto galvanized efforts for reform. Others mockingly dubbed it the "manifesto of 343 sluts."

The manifesto came at the right time. A different kind of politics was in the air. While the French media buzzed with the scandal of immigrant housing following a fire in a suburban temporary housing for African workers that proved deadly for five of them, sociologists and political leaders spoke of a "new society."[18] Some endeavored to bring this to light. It seemed especially urgent, in the wake of former President de Gaulle's death at the end of 1970, and the arrival of a new generation of politicians. Feminist politics also took a different turn. The MLF organized grassroots campaigns that rallied many women across the political spectrum. What became known as "second-wave feminism" agitated not just in France but also in Germany, Britain, Italy, and the United States where, Beauvoir noted with satisfaction, many feminist leaders had read *The Second Sex*.[19] Everywhere in the West, women were demanding recognition of their rights.

The following month, in May 1971, some MLF members published the first issue of a self-financed, self-proclaimed feminist newspaper, *The Towel is Burning* (*Le Torchon Brûle*). It was not composed by professional journalists and was designed to be the voice of grassroots feminism. Its editorial committee changed with every issue. While Beauvoir was delighted by these efforts, her own feminist activism built upon the strategies she had used during the Algerian War. She joined forces with her long-time friend and political ally, the lawyer Gisèle Halimi who, almost a decade earlier, had asked her to help publicize Djamila Boupacha's case. Together, they founded the nonprofit organization and feminist group To Choose (Choisir) in June 1971.[20] Beauvoir became its president. Its aim was to fight for the legalization of abortion. The issue came to a head with the Bobigny trial, which took place the following year, in the winter of 1972.

On October 11, 1972, seventeen-year-old Marie-Claire Chevalier was tried for having undergone an abortion. Her story embodied the contradictions of French abortion laws. Marie-Claire was a student in a technical school. Her single mother, a subway driver, raised her and her two younger sisters in a working-class Parisian suburb. During the trial, Marie-Claire recounted how she had become pregnant after one sexual encounter with a young man who, she explained, had forced himself on her. In short, she had been raped. She testified this had been the only time she had had sex. Upon discovering her pregnancy, her mother brought her to doctors who agreed to abort her fetus but whose fees were prohibitively expensive. She then went to "see someone who had learned how to do abortions by having to do them for herself."[21] (Marie-Claire was not the only one being tried, so was her mother, and her mother's friends.) Still, despite the risks involved, Marie-Claire told her judges that, as a young underage and unmarried woman, she chose abortion over the prospect of abandoning her child to the government: she "was not sorry [she] had an abortion because that child would have been looked after by [the state's] Public Assistance (Assistance Publique) and would have been unhappy."[22]

To Choose took on the case, and Halimi became Marie-Claire's lawyer at her mother's request. Marie-Claire's mother had read Beauvoir and Halimi's book on Boupacha and had thought of contacting them. Halimi and Beauvoir did just what they had done with the case of Djamila Boupacha ten years earlier. They knew publicizing the issue was essential and set out to do just that. The trial was featured heavily in the news. Women demonstrated outside the courthouse during the proceedings. Beauvoir was among them. Prominent personalities publicly supported Marie-Claire.

FIGHTING "CRIMINAL" LAWS. *Simone de Beauvoir demonstrating with other feminists in front of the courthouse during the Bobigny trial (Nov. 1, 1972).*

Rather than focusing on defending Marie-Claire's choice to have an (illegal) abortion, Halimi decided to denounce the 1920 law, which criminalized abortion. Abortion was now a political issue that could no longer be ignored.

This time, however, the trial had a different outcome than the Boupacha case. Marie-Claire was acquitted (as was her mother) because, the proceedings declared, she "was not pre-pared for the conditions in which she found herself, not aware of the risks she was running, and did not freely and deliberately choose to commit the act with which she is charged."[23] The court concluded that "she was subjected to the pressures of a moral, familial, and a social nature that she was not able to resist."[24] The judgment was paradoxical. On the one hand, Marie-Claire was cleared of all charges. This was a huge victory for feminists calling for the reform of the 1920 law. But the judge's argument reproduced gendered stereotypes to justify his ruling. It emphasized the young woman's inability to act as a rational and autonomous individual, thus reiterating the myth of women as childlike and impressionable.

However, the publicity about the trial did not end there. Contesting the grounds for the judge's ruling, To Choose pub-lished full transcripts of the proceedings a few weeks later. Beauvoir penned a short and impassioned preface. Just as Halimi had put the law itself on trial during her closing remarks, Beauvoir explained that it was the 1920 law, and not abortion itself, that was a "crime." She wrote that, for the vast majority of women, "termination is performed . . . by unqualified people under bad conditions—so bad, in fact, that the most elementary hygienic precautions are not observed. It is for this reason that so many women who have had abortions die," and others are left "sterile, sick or handicapped."[25] Because of this, and the difficulties in ob-taining an abortion, Beauvoir added, these women experience "fear," "humiliation," despair, and "guilt." To make matters worse, it is "the poorest [women] who pay the highest price."[26] After dismantling arguments commonly leveled against the legalization of abortion, Beauvoir concluded that, "once a woman has mastery over her body, and [is] no longer poisoned by fear or remorse, she will be ready for other struggles."[27] Thirty thousand copies of the To Choose transcripts were sold in those first few weeks. The campaign gained traction.

Even as Beauvoir embraced feminist militancy, she embarked on another major project. She had always written her memoirs, reflecting on her life and self while being involved in the crucible of politics. This time, too, she started writing what would be her last memoir while involved in the Bobigny trial. The title was ominous, *All Is Said and Done* (*Tout compte fait*), hinting at a final summing up of her life. The tone, however, was neither bleak nor pessimistic. As she had always done, she dedicated it to the person she cherished the most, or had an important place in her life: this time, she dedicated it to Sylvie Le Bon, who had become her companion. Beauvoir opened the memoir with the account of their meeting, tentative friendship, and blossoming relationship. Beauvoir wrote that her ultimate goal had been "to tell the truth" in her books. But as she usually did in her memoirs, despite her profession of truthfulness, she left some things out: Beauvoir, uncharacteristically, remained rather discreet on the nature of her relationship with Sylvie. Le Bon explained years later Beauvoir's choice had been at Sylvie's request.

The memoir, unlike her previous ones, did not follow a traditional chronological order. Instead, it was a compendium of Beauvoir's thoughts on what mattered to her: her relationship to literature, the books she loved, the films she enjoyed and, of course, the business of politics and her engagement in the world. She told the story of her involvement with the MLF and her newfound feminism. She memorialized her dear friend Violette Leduc, whose life "had closely been mingled" with hers the last ten years, and who had suddenly died of cancer in May 1972, while Beauvoir "corrected [the] proofs" of her memoir.[28] Leduc, who had always considered Beauvoir her "literary mentor," had designated her as the guardian of her unpublished work. Beauvoir followed her wishes and published Leduc's last autobiography, *Hunting for Love* (*La chasse à l'amour*) the following year, in 1973.[29]

Beauvoir remained silent, however, on what was a major source of anxiety in these years: Sartre's failing health, which had taken a turn for the worse in 1970. When it came to herself, Beauvoir seemed disinclined to think of illness or death, as she had done in her 1963 *The Force of Circumstance*. This time, she refused the fate of old age and was uninterested in contemplating her own death. She concluded her memoirs explaining that, while she had had "many enemies," she had also "gained many friends among her readers." This time, she finished, and in spite of the title she had given her memoir, "she would not offer any summing up to her life," but "leave it to the reader."[30] There was more in the world that awaited her.

"WOMEN ARE STUBBORN," 1973–1975

The 1970s brought great social and political upheaval. In many ways, these were the consequence of the previous decade's developments: decolonization, the baby boom, and popular movements. Feminist campaigns were traction in the West. European societies changed in the wake of the end of empires. Since the late 1950s, a growing number of immigrants, most from former colonies, entered Europe. As Europe rebuilt itself and grew economically, it looked to former colonial subjects from Africa and Asia to provide a cheap labor force. Immigration became a political issue in the 1960s, as some Europeans felt unsettled by these arrivals. Postimperial nations like France experienced a resurgence of racism directed against these immigrant workers. At the same time, the welfare state's provisions for its citizens, and new technologies (such as cars or TVs) had profoundly reshaped Europeans' lives. A new affluence was now available to many working-class families by the early 1970s. That prosperity, however, suddenly came to a halt in 1973.

On October 6, 1973, on the eve of the Jewish holy day of Yom Kippur, a coalition of Arab states attacked Israel. Led by Egypt and Syria, the coalition was intent on reclaiming territories lost during the 1967 Six Day War. Egypt crossed the Suez Canal and settled in the Sinai, while Syria moved into the Golan Heights. Israel reacted swiftly. Despite the coalition's early military successes, Israel managed to fend off these attacks and turn the tide of the conflict. The Arab-Israeli conflict came to an end when a ceasefire was negotiated under the aegis of the United Nations on October 25. What became known as the Yom Kippur War changed the face of diplomatic relations and had unexpected economic consequences. Egyptian President Anwar al-Sadat became the first Arab leader to recognize the legitimacy of Israel. Middle Eastern politics, Europeans learned, had a direct impact on their lives. In response to military defeat, Middle Eastern oil-producing countries decided to limit their exports of oil to the United States and its European allies that had supported Israel. The price of oil rose, and the unexpected inflation that followed fueled a recession that took the West by surprise. This caused a worldwide ripple as the West was forced to realize its dependence on these resources.

The Yom Kippur War reminded the world it was embroiled in a global network few could escape, even if the Cold War was receding. Furthermore, it also resurrected long-standing debates for the European left. Again, Beauvoir commented on the debate. In the wake of a special *Modern Times* issue on the conflict published in November, barely a month later, Beauvoir published an article, which explored the *Modern Times'* chosen theme of reflection, "War and Peace." The French left overall supported the Palestinian cause for independence, pointing to the ways Israel had become a colonial power. Beauvoir reiterated her support for Palestinians but insisted that Israel, too, had the right to continue existing. She argued for a "middle-ground" that involved support for both sides.

While Sartre founded the leftist weekly newspaper, *Libération*, Beauvoir continued with her feminist work.[31] Indeed, Beauvoir and her MLF companions had not stopped after the Bobigny trial. In 1974, Beauvoir became the president of the newly created League for the Rights of Women. At the same time, she supervised a special issue of *Modern Times* devoted to feminist questions. It was published in the spring of 1974 with a preface she authored entitled "Women are Stubborn" ("Les femmes s'entêtent"). Beauvoir continued publishing articles even though she had slowly disengaged from the daily work of running *Modern Times*.

Denouncing injustice mattered to Beauvoir. That year, French readers found themselves riveted by Alexander Solzhenitsyn's newly translated book, *The Gulag Archipelago*, which detailed the totalitarian doctrine and repressive practices of the Soviet communist regime. Beauvoir, too, was horrified by the Russian novelist's account of the "gulags," these work camps in the remote lands of Siberia where anyone suspected of opposition to the regime was sent. Nonetheless, she still cared about the topic of inequalities produced by an unfair capitalist order. Though she agreed with Sartre and other fellow intellectuals' denunciation of French society's racism, she spent little time on that issue; just as in the 1940s, Beauvoir was quicker to denounce racism elsewhere in the world. She had denounced the Vietnam War and, in 1973, applauded the US withdrawal of troops from Vietnam. Her political activism had increased, but her political concerns remained focused on what she now believed to be the most urgent cause. Feminism remained her priority. While the MLF kept on lobbying and campaigning, Beauvoir gave many interviews to the French and foreign press on the question of feminism, women's rights, marriage, and prostitution.

When the centrist Valéry Giscard d'Estaing came to power on May 19, 1974, he promised reform and change. These seemed much needed since, in the wake of the 1973 oil crisis, unemployment had almost doubled throughout most of Europe. France was hard-hit by the recession. The government embarked on a series of widespread reforms. For the first time, women's issues figured at the forefront. Giscard D'Estaing appointed Simone Veil, a

French Jewish lawyer who had survived deportation at the women's camp of Ravensbrück and had also been involved in issues surrounding FLN prisoners during the Algerian war. This was the first time a woman had become a full government minister (in 1936, the left-wing Popular Front coalition leader Léon Blum had appointed two women to lesser positions in his cabinet). Giscard also nominated Françoise Giroud, former co-editor of *L'Express*, to a state cabinet devoted to women's affairs (that, in fact, had little effective power). Thanks to the relentless campaigning of French feminists, the government decided to tackle the issue of abortion. After all, there had been growing public protest in the last three years, not just in the streets but coming from the medical establishment itself and with the direct disobedience to the law proclaimed by the Family Planning, which had declared in 1973 it would provide abortions.[32] In this, the French government was also following and participating in what was happening elsewhere: in 1973, the US Supreme Court had overturned restrictions on abortion in *Roe v. Wade*, a year after Eastern Germany had done the same, and seven years after Great Britain had legalized abortion. This time, under the leadership of a president committed to reform, change seemed possible. Veil proposed a law legalizing voluntary abortion. After many heated debates in parliament where she weathered personal attacks, the law legalizing abortion was passed in 1975 with the support of socialists and communists (it was fully made permanent four years later, in 1979). France was not alone in making such changes. West Germany also legalized abortion in 1974, but rescinded the law a year later before reinstating it in 1976 under limited circumstances. Italy followed four years later in 1978. Finally, Beauvoir witnessed substantial changes for women.

By 1975, Beauvoir had become a worldwide celebrity, and her work as writer and as novelist was receiving accolades everywhere. In January, she was awarded the Jerusalem Prize for the Freedom of Society.[33] Created in 1963, it was designed to recognize "a writer whose work best expresses and promotes the freedom of the individual in society."[34] Nobel Prize–winner British philosopher Bertrand Russell had been its first recipient in 1963. Novelist Jorge Luis Borges and playwright Eugene Ionesco had received it in 1971 and 1973. Beauvoir was the first woman awarded the prize. In her speech, Beauvoir reminded her audience that "it is not necessary to have personal ties with someone to feel the horror of the Holocaust, but it happens that I had a few Jewish friends, almost all of them are gone. They were deported, never to return."[35] It was published later that year in a French left-wing Jewish magazine under the title, "Solidarity with Israel: A Critical Support." The ability to care for someone other than oneself in a world where each and every one was bound to others was a principle Beauvoir had first elaborated in her definition of existentialist philosophy in the wake of World War II. Three decades later, it still shaped her understanding of the world. As she had learned since then, it also required never renouncing one's ability to be critical. Blindly serving a cause was foolish. Her support for Israel illustrated this conviction: she signed the manifesto of French intellectuals protesting the UNESCO decision to exclude Israel from its organization but was also critical of the Israeli government's policies. She called for recognition of Israeli and Palestinian rights and argued for a "two-state solution." She never wavered in this position.

As the Vietnam War finally came to a close, two years after the US military withdrawal of its troops, Beauvoir resumed her public work on behalf of feminism. The French literary journal *L'Arc* published in 1975 a special issue, "Simone de Beauvoir and the Women's Struggle."[36] It included Beauvoir's lengthy interview of Sartre on that very question. Because they were known to the world as a literary and political couple, Sartre and Beauvoir had often published or been filmed in conversation. Beauvoir's questions were blunt and unsparing: she opened the interview by asking him why, since he had written about racism, antisemitism, and the oppression of workers, he had "never spoken about" the oppression of women.[37] Sartre's responses were candid. He explained he had probably been conditioned by his own childhood and education. Beauvoir insisted he, like others, had harbored "sexist" ideas and attitudes, and asked him to explain how he could have remained so "blind" to this. Sartre responded that his own sexism had been invisible to him because, as a young man, he had naively believed that "man's superiority" did not mean refusing equality between men and women.[38] Beauvoir asked him to reflect on the intersection of class and gender: could socialism emancipate women? Ultimately, Sartre agreed with her that there was "something specific" and unique to women's oppression that must addressed as such.[39] The interview was reprinted the following year in a collection of Sartre's writings on his relationship to politics and the self. Beauvoir, however, confessed a few years later that she had been rather disappointed with the interview. It is true, he had "answered with the greatest good will but rather superficially."

BEING AN ICON, 1975–1980

That same year, in 1975, French people in their living rooms witnessed an unusual event. Television sets were now a common feature of French family life, and evenings spent watching interviews of philosophers, authors, and artists were a regular occurrence in France. The government had recently ended its monopoly of TV and radio. One evening, the dashing and serious interviewer Jean-Louis Servan-Schreiber welcomed Beauvoir. As he informed viewers, she had, until then, refused to appear on TV, thus reminding viewers this was indeed a historic moment. (She had been on TV before, but only in documentaries or with Sartre.) The title of the show that evening was unambiguous: "Why I'm a feminist." The setting was subdued and simple. Beauvoir sat on a brown leather couch across from her interviewer. In typical fashion, she was well dressed. Her austere yet striking dress in variations of blue, navy, and turquoise echoed her distinctive accessory, a blue turban. Beauvoir responded to questions in a clipped and fast-paced voice. She began by stating very forthrightly that what her controversial 1949 work, *The Second Sex*, had tried to reveal was this simple fact: "Woman is not a natural given. There is no biological destiny to being a woman. She has been forged by history." Beauvoir's physical presence emphasized her clear and blunt pronouncement. The interview was a sensation, and extracts were reprinted in newspapers the following days.

Despite her age, as viewers had witnessed on their television screens, Beauvoir was neither an outdated thinker nor an icon frozen in time. She had understood the new media were important in publicizing issues. In 1954, only 1 percent of French households owned a television set. By 1974, 80 percent did. This had motivated her TV interview. It also motivated the interviews and speeches she gave in different venues. She no longer left the public work of an engaged intellectual to Sartre. In May 1975, she gave a speech to the left-wing Jewish group, the Cercle Bernard Lazare, reiterating her belief that Israel was a legitimate state but that the Palestinians should neither be oppressed nor displaced.[40] Two months later, in July, the American feminist magazine *Ms.* published an interview she had given to German journalist Alice Schwarzer whom she had first met three years earlier in 1972. Over the following years, the two writers regularly published their discussions. She also wrote a preface to a *History of the MLF* authored by two feminists whose pseudonyms paid homage to the Renaissance writer Christine de Pizan and the nineteenth-century feminist Flora Tristan. She went to Lisbon with Sartre in support of the "Carnation Revolution" that erupted in the spring of 1974 and had brought down the authoritarian and fascist-inspired dictatorship, which had ruled Portugal since 1933. Back in Paris, on June 21, 1976, she and Sartre attended a gathering organized to support Soviet and Eastern European dissidents that brought together some of the most preeminent of France's intellectuals including Michel Foucault, Roland Barthes, and Gilles Deleuze.

Sexuality became a pressing and much-debated issue in the mid- to late-1970s. In part, this was the result of the evolution of the activism that had emerged in the late 1960s, feminists' arguments and campaigns, and the general cultural shift that was taking place across the West. Just as feminists had challenged the oppression of women in the wake of May '68, gay activists had also denounced their particular oppression. In 1968, the World Health Organization still considered homosexuality to be a mental illness.[41] Homosexual acts were still criminalized in many European countries. In France, heterosexual men and women were considered consenting adults as soon as they reached fifteen. However, the age of consent for gay men and women was twenty-one. Being caught engaging in sexual acts or relationships before that was considered a misdemeanor and punishable with prison.[42] For these gay men and lesbians, the end of stigmatization, discrimination, and persecution was an urgent matter. A number of them had come together in March 1971 to create an organization they named the Gay Front for Homosexual Action (Front Homosexuel d'Action Révolutionnaire), or FHAR.[43] Taking their inspiration from the Black Panthers and the American Gay Liberation Movement, they called for a sexual revolution.[44] The organization disbanded in early 1973 as lesbians and gay men focused on different questions. One of the points of division was the question of sexual violence (for women) and the role of racism in sexual politics.

Legal reforms continued in the 1970s. Three years after the legalization of abortion, divorce by mutual consent was made legal. Feminists now turned their attention to sexual violence and rape. They were galvanized in part by the controversies surrounding a recent spate of films that systematically associated sexuality with violence and offered negative portrayals of female sexuality. The scandal had first started with Bernardo Bertolucci's 1972 *Last Tango in Paris* which depicted the anonymous encounters between a widowed American (played by Marlon Brandon) and a young French woman who, after shooting him, claimed he had raped her. The film was censored but was still a huge success to French feminists' dismay since it belittled women's claims of sexual assault. Two years later, Italian director Liliana Cavani released *The Night Porter* where she depicted a female Jewish survivor engaging in a masochistic relationship with her former Nazi guard in postwar Europe. In 1975, a Franco-German adaptation of the 1954 pornographic novel *The Story of O* was released.[45] Though originally written by a woman, the publicity for the film portrayed a passive and subservient heroine. At the same time, the far-right press increasingly focused on North African immigrants who they portrayed as lustful, excessive, and animalistic and thus in need of control. In newspapers and speeches, the far-right warned against the "invasion" of Algerian men left to their own devices on French soil.[46] The government's decision to end all legal immigration in 1974 only strengthened these racist myths. These controversies provided the context to feminist campaigns to battle sexual violence and criminalize rape.

Again, the campaign began with a trial. In February 1976, Halimi defended two young Belgian women who had been raped a couple of years earlier. Though considered a crime, rape was usually tried as a "misdemeanor assault" rather than in criminal courts as a "felony."[47] She succeeded in moving the case to criminal court. The campaign was waged publicly in almost all newspapers and magazines of the period. Beauvoir published an article on March 1, 1976, in the *Nouvel Observateur*, calling for the serious consideration of rape, three days before an International Tribunal for Crimes Against Women took place in Brussels.[48] The MLF published a "Manifesto Against Rape" in *Libération*, on June 16, 1976. Ten days later, a demonstration entitled "Ten Hours Against Rape" took place in a Parisian meeting hall, bringing together several thousand women.[49] Beauvoir was involved since the two organizations she presided, To Choose and the League of the Rights of Women, were lobbying for a reform of the law.

Sexuality was indeed at the forefront of public discussions. In 1976, Michel Foucault published his first volume of the *History of*

Sexuality where he explained that sexuality was a matter of power that no one escaped. As Beauvoir had done, he criticized both the psychoanalytic account of sex (that individuals are repressed) and the Marxist version (that people are oppressed from above by economic and class structures and only need to revolt). But sexual liberation was a complicated issue. The 1977 film of a teenage girl's coming of age in the early 1960s, *Peppermint Soda* (*Diabolo Menthe*), dramatized some of these issues as it highlighted the ways in which female sexuality was still ensconced in the confines of conservative impulses. The film was a huge box-office success. In politics, however, reforming laws about sex and sexual violence proved more difficult. As other rape trials took place, feminists arguing for the criminalization of rape were accused of embodying conservative forces. Far-left gay activists argued that feminists were interested only in the repression of sexual desire. Because those who stood accused were Algerian working-class men, feminists were accused of being "bourgeois" and racist.[50] Among feminists themselves, there were profound divisions: some wanted to argue that male sexuality was inherently violent and "fascist" while others argued that once society faced its sexism, the question of sexual violence would recede. Others decried the oppressive nature of heterosexuality. Many felt uncomfortable with the judicial system's severe punishment of North African men while so many European men escaped any penalty.

In the midst of these "rape debates," a group of radical feminists created an academic and political magazine to address these discussions. Its editorial committee included many of those who had been involved in early feminist actions and in the FHAR. It included Christine Delphy, Emmanuelle de Lesseps, Nicole-Claude Mathieu, and Colette Guillaumin, later joined by Monique Wittig. They were thinkers as well as activists. Beauvoir embraced it wholeheartedly and provided her name, prestige, and influence to the magazine, becoming its director. The first issue of *Feminist Questions* was published in 1977. Delphy wished to promote what she termed "materialist feminism," a feminist politics that aimed to build upon Beauvoir's early insights in *The Second Sex* and took up the challenge of articulating a feminism that considered the material conditions of women's oppression and salvage socialist thought from its blindness to gender and women's condition. While in conversation with British and American feminists, the *Feminist Questions* writers tackled issues such as the relationship between "Sexism and Racism" and "Heterosexuality and Feminism." The law making rape a crime rather than a misdemeanor finally passed in 1978; the *Feminist Questions* collective continued its feminist academic work, all the while supported by Beauvoir.

By then, Beauvoir had become a reference point and a model to most feminists in the 1970s, whatever their political differences. She was asked to intervene by both reformist and radical feminists. Her presence was actively sought everywhere either as author or activist. She had become an "icon" in her own right. The documentary that Josée Dayan and Malka Ribowska made about her in 1979 (they had already approached her in 1976 to make a TV adaptation of *The Woman Destroyed*, which Beauvoir had enjoyed) embodied that evolution.[51] When the filmmakers were interviewed on French TV, Beauvoir was described as "the most famous Frenchwoman," suggesting her fame was far greater than that of film stars Brigitte Bardot and Catherine Deneuve. In the documentary, when asked why she had agreed to participate in it, Beauvoir explained it was partly out of "vanity": this way, people who did not read her works might get to know her and her works. It was also partly out of a desire for "recognition" and "truth": she wanted to correct the false and misguided impressions that some people, she felt, had about her since so much had been written about her. The success of this film also signaled another success for Beauvoir. At the same time as she was memorialized in the documentary as an inspiration and icon, she was able to finally see her first-ever completed collection of stories published. *When Things of the Spirit Come First* had been turned down in 1937 when she was still an aspiring novelist. Four decades later, she could share it with her readers.

PUBLIC DEATHS, POLITICAL SCANDALS, 1980–1986

While she continued monitoring Sartre's health and saw him regularly, over the previous decade her life had slowly become less entwined with his. He still joined Beauvoir and Sylvie for holidays in Italy, Venice, Greece, or Crete. But their daily lives were no longer as connected. Sartre "regularly saw long-established women friends" and spent two nights a week at his adopted daughter's house, Arlette Elkaïm.[52] He also enjoyed the company of many young women who flocked to him, exclaiming with delight, as Beauvoir recounted, that he had never been "so surrounded by women."[53] In 1973, Sartre had also made his young collaborator, Benny Lévy, his personal secretary.[54] Lévy was a stateless refugee from Egypt who had been one of the leaders of the Gauche Prolétarienne under the name Pierre Victor. As time went on, though, Beauvoir felt Lévy exercised undue influence over Sartre who was physically diminished. For the first time, she remembered with some sadness, one of Sartre's close friends was not also her own.[55] After the publication of an interview Lévy had conducted with Sartre in the *New Observer* in 1980, Beauvoir thought Lévy "made Sartre adopt" Lévy's own opinions, which involved "turn[ing] toward God."[56] Beauvoir's judgment was not kind. She was angry at what she perceived to be Lévy's exclusive control of Sartre and the ways he seemed to steer him to causes and topics that, she thought, were not truly his own. But she also said she knew Sartre was attempting to live his passion for politics in his dialogues with Lévy and, even while beset by ill health and failing eyesight, Sartre could still live vicariously. Soon after, in the spring of 1980, Sartre died.

Beauvoir was not surprised by his death, but her shock and sadness were still immense. She spent the next few days in a daze, "her mind a blank."[57] She barely registered the thousands who had come to join the funeral procession. His funeral was a national event. Beauvoir spent the next two weeks in bed with a sudden bout of pneumonia. She then resolved to do what she did best, publish an homage to Sartre. She had crafted her own 1972 memoir as a self-conscious "testament" to her life, while still alive and more involved in the world than ever before. Now, she set out to craft the testament to her lifelong partnership with Sartre.[58] She opened the volume with moving words, speaking directly to her now-deceased companion: "This is the first of my books—the only one no doubt—that you will not have read before it is printed. It is wholly and entirely devoted to you; and you are not affected by it."[59] Predictably, this was neither a traditional eulogy nor sentimental memoir. The first part was Beauvoir's account of the final ten years of his life—a kind of diary. She wrote about their times together, sometimes with nostalgia, a feeling that Beauvoir rarely exhibited in her writings. The second half was the transcription of a conversation they had had in the summer and fall of 1974 in Rome and Paris.

The book caused a scandal when it came out in November 1981, less than two years after Sartre's death. As one journalist commented, Beauvoir had refused to turn her homage into the fantastic and idealized love story readers might have wished for.[60] In fact, Beauvoir did not hesitate to recount in detail the often embarrassing physical degradation that characterized Sartre's last ten years: vertigo, strokes, high blood pressure, tooth abscesses, dentures, memory loss, and incontinence. She described the ill effects of his excessive drinking against doctors' advice and the moments when he could no longer fully function as he stumbled, weakened, dozed off during lunches and meetings, and most devastating of all, how he lost his eyesight.[61]

To readers familiar with Beauvoir's writings and philosophical principles, such a detailed and unvarnished account was unsurprising. Beauvoir had never hesitated to recount her own physical ailments and failing body in her memoirs. This was after all the indignity of old age that Beauvoir had talked about in her 1970 study, *The Coming of Age*, and that society refused to recognize. She had always engaged with the materiality of the body in her novels and in *The Second Sex*. In *All Said and Done*, she had described her friend Violette Leduc's mental breakdown, psychiatric stay, hallucinations, and irrational moods—just as she did other women she had been friends with.[62] In *Farewell to Sartre* (*La cérémonie des adieux*), however, Beauvoir was not describing a woman's body and failing mind but the "great man" that Sartre was in the eyes of the public. She had shown this great mind to be a vulnerable, weak, and fragile body. This time, the shame and indignity were too great for his friends, critics, and readers. They accused Beauvoir's text of being voyeuristic and tasteless. Even now Beauvoir did not hesitate to transgress conventions in order to follow her deeply held conviction that a conscience was always embodied and that this embodiment mattered.

Her *Farewell to Sartre* was Beauvoir's last substantial "new" writing. After her 1972 memoir, *All Said and Done*, however, she did not publish any more fiction, philosophy, or memoirs. Writing, Beauvoir never tired to repeat, had always been her one and only commitment. In the previous decade, she devoted herself to many new political ventures, and as she delved deeper into public and political life, Beauvoir stopped writing new books. Writing in such a way was no longer her only passion. She focused on different formats and on a different sets of issues, publishing op-ed pieces, articles, commentaries, and prefaces—all of them mostly focused on contemporary and urgent political issues. She had used her writing to "reflect" on the world but now was occupied with acting in the world.

Being involved in the world was indeed what mattered, especially now that she stood for the first time without Sartre. 1981 was an eventful personal and political year. Beauvoir decided to adopt her companion, Sylvie Le Bon, who became her "daughter" in the eyes of the law. Beauvoir's decision ensured that her legacy would live on as Sylvie was entrusted with her life's works. It also brought to life a belief she and Sartre had long held, namely that the bonds of kinship are created, forged through friendship, and that these bonds were often more enduring than biological ones. With Sylvie by her side, Beauvoir still enjoyed the company of her friends. And just as feminist activism had engulfed her life, it also dominated her social life. The dinners she organized were dominated by either her long-time *Modern Times* friends or those she knew through her feminist involvement. The private fed into the political, and the political also shaped the private.

Beauvoir's hopes were finally realized when she witnessed the victory of left-wing candidate Francois Mitterrand in the May 1981 presidential elections. Now that the communists had lost their influence among the working classes and the young, the left had assembled and united under the banner of the Socialist Party. The 1981 victory was as momentous to most French people as the 1936 election of the Popular Front coalition had been. To the French citizens who voted for Mitterrand, reformist socialism might bring to life their hopes for justice, equality, and reform.

It certainly signaled, at first, a different era for women. Long-time socialist and feminist activist, Yvette Roudy, who had worked alongside Beauvoir in the League for the Rights of Women, was appointed minister for Women's Rights. This was an extension of the position that Giroud had presided over in the early 1970s: the ministry had its own budget and became fully permanent in 1984. Roudy soon asked Beauvoir to preside over a "Commission on Women and Culture" designed to study and draw up recommendations on how best to eradicate sexism in culture. Paradoxically, while feminism seemed to have become legitimate within formal politics, feminist grassroots politics were profoundly shaken. A group of MLF members, led by psychoanalyst Antoinette Fouque, had broken off in the early 1970s. The intellectual group that Fouque led, and which included thinkers Luce Irigaray, writer Hélène Cixous and Julia Kristeva, deemed equality a secondary rather than primary goal for women. Instead, they claimed, women's inherent "difference" needed to be valorized. Rather than abolishing the constraints of motherhood as Beauvoir had long argued, they argued culture and society needed to value femininity. There was a "nature" specific to women, they claimed.

Theoretical and political differences among feminists had existed since the early 1970s. Even while the Bobigny trial was going on, some MLF members criticized To Choose's reliance on publicity and celebrity. These divisions returned with great force when a scandal shook feminists in 1980. Most French reformist and radical feminists were shocked to discover that Fouque had, the previous year, copyrighted the acronym "MLF," thus registering it as a brand that only she controlled. She had also registered the organization as one that she was responsible for. Those who had been involved in the MLF since 1970 could no longer publish, demonstrate, or lobby under the banner of what had, so far, been one of the most popular twentieth-century grassroots movements.

Feminists denounced what Beauvoir called, in a 1981 article, an "usurpation." This scandal solidified divisions that most participants often articulated in terms of their relation to Beauvoir's philosophical work. In all of these debates and divisions, her work had become a reference that some challenged and others embraced. While Fouque and others explained they sought to free themselves from the shackles of Beauvoir's and Sartre's thought, others identified Beauvoir as the feminist thinker they were building upon. At the same time, the radical *Feminist Questions* collective split up over fundamental theoretical divisions regarding the role of sexuality in individuals' lives and in politics. When a few former members started another magazine, under the title *New Feminist Questions*, the remaining members took them to court asserting it was a violation of their earlier agreement not to use any part of their former name. Again, Beauvoir was involved. She wrote on behalf of Delphy and the *New Feminist Questions* editorial committee. They won the trial which, like the MLF copyright, hardened differences and divisions.

Despite these scandals and her weakening health, Beauvoir did not slow down her pace. In 1983, she visited a Palestinian refugee camp in Beirut and published an impassioned editorial in the November issue of *Modern Times* where she compared the 1982 Sabra and Chatila massacres with the Nazi massacre of the small French town of Oradour-sur-Glane in 1944. While Roudy spearheaded and passed a law designed to fight sexism, Beauvoir embarked on another major project. She published a large volume that contained the thousands of letters that Sartre had written her over the course of his life. They had written to each other almost daily. This time, however, she edited many of the letters (something she had not done in *Farewell to Sartre*). Beauvoir was all too aware that the issue of their complicated emotional and erotic lives fascinated many but was also a source of controversy. She had often rewritten episodes in her memoir or omitted certain facts. As she put together Sartre's letters to her, she was also concerned with not wounding (too much) some of their friends, former lovers, and even acquaintances. The letters were published under the title, *Letters to the Beaver* (*Lettres au castor*), in reference to the nickname Sartre had given her when they first met in 1929. She also knew how to dramatize her life, and when journalists and readers asked about her letters to Sartre, Beauvoir usually answered that she did not know where they were.

In 1985, Beauvoir once again lent her name to a preface, this time to a film rather than a book. Beauvoir had long held that cinema could not describe the world the way literature could.[63] However, she revised that judgment upon watching Claude Lanzmann's documentary film *Shoah* released that year. Beauvoir was well acquainted with the arduous work it had required. Lanzmann had started working on this project eleven years earlier, in 1974. He went to Poland, filmed the ruins of extermination camps like Auschwitz and the abandoned overgrown fields where others had been built, like Chelmno. He traveled to New York, Tel Aviv, and Germany to interview survivors, perpetrators, and bystanders—a choice inspired by his reading of historian

"I Am a Feminist". *Simone de Beauvoir being interviewed at her home for a documentary about her 1949 book* The Second Sex *(Oct. 15, 1983).*

Raul Hilberg's 1961 pioneering work *The Destruction of European Jews* (who was also interviewed in the film). Out of the three hundred and fifty hours of footage, Lanzmann edited the film to nine grueling hours. Unlike Resnais's thirty-minute *Night and Fog*, which universalized the concentration camp experience,

Lanzmann's *Shoah* focused on the Nazi extermination project, its Jewish victims, and what Beauvoir called "the technicians of death."[64] Beauvoir called it a "masterpiece."[65] She explained that reading testimonies and history books had "moved" her but had not "brought the experience closer." Lanzmann's film, which "blended past and present," succeeded in "having faces translate what cannot be said" and allowed viewers like her "to feel this in their head, heart, and flesh."[66]

This was not Beauvoir's last published text. Barely a year later, she provided the preface to a novel, *Milhoud*, chronicling a gay love affair written from the point of view of an AIDS sufferer.[67] As Beauvoir usually did, she tackled some of the most important issues of the 1980s, namely sexuality and, in the early 1980s, the rumors, fears, and uncertainties surrounding the discovery of a disease, AIDS, that many mistakenly believed at the time afflicted only gay men and that was, at the time, 100 percent fatal.

Unfortunately, after that preface Beauvoir did not have time to pursue the topic any further. She suddenly succumbed to pneumonia on April 14, 1986 at the age of seventy-eight. She was buried five days later. The funeral procession was immense. More than five thousand people gathered to pay their last respects. Her ashes were placed in the Montparnasse cemetery, in the neighborhood she had always lived in, next to Sartre, with whom she had shared most of her life.

CONCLUSION

In 1972, Beauvoir wrote, "The way of the world had become the texture of her life."[68] She had first experienced this when World War II began. The Algerian War had demanded she follow through on this realization, and she had then, for the first time, intervened in the world as an intellectual. Ambivalence and contradictions characterized the 1960s. In the following decade, she decided to become engaged in collective struggles and activism. While the fate of women had preoccupied her for a long time and had been the topic of her novels and her philosophi-cally inspired studies, she had never until then translated her ideas into her politics. In the 1970s, Beauvoir became a feminist. During these decades, she published profusely in almost every genre. Her writings stirred controversy, often causing scandals. She had also enchanted thousands of readers who, over the years, devoured her memoirs and paid attention to everything she published.

Beauvoir was not always completely truthful, despite her claims of radical honesty. She wrote, "I am neither a slave to my past nor am I haunted by it."[69] This was not quite true. Some events had affected her more than others. The Algerian War had shaped her relation to politics and challenged her understanding of the writer's role in the world. It is World War II, however, that remained a defining moment for Beauvoir. It had turned her into an adult and led her to begin thinking for the first time about justice, ethics, and equality. It had also been the time when she first became a recognized novelist. Four decades later, it still provided her with the vocabulary with which she described the injustices and horrors of the world. Amidst political turmoil, changing societies, and wars, Beauvoir always held fast to what, ultimately, she felt had provided her the most happiness: "My relations with others—my affections, my friendships," she wrote, "hold the most important place in my life."[70]

PRIMARY SOURCE EXCERPTS
AND STUDY QUESTIONS

THE BOOK HAS FOCUSED ON some of following themes: the question of political involvement, what it means to be an intellectual, the role of phenomenology (philosophy of embodied consciousness) in Beauvoir's thought, and the contradictions that existed in her life and in her thought. Keep these in mind as you read the following primary sources.

I.
"AN EYE FOR AN EYE" (1946)

This essay was published in February 1946 in the magazine Beauvoir and Sartre created, Les Temps Modernes. *It focuses on the meaning of justice and revenge, themes that preoccupied many in the wake of the "purge" of intellectuals, like Robert Brasillach, who were accused of treason for collaboration with the Nazi occupier.*

"Our executioners have corrupted our morals," noted Gracchus Babeuf with regret.[a] We too, under Nazi oppression, when faced with traitors eager to compromise themselves, felt murderous impulses arise in our hearts, sentiments for which we'd never developed a taste. Before the war we never wished ill of our

---

[a] **Babeuf** (1760–1797) was a journalist and radical political activist during the French Revolution. He was seen as a radical especially when the revolution took a "conservative" turn after the end of the Terror in the mid-1790s, a period of great violence. He argued, among other things, for the abolition of private property and the protection of society's poorest.

countrymen; words of vengeance and expiation had no meaning for us. We scorned our political or ideological adversaries more often than we detested them. And as for those individuals who society condemned as harmful, such as murderers and thieves, we didn't consider them our personal enemies; their crimes appeared in our eyes as accidents provoked by a social order that didn't give everyone a fair chance, but they certainly didn't compromise our own cherished values. We couldn't have pressed charges against a thief, before we don't feel entitled to our possessions; a murderer might have inspired horror, but not resentment: conscious of our own privileges, we wouldn't have dared demand that someone forced by poverty or birth to live outside the human community should respect our lives. We wouldn't have wanted to be complicit with a justice system that tenaciously upheld an order that we deplore.

But since June 1940, we have learned both rage and hate. We've wished for the humiliation and the death of our enemies. And today, each time a tribunal condemns to death a war criminal, a betrayer, a collaborator, we hold ourselves responsible for the verdict. Since we have desire this victory, since we have demanded this punishment, it's in our name that one judges and punishes; we are the selfsame public opinion that is expressed in newspapers and notices, in meetings, and which special bodies have been set to gratify; we are overjoyed by the death of Mussolini, the hanging of the killings of Kharkov, the tears of Darnand:[b] in this way, we have played a part in their condemnation. Their crimes have struck at our very hearts; it's our values, our justification for living that we reaffirm in punishing them. . . .

---

[b] **Benito Mussolini** (1883–1945) was Italy's fascist dictator and Nazi Germany's ally. He was arrested while trying to escape in April 1945 and summarily executed by Italian partisans. The **killings of Kharkov** refers to the deaths brought about the German's military takeover of the city against Soviet forces in October 1941. The face-off between Nazi and Soviet forces lasted until August 1943. Thirty thousand civilians (half of whom where Jewish) were murdered by the Nazis. **Joseph Darnand** (1887–1945) was a prominent French collaborationist. A fascist sympathizer and far-right activist before the war, he worked during the Vichy regime to create its paramilitary force, the Milice, fighting the Resistance and hunting French and foreign Jewish civilians to deport them. He joined the Waffen-SS in August 1942, was captured at the end of the war, and executed.

It is no small thing suddenly to discover ourselves judges and executioners. During the Occupation, we took up this role with enthusiasm. Hate was easy then. When we read the articles of *Je Suis Partout*, when we listened to the voices of Ferdonnet or Hérold Paquis on the radio, when we thought of the murderers of Oradour, of the torturers of Buchenwald, of the Nazi leaders and their accomplices, the German people, we would say in voices full of righteous indignation, "They will pay."[c] And our anger would feel like a promise of joy so profound that we hardly believed we could endure it. They have paid, they are going to pay, they pay daily, and yet the joy does not fill our hearts.

No doubt our disappointment is due, at least in part, to circumstances: the purges were not aboveboard. Many great war criminals met with such brutal ends that it was hard to see their deaths as atonement. Others remain at liberty to this very day. The dejection of the German people also tempers our hatred. But nothing sufficiently explains why this revenge so ardently desired leaves a taste of ashes in our mouths.

The very idea of punishment is distasteful. The moment we grasp in their actual reality the feelings, the attitudes represented by the words *vengeance, justice, pardon, charity*, they are reclothed in a new meaning that both astonishes and disquiets us. Punishment no longer appears as simple disciplinary measures casting a reflection of some past mystique. We've all felt the effects, to some degree, of the need to punish, to avenge ourselves, and we'd like to understand what this means today: is this need well founded, can it ever be gratified? To answer these questions, we must examine both the world and our consciences. . . .

---

[c] *Je Suis Partout* was a far-right newspaper that openly supported the Nazis and promoted antisemitism. Its editor in chief was Robert Brasillach. **Paul Ferdonnet** (1901–1945) was an antisemitic journalist and Nazi sympathizer who moved to Germany in the 1930s to work for the Nazi state radio. **Jean Hérold-Paquis** (1912–1945) was a journalist who joined the Spanish fascist forces and fought for Franco during the Spanish Civil War. During the war, he was a broadcaster for the official Vichy state radio. Like Ferdonnet, he was executed for treason in 1945. **Oradour** refers to the massacre of 642 men, women, and children by the Nazis in the small village of Oradour-sur-Glane on June 10, 1944.

This is why society doesn't authorize private vengeance; it can't allow it except in exceptional cases and never officially legitimizes it. The very day after the Liberation, an ordinance severely forbid individual score-settling. It invested in special bodies the responsibility to punish; the inflicting of vengeance was replaced by the imposition of punishment, which was elevated to the status of an institution and severed from its personal base: one declared that it was necessary to punish without hate, in the name of universal principles. If private vengeance inevitably ended up being thwarted, wouldn't social justice be better served? . . .

These are the reasons why I found myself unable to sign the petition in favor of pardoning Robert Brasillach. I believe that in the course of his trial I understood, by and large, how his political attitude fit in the whole of his life, and I know that in leaving the court of assizes I did not desire his death, because during that long and sinister ceremony his behavior merited esteem and not hate. Finally, I cannot envision without anguish how an affirmation of the principle "traitors must be punished" must end, one gray morning, with the flowing of actual blood. But I did not sign. Above all, to understand is not to excuse, and one can never understand a situation in which someone freely will to do wrong. The decision itself would have to be different than it was. To grasp the coherence of a life, its rapport with the given world, the logic of its development, none of this prevents the wrongful act from appearing as a choice. . . .[1]

1. Who is the "we" that Beauvoir refers to in her text? Who is her audience? How does this text reflect the particular postwar situation in France?

2. Why does Beauvoir make a distinction between "ordinary crimes" and war crimes? How is this distinction important for her analysis of the role of punishment?

[1]   Simone de Beauvoir, *An Eye for an Eye*, trans. Lisa Lieberman (Now and Then Reader, 2012), 16–76, Kindle edition.

3. Why does Beauvoir emphasize the power of feelings (rage, hate, resentment) and their role in wartime and postwar society?

4. How do Beauvoir's philosophical framework (phenomenology, existentialism) and political principles shape her analysis?

5. How does this text illustrate Beauvoir's own blind spots?

II.
INTRODUCTION TO *THE SECOND SEX* (1949)

The introduction to the first volume of The Second Sex *lays out the rationale, and the philosophical and political framework for the study of women, as well as the influences that shaped Beauvoir's thinking.*

I have long hesitated to write a book on woman. The topic is irritating, especially for women; neither is it new. Feminist quarrels have provoked much debate, and these have now been settled: let's not discuss it further. And, yet, there is still talk about it. Is there a "problem" after all? And what might this problem be? Do women even exist? Admittedly, many still believe in the "eternal feminine." Some whisper, "Even in Russia, at least, women are still womanly";[d] but others who claim to be well-informed—and they are sometimes the same people—bemoan that "womanliness is being lost, woman will be lost." One no longer truly knows whether women still exist, whether they will exist in the future, whether one should wish for their survival, what place they occupy in the world, and what place they should occupy. "Where are women?" a magazine's recent headline asked. But, first, what is a woman? One remarks: "*Tota mulier in utero*: it is a womb."[e]

---

[d] This is a reference to Soviet Russia. Some Western observers had criticized Soviet insistence on equality above all.

[e] Latin expression, commonly used by eighteenth-century medical doctors, meaning: "All of woman is in her womb."

Nonetheless, others who proclaim themselves experts decree upon commenting on some women, that "these ones are not women" although they possess, like others, a uterus. Everyone seems to agree that the human species contains females: they make up today, as they have yesterday, more or less half of humankind; and yet, we are told that, "femininity is endangered;" we are urged to "be women, stay women, become women." Does this mean that every female human being is not necessarily a woman? She must participate in this mysterious and imperiled fact of femininity. Is femininity a product of one's ovaries? Or frozen within a Platonic sky? Would one merely need a rustled skirt to make it come down to earth? Although many women strive to embody [this femininity], it has never been copyrighted. Instead, it is described in vague and shimmering terms almost borrowed from a fortune-teller's vocabulary. . . . Social and biological sciences no longer subscribe to the belief in immutable and fixed concepts that determine the characteristics of beings like Woman, the Jew, the Black; they deem one's character to be the secondary reaction to a *situation*. If there isn't any femininity nowadays, that is because it has never existed. Does this mean that is any substance to the word "woman?" . . . Surely, woman is, like man, a human being: but such a claim remains abstract; the fact of the matter is that every real human being is always individually situated. To reject the notion of an eternal feminine, a black soul, a jewish character does not mean denying that Jews, Blacks, and women exist; this denial only means for those concerned an inauthentic flight, rather than emancipation. It is obvious that no woman can pretend to be beyond her sex, unless she is of bad faith. . . .

The category of the Other is as old as consciousness itself. One can find a duality of the Same and the Other in the most primitive societies and in the most ancient mythologies; Originally, this division was not placed under the sign of sexual difference and did not depend upon empirical facts: this is what the works of Granet on Chinese thought, Dumézil on India and Rome have shown. No feminine element is identified in the couples Varuna-Mitra, Ouranos-Zeus, Sun-Moon, Day-Night;[f] neither does it appear in the opposition between Good and Evil, auspicious and harmful principles, left and right, God and Lucifer. Otherness is an essential category in human thought. No collectivity will define itself as One without first expressing that there is an Other it faces. One only needs to put three travelers together in a same train car for the rest of the train's travelers to be considered vaguely hostile "others." Villagers consider all those who do not belong to the village as suspicious "others;" a country's native resident will look at other countries' inhabitants as "foreigners;" the anti-Semite believes Jews are "others," American racists do the same with Blacks, as do colonizers with indigenous people, and the owning classes with the working classes. . . .[g]

There have been cases when, for a while, a category of people was able to dominate another completely. This privilege has often been the result of numerical inequality: the majority imposes its law upon a minority, and even persecutes it. But women are not a minority like American Blacks or like Jews: there are as many women as men on earth. Often, at first, these two groups existed independently: they sometimes ignored one another, or each recognized the other's autonomy; and one was subordinated to the other through a historical event: the Jewish diaspora, the introduction of slavery in America, colonial conquests—these are historical facts. In these cases, those oppressed can point to a *before*: [as a group,] they have a common past, tradition, sometimes a religion,

---

[f]   **Marcel Granet** (1884–1940) was a French sociologist and ethnologist specializing in the study of China. **Georges Dumézil** (1898–1986) was a world-renowned philologist specializing in the study of ancient Indo-European myths. **Veruna and Mitra** are Indian gods, and **Oranous and Zeus**, Greek gods.

[g]   Beauvoir uses the term "proletarians" and "proletariat" rather than working classes as a way of indicating her use and understanding of Marxist theory. She also uses the term "Black" as was common then, and as did her friend African-American novelist Richard Wright.

or culture. Maybe it is the comparison between woman and the working classes that Bebel first made that might be the most appropriate: proletarians are not numerically inferior, nor are they a separate group. It was not so much *one* event, but rather a historical development that explains their existence as a class and that sheds light on the subjection of *these* individuals within this particular class. There have not always been proletarians: there have always been women; they are women because of their physiological structure; and, as long as one goes back in history, women have been subordinated to men: . . . it is in part because this [subordination] does not seem to have come about as the accidental result of historical events that otherness here appears like an absolute. After all, a situation created over time can be undone over time: Haitian Blacks have clearly proved it;[h] whereas, it seems, on the contrary that a natural condition cannot change. However, in truth, like history, nature is not an unchanging fact. . . .[2]

1. What is the tone of Beauvoir's text? Does it change? What does it tell us about her intent and purpose?

2. Why does she focus on the question of otherness? What point is she trying to make?

3. Why does she compare women to "Jews," "Blacks," and workers?

4. How does Beauvoir conceive of power relations in society?

5. What does Beauvoir suggest is the role of history in shaping societies and relations?

6. How does Beauvoir think of biology? What is, according to her, the relationship between nature and history?

---

[h] Beauvoir refers to the Haitian 1791 slave revolution where, for the first and only time in history, slaves in the French colony of Saint-Domingue (present-day Haiti) took up arms and rebelled, demanding freedom and reform. Over the following years, war broke out and the French Republic was forced, as a result, to abolish slavery in 1793. Napoléon failed to reestablish his rule and slavery in St.-Domingue, and the first "Black Republic" of Haiti was proclaimed in 1804.

[2] Translated by Sandrine Sanos.

III.

INTRODUCTION TO *DJAMILA BOUPACHA*— *THE STORY OF THE TORTURE OF A YOUNG ALGERIAN GIRL WHICH SHOCKED LIBERAL FRENCH OPINION* (1962)

Beauvoir first published an article on June 3, 1960, in the respected left-leaning newspaper Le Monde *at lawyer Gisèle Halimi's request. The article caused a scandal. Two years later, she wrote the introduction to a book regarding Djamila Boupacha's ordeal, which included Halimi's account of her torture and trial, a reprint of Beauvoir's article, "In Defense of Djamila Boupacha," and reprints of testimonies by French and Algerian citizens who had also been tortured.*

An Algerian girl of twenty-three, an FLN liaison agent, illegally imprisoned by French military force, who subjected her to torture and deflowered her with a bottle: it is a common enough story. From 1954 onwards we have all compounded our consciences with a species of racial extermination that—first in the name of "subjugating rebellious elements" and later in that of "pacification"—has claimed over a million victims. Men and women, old folk and children, have been machine-gunned during "mopping up operations," burnt alive in their villages, had their throats slit or their bellies ripped open, died countless sorts of martyrs' deaths. Whole tribes have been bundled off to so-called rehabilitation or "regroupment" centres, where they were starved, beaten, and decimated by exposure and epidemics. Such places are in fact death camps, though they have a subsidiary function as brothels for the crack regiments. Today more than five hundred thousand Algerians are confined in them. During the last few months even our most circumspect papers have been full of horror stories: murders, lynchings, *ratonnades* and man-hunts through the streets of Oran [Algeria], dozens of corpses strung up from trees in the Bois de Boulogne, beside the Seine, in the very heart of

Paris;[i] endless cases involving maimed limbs or broken skulls. Algeria has become a second Haiti. Can we still be moved by the suffering on one young girl? After all—as was delicately hinted by M. Patin, President of the Committee of Public Safety, during an interview at which I was present—Djamila Boupacha is still alive, so her ordeal cannot have been all that frightful. M. Patin was alluding to the use of bottle on Djamila when he declared: "I feared at first that she might have been violated *per anum*, as was done on occasion with the Viets in Indochina: such treatment results in perforation of the intestines, and is fatal. But this was something quite different," he added, smiling: clearly nothing of the sort could ever happen to *him*.

In telling this story Gisèle Halimi is not attempting to convert those whose hearts still remain stubbornly impervious to the deep shame most of us feel because of it. The paramount interest of her book lies in its detailed exposure of a lying propaganda machine—a machine operated so efficiently that during the past seven years only a few faint glimmers of truth have contrived to slip past it. . . .

A man is tortured. He breaks under pressure, and is killed, or commits suicide. His body is spirited away. No corpse, no crime. Sometimes a father or a wife will make inquiries, to be met with the brief formula: disappeared, after which silence closes in once more. There was the case of a French university student called Audin, who had numerous friends, and whose "disappearance" provoked considerable comment.[j] Yet here rumor achieved nothing: his murderer received the Legion of Honour, and there were no reprisals. After the spectacular "suicide" of Boumendjel, numerous voices were raised in loud and vigorous protests, though again without result. As for all those unknown Algerians listed

---

[i] *Ratonnade* was a colloquial and pejorative term, referring to physical violence specifically directed at North African peoples, perpetrated by official authorities or civilians.

[j] **Maurice Audin** (1932–1957) was a communist university professor who was arrested in 1957 during the Battle of Algiers by the French army, tortured, and murdered. His "disappearance" was mentioned by Henri Alleg, who was also arrested and tortured, in his 1959 book on torture in Algeria, *The Question*. This became known as the "Audin affair" and was never recognized by the French state.

in the *Cahier Vert* (not to mention the much greater number of whom no record has been kept anywhere), public opinion is utterly indifferent to their fate, and of the agony they suffered no tangible trace survives.[k]

What of the victim who comes through such an ordeal? Though found innocent and released, he remains gagged by threats the effectiveness of which he knows all too well. In the normal course of events, too, and as an extra security measure, his place of residence is laid down for him, and this his gaolers guarantee that he will hold his tongue. If, on the other hand, he is found guilty, it is generally too late for him to lodge a complaint after the verdict has been pronounced. But, you may ask, does he not get a chance to speak out at the preliminary hearing? Far from it: he knows very well that if his testimony is dismissed, he will be "interrogated" all over again. Sometimes his torturers are actually waiting for him outside the magistrate's court. In Algeria, judges, doctors and barristers alike all regard such defendants as "the enemy," and it is on this tacit professional collusion that the entire system rests. A verdict of "guilty" is inevitable. The sentence has been decided in advance, and the only purpose of the trial is to camouflage the arbitrary nature of the proceedings. In this respect Djamila's case is instructive. . . .

. . . The alternatives are simple and clear-cut. Either—despite your willing and facile grief over such past horrors as the Warsaw ghetto or the death of Anne Frank—you align yourselves with our contemporary butchers rather than their victims, and give your unprotesting assent to the martyrdom which thousands of Djamilas and Ahmeds are enduring in your name, almost, indeed, before your very eyes; or else you reject, not merely certain specific practices, but the greater aim which sanctions them, and, for which they are essential. In the latter case you will refuse to

---

[k] **Ali Boumendjel** (1919–1957) was a journalist and lawyer who joined the FLN in 1955. He was arrested, tortured, and murdered in 1957. The army, at the time, claimed he had committed suicide and only recognized in 2000 that this was not the case. The *Cahier Vert* was published in 1959 by lawyer Jacques Vergès (who had defended FLN activist Djamila Bouhired in 1957), Michel Zavrian, and Maurice Courrège. Conceived with the Committee Maurice Audin, it was titled *The Disappeared*.

countenance a war that dares not speak its true name—not to mention an Army that feeds on war, heart and soul, and a Government that knuckles under to the Army's demands; and you will raise heaven and earth to give this gesture of yours effective force. There is no alternative, and I hope this book will convince you of this fact. The truth confronts you on all sides. You can no longer mumble the old excuse "we didn't know": and now that you *do* know, can you continue to feign ignorance, or content yourselves with a mere token utterance of horrified sympathy? I hope not.[3]

1. What is Beauvoir denouncing about the Algerian War?

2. How does Beauvoir try to elicit empathy from her readers? What kind of language does she use?

3. What is she criticizing?

4. Compare her argument with that made in her 1946 piece "An Eye for an Eye" regarding the role of justice. What is the problem in the case of the Algerian War?

5. Who are those she holds responsible for the shocking character of the Algerian War?

6. Why does Beauvoir compare the "past horrors" with present events? What is she pointing to?

IV.
CHAPTER 7 FROM *THE FORCE OF CIRCUMSTANCE* (1963)—EXCERPT

Beauvoir began writing this memoir, her third, in 1962. It covers the period from the Liberation of France in 1944 to the end of the Algerian War of Independence in 1962. While she used her letters and diaries, it was written with the knowledge of the outcome of the war. Like her previous memoirs, it was a huge

[3] Simone de Beauvoir, *Djamila Boupacha*, trans. Peter Green (New York: Macmillan, 1962), 9–21.

success, although Beauvoir felt her readers misunderstood her
and especially the politics and feelings she had tried to convey.

I did not willingly or even joyfully let the Algerian war invade my
thoughts, my sleep, my moods. After all, no one was more inclined
to follow [Albert] Camus' advice –to always and regardless protect one's happiness—than myself. There had been Indochina,
Madagascar, the (Tunisian) cap Bon, Casablanca: I had always
managed to recover my calm. After the [1956] capture of Ben Bella
and the Suez coup, I lost my tranquility: the government was stubbornly holding on to this war.[l] Algeria would become independent: but not for a long time. The truth of "pacification" revealed
itself at the very moment when I could not foresee the end of the
war. Some conscripts began talking; information started flooding
out: conversations, letters I received, that my friends received, foreign news accounts, reports that were to be more or less secret
were released by small groups. We did not know everything, but
we knew a lot, too much. My own situation in my country, in the
world, and in the relation I had to myself, was turned upside down.

I am an intellectual, I value words and truth: I had to endure
every day, endlessly and repeatedly, the assault of lies that all
these mouths spat out. Generals and colonels explained that they
were leading a generous and even revolutionary war. We witnessed a phenomenon akin to a circus: a thinking army! Pieds-
noirs were clamoring for their integration when the very idea of a
unique Collège made them jump in horror.[m] They asserted that,
aside from a few ringleaders, they were loved by the [Algerian]
population. However, during the *"ratonnade"* that followed

---

[l] **Ahmed Ben Bella** (1916–2012) was a FLN leader. He was arrested by the French in 1956 and only released at the end of the war in 1962. He became president of Algeria between 1963 and 1965. **The Suez
coup** is a reference to the 1956 Suez crisis when Israel invaded Egypt, with the support of the British and
the French. The invasion was condemned by the United States and a UN resolution.

[m] **Pied-noir** is a term used to refer to "European Algerians." Though it had been in used since the late nineteenth century, it became widespread especially after the end of the Algerian war. The Algerian population
was organized into two parliamentary-style bodies, electoral **collèges:** there were two, one comprised of
"Europeans" and the second of Algerian "Muslim" men, ensuring the domination of "European settler"
political voice.

Froger's funeral, they made no distinction between *good* Muslims, *their* Muslims, and the others: they lynched every single one they could get their hands on.[n] The media had become a counterfeiting machine. It did not say a word about the slaughter caused by Fechoz and Castille, but screamed at the bombings that started the Battle of Algiers.[o] Paratroopers shut down the Casbah, terrorism was stopped: we were not told how. Newspapers did not only fear seizures and judicial proceedings, but their readers' loss of interest: they said what their readers wanted to hear.

Because, as long as it was disguised, the country happily agreed to this war. . . .

I wanted to shatter my complicity with this war, but how? To speak in gatherings, to write articles: I would have explained the same things as Sartre but not as well. It seemed ridiculous to follow him like a shadow to the silent demonstration he joined with [François] Mauriac.[p] Today, [in 1961], I would have no other choice than to throw myself into this conflict, even if my presence weighs little. Before then, I had wanted to make sure my efforts meant something, even before I started trying.[4]

1. How does Beauvoir describe her response to the Algerian War? How is this influenced by her philosophical outlook? What effect does it have on readers?

2. What is especially shocking to her?

3. Beauvoir describes herself as an "intellectual" rather than a writer. Why does this distinction matter? How does she see her relationship to public involvement, especially as opposed to Sartre?

---

[n]   **Amédée Froger** (1882–1956) was the pied-noir mayor of the Algerian town of Boufarik. He was assassinated on December 28, 1956, by FLN activist Ali La Pointe.

[o]   Beauvoir refers to the bombs left by "French Algeria" supporters Michel **Fechoz** and Philippe **Castille** in the Algerian Muslim neighborhood of the Casbah (as opposed to the FLN-orchestrated bombs that inaugurated the Battle of Algiers). The **Battle of Algiers** is the face-off between the French army and the FLN between January and March 1957, which ended in the military defeat of the FLN.

[p]   **François Mauriac** (1885–1970) was a Catholic and conservative novelist who won the Nobel Prize for literature in 1952. He was among the minority of intellectuals denouncing torture from 1955 on.

[4]   Translated by Sandrine Sanos.

4. Why does she describe how she came to change her mind?

5. Compare this text to her text on the Djamila Boupacha affair. She wrote this text in 1962, almost two years after her Boupacha article. What are the differences and similarities in tone and in argument?

6. Is Beauvoir being "truthful" in her memoir about her own involvement?

V.
INTRODUCTION TO *THE BOBIGNY AFFAIR REPORT* (1973)

In 1972, Beauvoir joined forces with Gisèle Halimi to found the organization To Choose (Choisir), which would campaign for the legalization of abortion. After the trial of Marie-Claire Chevalier, her mother, and friends had ended with acquittal (she had been prosecuted for having had an abortion), To Choose published the transcript of the court proceedings, under the title "A Law on Trial," with an introduction by Beauvoir.

On the surface, this book appears to be like a lot of others. It is, however, completely out of the ordinary. Never before have the proceedings of a trial dealing with abortion been brought to the knowledge of the public. If the association Choisir has decided to have them printed in full it is for the simple reason that this particular trial bears no resemblance whatsoever to any of those which preceded it. It is not Mrs. Chevalier on whom judgment has been passed; rather it is the law under which she appeared before the court.[q] Women and men have followed one another into the witness box to indict a law which France appears to be one of the most reactionary nations of our time: a law which is

---

[q] Marie-Claire, who was then a minor, was not the only one tried. So was her mother, Michèle Chevalier and four other women. Marie-Claire was called as a witness in her mother's trial.

totally out of phase with the facts since it is broken every year by almost a million Frenchwomen. Judge Casamayor wrote, quite rightly:[r]

> When in a country, daily practices move too far away from what is in the legal code, there is then a grave threat to the stability and to the general mental health of that society. Experience shows that the legal code has no influence whatever on what is actually done: it is the law, then, that must be changed.

I have no hesitation in calling [this law] criminal. A properly performed abortion is an operation as minor as the extraction of a tooth: less dangerous than childbirth. In England, the percentages are 21 deaths out of 100,000 abortions and 24 out of 100,000 live births. In the State of New York where for two years now any woman less than 24 weeks pregnant may freely have an abortion, the results, according to the official pronouncement of the Director of the Health Department, have been an "enormous success." . . . There is only a minute number of doctors, of midwives and of nurses who are prepared to perform illegal terminations of pregnancy: termination is performed in the vast majority of cases by unqualified people under bad conditions—so bad, in fact, that the most elementary hygienic precautions are not observed. It is for this reason that so many women who have had abortions die; it is why a large number of them subsequently find themselves to be sterile, sick, or handicapped. The desperate quest to find an "address," the humiliation, the lies and subterfuge, the worry and the fear make abortion very often a traumatic experience. All the more so in that they are breaking the law, a lot of women are in awe of it or even have respect for it. They feel guilty and this contradiction sometimes gives rise to neurosis. And quite obviously, the risks of death and mutilation, the anxieties, are not shared equally by all the women. It is the poorest who pay the highest prices. And it is

---

[r] **Casamayor** was the pseudonym used by Serge Fuster (1911–1988) who was a judge and a writer.

always from this group that "justice" chooses its victims for repressions. You never see in the dock the wife of a magistrate or of a Minister, but rather salesgirls and secretaries. Mrs. Chevalier works in the Metro and is an unmarried mother. . . .[s]

The association Choisir has undertaken the struggle for the dissemination of contraceptive knowledge and for abortion on request. This struggle has more than one goal and there is more than one level to it. It is concerned in the first place to make abortion unnecessary by widening the use of those methods of contraception which are officially allowed but which only 7 percent of Frenchwomen use. It is concerned with defending women who have abortions and defending their "accomplices" too, against a society which, to breathe a semblance of life into a moribund law, arbitrarily decides to prosecute those who are the most disadvantaged. It is concerned with arousing public opinion, with putting pressure on the Government, in the furtherance of its object— that abortion shall no longer be punished. To bring about this reform would also be to go a long way beyond it. When—thanks to the wider knowledge and use of contraception, and the right to have an abortion—a women has gained mastery of her body and no longer poisoned by fear or remorse, she will be ready for other struggles. She will understand that she must change simultaneously her own status and this society which has imposed it on her. She will fight; but I hope the day will come when she will win.[5]

1. How does Beauvoir undermine the legitimacy of the law forbidding abortion and, as a result, of the judicial proceedings under way? What is the purpose of this argument?

2. On what grounds does Beauvoir begin arguing for the legalization of abortion?

---

[s] Here, Beauvoir refers to Marie-Claire Chevalier's mother who was also being tried for having helped her daughter.

[5] Simone de Beauvoir, Introduction to *The Bobigny Affair Report*, trans. Beryl Henderson (Sydney: Wild and Woolley, 1973), 9–21.

3. Beauvoir suggests matters of sexuality are also matters of class. Why is this important?

4. How does Beauvoir rhetorical strategy echo the one she and Halimi used during the Djamila Boupacha affair?

5. Beauvoir argues Choisir (To Choose) has "more than one goal." What are they?

6. In what ways is the struggle for reproductive rights a central component of Beauvoir's feminism? How does it echo (or differ from) her argument(s) in *The Second Sex*?

FURTHER READING

BEAUVOIR'S WORKS—A SELECTION

L'invitée [*She Came to Stay*], 1943—novel

Pyrrhus et Cinéas [*Pyrrhus and Cineas*], 1944—philosophical essay

Le sang des autres [*The Blood of Others*], 1945—novel

Les bouches inutiles [*Useless Mouths*], 1945—play

Tous les hommes sont mortels [*All Men Are Mortal*], 1946—novel/essay

Une éthique de l'ambiguïté [*The Ethics of Ambiguity*], 1947—philosophical essay

L'Amérique au jour le jour [*America Day by Day*], 1948—travel writing

Le deuxième sexe [*The Second Sex*], 1949—essay/study

Les mandarins [*The Mandarins*], 1954—novel

La longue marche [*The Long March*], 1957—political essay

Mémoires d'une jeune fille rangée [*Memoirs of a Dutiful Daughter*], 1958—memoir

La force de l'âge [*The Prime of Life*], 1960—memoir

Djamila Boupacha, with Gisèle Halimi, 1962—political essay

La force des choses [*The Force of Circumstance*], 1963—memoir

Une mort très douce [*A Very Easy Death*], 1964—novel

Les belles images [*Beautiful Images*], 1966—novel

La femme rompue [*The Woman Destroyed*], 1967—short stories

La vieillesse [*The Coming of Age*], 1970—essay/study

Tout compte fait [*All Said and Done*], 1972—memoir

ENGLISH-LANGUAGE COLLECTIONS
OF ESSAYS AND ARTICLES OF INTEREST

Feminist Writings, edited by Margaret Simons, Marybeth Timmermann, and Sylvie Le Bon Beauvoir. University of Illinois Press, 2015.

Philosophical Writings, edited by Margaret Simons, Marybeth Timmermann, and Sylvie Le Bon Beauvoir. University of Illinois Press, 2005.

Political Writings, edited by Margaret Simons, Marybeth Timmermann, and Sylvie Le Bon Beauvoir. University of Illinois Press, 2012.

ON BEAUVOIR, HER LIFE,
AND HER WORKS

Judith Coffin. *Sex, Love, and Letters: Writing Simone de Beauvoir* (in progress).

Judith Coffin. "Beauvoir, Kinsey, and Mid-Century Sex." *French Politics, Culture, and Society* 28, no. 2 (Summer 2010): 18–37.

Judith Coffin. "Historicizing *The Second Sex*." *French Politics, Culture, and Society* 25, no. 3 (Winter 2007): 123–48.

Emily Grosholz, ed. *The Legacy of Simone de Beauvoir*. Clarendon Press, 2004.

Sonia Kruks. *Simone de Beauvoir and the Politics of Ambiguity*. Oxford University Press, 2012.

Toril Moi. *Simone de Beauvoir: The Making of an Intellectual Woman*. 2nd ed. Oxford University Press, 2008.

Toril Moi. "While We Wait: The English Translation of *The Second Sex*," *Signs* 27, no. 4 (Summer 2002): 1005–35.

Margaret Simons. *Beauvoir and the Second Sex: Feminism, Race, and the Origins of Existentialism*. Littlefield and Rowman, 2001.

Judith Surkis. "Ethics and Violence: Simone de Beauvoir, Djamila Boupacha, and the Algerian War." *French Politics, Culture, and Society* 28 no. 2 (Summer 2010): 38–55.

Ursula Tidd. *Simone de Beauvoir: Gender and Testimony.* Cambridge University Press, 1999.

BOOKS IN FRENCH

François Azouvi. *Le mythe du grand silence: Auschwitz, les Français, la mémoire.* Fayard, 2014.

Raphaëlle Branche. *La torture et l'armée pendant la guerre d'Algérie: 1954–1962.* Gallimard, 2001.

Sylvie Chaperon. *Les années Beauvoir 1945–1970.* Fayard, 2000.

Annie Cohen-Solal. *Sartre, 1905–1980.* Gallimard, 1999.

Danièle Sallenave. *Castor de guerre.* Gallimard, 2008.

THE INTERWAR YEARS

Jennifer A. Boittin. *Colonial Metropolis: The Urban Grounds of Anti-Imperialism and Feminism in Interwar Paris.* University of Nebraska Press, 2015.

Caroline Campbell. *Political Belief in France, 1927–1945: Gender, Empire, and Fascism in the Croix de Feu and Parti Social Français.* Louisiana State University Press, 2015.

Jeffrey Jackson. *Making Jazz French: Music and Modern Life in Interwar Paris.* Duke University Press, 2003.

Roxanne Panchasi. *Future Tense: The Culture of Anticipation in France between the Wars.* Cornell University Press, 2009.

Mary-Louise Roberts. *Civilization Without Sexes: Reconstructing Gender in Postwar France, 1917–27.* Chicago University Press, 1994.

Sandrine Sanos. *The Aesthetics of Hate: Far-Right Intellectuals, Antisemitism, and Gender in 1930s France*. Stanford University Press, 2012.

Tracy Denean Sharpley-Whiting. *Negritude Women*. University of Minnesota Press, 2002.

Tyler Stovall. *Paris Noir: African-Americans in the City of Light*. Houghton Mifflin, 1996.

Gary Wilder. *The French Imperial Nation-State: Negritude and Colonial Humanism between the Two World Wars*. University of Chicago Press, 2005.

WORLD WAR II

Sarah Farmer. *Commemorating the 1944 Massacre at Oradour-sur-Glane*. University of California Press, 2000.

Shannon Fogg. *The Politics of Everyday life in Vichy France: Foreigners, Undesirables, and Strangers*. Cambridge University Press, 2011.

Julian Jackson. *France: The Dark Years, 1940–1944*. 2nd ed. Oxford University Press, 2003.

Eric Jennings. *Vichy in the Tropics: Pétain's National Revolution in Madagascar, Guadeloupe, and Indochina, 1940–1944*. Stanford University Press, 2004.

Alice Kaplan. *The Collaborator: The Trial and Execution of Robert Brasillach*. University of Chicago Press, 2001.

Daniel Lee. *Pétain's Jewish Children: French Jewish Youth and the Vichy Regime*. Oxford University Press, 2014.

Michael Marrus and Robert Paxton. *Vichy France and the Jews*. Basic Books, 1981.

Renée Poznanski. *Jews in France During World War Two*. Brandeis University Press, 2001.

THE POSTWAR YEARS

Tamara Chaplin. *Turning on the Mind: French Philosophers on Television*. University of Chicago Press, 2007.

Frederick Cooper. *Citizenship Between Empire and Nation: Remaking France and French Africa, 1945–1960*. Princeton University Press, 2015.

Richard I. Jobs. *Riding the New Wave: Youth and The Rejuvenation of France after the Second World War*. Stanford University Press, 2009.

Alice Kaplan. *Dreaming in French: The Paris Years of Jacqueline Bouvier Kennedy, Susan Sontag, and Angela Davis*. University of Chicago Press, 2013.

Steve Katz and Seàn Hands, eds. *Post-Holocaust France and the Jews*. Brandeis University Press, 2015.

Mary-Louise Roberts. *What Soldiers Do: Sex and the American GI in World War Two France*. Chicago University Press, 2014.

Daniel J. Sherman, *French Primitivism and the Ends of Empire, 1945–1975*. University of Chicago Press, 2011.

Rosemary Wakeman, *Heroic City: Paris, 1945–1958*. University of Chicago Press, 2009.

Gary Wilder. *Freedom Time: Negritude, Decolonization, and the Future of the World*. Duke University Press, 2015.

THE ALGERIAN WAR OF INDEPENDENCE, 1954–1962

Matthew Connelly. *A Diplomatic Revolution: Algeria's Fight for Independence and the Origins of the Post-Cold War Era*. Oxford University Press, 2002.

Martin Evans. *Algeria: France's Undeclared War*. Oxford University Press, 2012.

Fanon, Frantz. *The Wretched of the Earth*. Grove Press, 1960–reprint 2005.

Jim House and Neil Macmaster. *Paris 1961: Algerians, State Terror and Memory*. Oxford University Press, 2009.

James Le Sueur. *Uncivil War: Intellectuals and Identity Politics during the Decolonization of Algeria*. 2nd. ed. University of Nebraska Press, 2005.

Patricia M. E. Lorcin. *Imperial Identities: Stereotyping, Prejudice and Race in Colonial Algeria*. St. Martin's Press, 1995.

James McDougall. *History and the Culture of Nationalism in Algeria*. Cambridge University Press, 2006.

Todd Shepard. *The Invention of Decolonization: The Algerian War and the Remaking of France*. Cornell University Press, 2008.

THE 1960s

Margaret Atack. *May 68 in French Fiction and Film*. Oxford University Press, 1999.

Julian Jackson et al., eds. *May 68: Rethinking France's Last Revolution*. Palgrave Macmillan, 2011.

Martin Klimke. *1968 in Europe: A History of Protest and Activism, 1956–1977*. Palgrave Macmillan, 2008.

Samuel Moyn. *A Holocaust Controversy: The Treblinka Affair in Postwar France*. Brandeis Editions, 2005.

Kristin Ross. *May 68 and Its Afterlives*. University of Chicago Press, 2002.

Daniel J. Sherman et al., eds. *The Long 1968: Revisions and Perspectives*. Indiana University Press, 2013.

THE 1970s, 1980s, AND AFTER

Julian Bourg. *From Revolution to Ethics: May 68 and Contemporary French Thought.* McGills-Queen's University Press, 2007.

Michael Christofferson. *French Intellectuals Against the Left: The Anti-totalitarian Moment of the 1970s.* Berghahn Books, 2004.

Joan W. Scott. *Parité! Sexual Equality and the Crisis of French Universalism.* University of Chicago Press, 2007.

Joan W. Scott. *The Politics of the Veil.* Princeton University Press, 2009.

NOTES

INTRODUCTION

1. Alice Schwarzer, *Simone de Beauvoir Live* (DVD Emma Film edition, 1974).
2. Sabine Engel, "Interview with Alice Schwarzer," *Journal of French and Francophone Philosophy* (2003): 200–3, *jffp.pitt.edu/ojs/index.php/jffp*.
3. Engel, "Interview with Alice Schwarzer," 203.
4. Toril Moi, "While We Wait . . . Notes on the English Translation of *The Second Sex*," in Emily Grosholz, ed., *The Legacy of Simone de Beauvoir* (Oxford: Clarendon Press, 2006), 42.
5. Moi, "While We Wait," 38, 41.
6. See Further Reading at the end of the book.

CHAPTER I

1. Simone de Beauvoir, *The Force of Circumstance* (New York: Putnam & Sons, 1964), 648.
2. Simone de Beauvoir, *Memoirs of a Dutiful Daughter* (New York: World, 1959), 116.
3. Beauvoir, *Memoirs of a Dutiful Daughter*, 144–45.
4. Beauvoir, *Memoirs of a Dutiful Daughter*, 142.
5. Beauvoir, *Memoirs of a Dutiful Daughter*, 167.
6. Beauvoir, *Memoirs of a Dutiful Daughter*, 343, 355.
7. Ingrid Galster, interview with Jacqueline Gheerbrant, in *Beauvoir dans tous ses états* (Paris: Editions Tallandier, 2007), 48, 55.
8. Galster, *Beauvoir dans tous ses états*, 48.
9. Galster, *Beauvoir dans tous ses états*, 50, n.11, 58–59.
10. Galster, *Beauvoir dans tous ses états*, 50, 51, 56.
11. Galster, *Beauvoir dans tous ses états*, 53, 56.
12. Cited in Mary-Louise Roberts, *Civilization Without Sexes: Reconstructing Gender in Postwar France, 1917–1927* (Chicago: Chicago University Press, 1994).
13. Simone de Beauvoir, *The Prime of Life* (New York: World, 1962), 34.
14. Beauvoir, *Memoirs of a Dutiful Daughter*, 148.
15. Beauvoir, *The Prime of Life*, 24.
16. Beauvoir, *The Prime of Life*, 18.
17. Beauvoir, *The Prime of Life*, 35.
18. Beauvoir, *The Prime of Life*, 35–36.
19. Beauvoir, *The Prime of Life*, 28.
20. Beauvoir, *The Prime of Life* , 48.
21. Beauvoir, *The Prime of Life*, 48.

22. Beauvoir, *The Prime of Life*, 49.

23. On this movement, see Petrine Archer-Straw, *Negrophilia: Avant-Garde Paris and Black Culture in the 1920s* (London: Thames & Hudson, 2000); and Tyler Stovall, *Paris Noir: African Americans in the City of Light* (New York: Houghton Mifflin, 1996). On the inter-war cultural and political context, see Gary Wilder, *The French Imperial Nation-State: Negritude and Colonial Humanism between the Two World Wars* (Chicago: Chicago University Press, 2005).

24. Beauvoir, *The Prime of Life*, 17.

25. Beauvoir, *The Prime of Life*, 18, 22.

26. Beauvoir, *The Prime of Life*, 126.

27. Beauvoir, *The Prime of Life*, 255.

28. Beauvoir, *The Prime of Life*, 242, 255.

29. Beauvoir, *Memoirs of a Dutiful Daughter*, 251.

30. Beauvoir, *The Prime of Life*, 39.

31. Beauvoir, *The Prime of Life*, 40.

32. Beauvoir, *The Prime of Life*, 285.

33. Beauvoir, *The Prime of Life*, 285.

34. Annie Cohen-Solal, *Sartre. 1905–1980* (Paris: Gallimard, 1985), 232.

CHAPTER 2

1. Simone de Beauvoir, letter September 4, 1939, in *The Prime of Life* (New York: World, 1962), 295.

2. Cited in Ingrid Galster, *Beauvoir dans tous ses états* (Paris: Editions Tallandier, 2007), 80.

3. Simone de Beauvoir, *The Blood of Others* (New York: Penguin, 1964), 192, 198.

4. Beauvoir, *The Prime of Life*, 370.

5. Beauvoir, *The Prime of Life*, 473.

6. Rosemary Wakeman, *The Heroic City: Paris 1945–1958* (Chicago: University of Chicago Press, 2009), 22.

7. Beauvoir, *The Prime of Life*, 377.

8. Beauvoir, *The Prime of Life*, 369.

9. Shannon L. Fogg, *The Politics of Everyday Life in Vichy France: Foreigners, Undesirables, and Strangers* (New York: Cambridge University Press, 2009), 6.

10. Fogg, *Politics of Everyday Life*, 2.

11. Fogg, *Politics of Everyday Life*, 13.

12. Beauvoir, *The Prime of Life*, 369.

13. Julian Jackson, *France: The Dark Years, 1940–1944* (New York: Oxford University Press, 2001), 150.

14. Beauvoir, *The Prime of Life*, 365.

15. Beauvoir, *The Prime of Life*, 370.

16. Jackson, *The Dark Years*, 150–51.

17. Beauvoir, *The Prime of Life*, 374, 396.

18. Beauvoir, *The Prime of Life*, 370.
19. Beauvoir, *The Prime of Life*, 372.
20. Beauvoir, *The Prime of Life*, 381.
21. Beauvoir, *The Prime of Life*, 376.
22. Annie Cohen-Solal, *Sartre. 1909–1980* (Paris: Gallimard, 1985), 301.
23. Beauvoir, *The Prime of Life*, 395.
24. Beauvoir, *The Prime of Life*, 391.
25. Beauvoir, *The Prime of Life*, 384.
26. Beauvoir, *The Prime of Life*, 386.
27. Beauvoir, *The Prime of Life*, 295.
28. Beauvoir, *The Prime of Life*, 295.
29. Simone de Beauvoir, *She Came to Stay* (New York: World, 1954), 404.
30. Beauvoir seems to have noted the wrong date in her memoir, *The Prime of Life*, 406.
31. Galster, *Beauvoir dans tous ses états*, 84.
32. Beauvoir, *The Prime of Life*, 366.
33. Beauvoir, *The Prime of Life*, 407.
34. Jackson, *The Dark Years*, 218.
35. Beauvoir, *The Prime of Life*, 411.
36. Beauvoir, *The Prime of Life*, 411.
37. Beauvoir, *The Prime of Life*, 416.
38. Beauvoir, *The Prime of Life*, 366.
39. Galster, *Beauvoir dans tous ses états*, 82–83.
40. Beauvoir, *The Prime of Life*, 427–28.
41. Beauvoir, *The Prime of Life*, 440.
42. Beauvoir, *The Prime of Life*, 444.
43. Beauvoir, *The Prime of Life*, 444.
44. Beauvoir, *The Prime of Life*, 453.
45. Beauvoir, *The Prime of Life*, 453.
46. Beauvoir, *The Prime of Life*, 421.
47. Beauvoir, *The Prime of Life*, 418, 456. She always referred to him as a Spanish Jew but, in an interview decades later, she conceded he had not been Spanish but Algerian.
48. She wrote about Bourla's death in the novel she began writing after the war, *Les mandarins* (*The Mandarins*) published in 1954.
49. Beauvoir, *The Prime of Life*, 463.
50. Cited in Wakeman, *Heroic City*, 31.
51. Richard I. Jobs, *Riding the New Wave: Youth and the Rejuvenation of France after the Second World War* (Stanford, CA: Stanford University Press, 2007), 19.
52. Simone de Beauvoir, *The Force of Circumstance* (New York: Putnam's Sons, 1964), 10.
53. Beauvoir, *Force of Circumstance*, 10.
54. Cited in Galster, *Beauvoir dans tous ses états*, n.75, 93.
55. Beauvoir, *The Prime of Life*, 474.
56. Beauvoir, *The Prime of Life*, 373.
57. Beauvoir, *The Prime of Life*, 373, 474.

58. Beauvoir, *The Prime of Life*, 473.

59. Beauvoir, *The Prime of Life*, 479.

CHAPTER 3

1. Simone de Beauvoir, *The Force of Circumstance* (New York: Putnam & Sons, 1964), 13.

2. Beauvoir, *Force of Circumstance*, 14.

3. Annie Cohen-Solal, *Sartre. 1905–1980* (Paris: Gallimard, 1985), 436–37.

4. Jean-Paul Sartre, *Les Temps Modernes*, October 1945, no. 1, reprinted in *Situations II* (Paris: Gallimard, 1948).

5. Throughout the text, I will use the masculine pronoun in keeping with the conventions and habits of French philosophy and language. In French, the universal category of the "individual" or "human" is referred to, grammatically, as masculine. Only recently have critics and philosophers challenged this usage.

6. Beauvoir, *Force of Circumstance*, 8.

7. Beauvoir, *Force of Circumstance*, 9.

8. Beauvoir, *Force of Circumstance*, 9.

9. Beauvoir, *Force of Circumstance*, 8.

10. Julian Jackson, *The Dark Years: 1940–1944* (New York: Oxford University Press, 2001), 578.

11. On Brasillach's trial, see Alice Kaplan, *The Collaborator: The Trial and Execution of Robert Brasillach* (Chicago: Chicago University Press, 2001).

12. Simone de Beauvoir, "An Eye for an Eye," trans. Lisa Lieberman (Now & Then Reader – kindle edition, 2012), 56.

13. Beauvoir, "An Eye for an Eye," 18.

14. Beauvoir, "An Eye for an Eye," 41.

15. Beauvoir, "An Eye for an Eye," 76.

16. Beauvoir, *Force of Circumstance*, 21.

17. Simone de Beauvoir, *The Prime of Life* (New York: World, 1962), 398.

18. Beauvoir, *Force of Circumstance*, 22.

19. Ingrid Galster, *Beauvoir dans tous ses états* (Paris: Tallandier, 2007), 78.

20. Beauvoir, *Force of Circumstance*, 20.

21. Beauvoir, *The Prime of Life*, 290.

22. For an account of Violette Leduc's life, see Carlo Jansiti, *Violette Leduc. Biographie* (Paris: Grasset, 2013).

23. Simone de Beauvoir, "What Can Literature Do?" Conference Talk, December 9, 1964, cited in Toril Moi, "What Can Literature Do? Simone de Beauvoir as Literary Theorist," *PMLA* 124, no. 1 (2009): 189–98.

24. Because the English edition is out of print, all references will be made to the French text: Simone de Beauvoir, *Tout compte fait* (Paris: Gallimard, 1972), 62.

25. Beauvoir, *The Prime of Life*, 43.

26. Beauvoir, *Force of Circumstance*, 17.

27. Beauvoir, *Tout compte fait*, 291.

28. Simone de Beauvoir, *America Day by Day* (Berkeley: University of California Press, 1999), 3.

29. Beauvoir, *America Day by Day*, 13.

30. Beauvoir, *America Day by Day*, 14.

31. Beauvoir, *Force of Circumstance*, 52, 68–69.

32. Simone de Beauvoir, *Lettres à Nelson Algren: Un amour transatlantique 1947–1964* (Paris: Gallimard, 1997).

33. Simone de Beauvoir, July 19, 1948, letter, in Beauvoir, *Lettres à Nelson Algren*, 315–16.

34. Simone de Beauvoir, *The Mandarins* (New York: Harper Perennial, 2005).

35. On this, see Rosemary Wakeman, *Heroic City: Paris 1945–1958* (Chicago: University of Chicago Press, 2009).

36. Colette Audry, "Notes pour un portrait de Simone de Beauvoir," *Les Lettres Françaises*, December 17–24, 1954, 5.

37. Audry, "Notes pour un portrait," 5.

CHAPTER 4

1. Susan Weiner, *Enfants Terribles: Youth and Femininity in the Mass Media in France, 1945–1968* (Baltimore: Johns Hopkins University Press, 2001), 22; Sylvie Chaperon, *Les années Beauvoir 1945–1970* (Paris: Fayard, 2000), 31.

2. Cited in Weiner, *Enfants Terribles*, 23.

3. Cited in Weiner, *Enfants Terribles*, 23.

4. Colette Audry, "Notes pour un portrait de Simone de Beauvoir," *Les Lettres Françaises*, December 17–24, 1954, 1.

5. Simone de Beauvoir, *The Prime of Life* (Cleveland: World, 1962), 16.

6. Beauvoir, *The Prime of Life*, 400.

7. Fabrice Virgili, *La France virile: Des femmes tondues à la Libération* (Paris: Petite Bibliothèque Payot, 2004), 8.

8. Virgili, *La France virile*, 27–29.

9. Virgili, *La France virile*, 250.

10. Jean Elizabeth Pedersen, "Regulating Abortion and Birth Control: Gender, Medicine, and Republican Politics in France, 1870–1920," *French Historical Studies* 19, no. 3 (Spring 1996): 676; see also Mary-Louise Roberts, *Civilization Without Sexes: Reconstructing Gender in Postwar France, 1917–1927* (Chicago: Chicago University Press, 1994), 98–119.

11. Weiner, *Enfants terribles*, 23. The law's provision on divorce was annulled April 12, 1945, see Chaperon, *Les années Beauvoir*, 19. On the Vichy regime's gender ideology, see Miranda Pollard, *Reign of Virtue: Mobilizing Gender in Vichy France* (Chicago: University of Chicago Press, 1998).

12. Beauvoir, *The Prime of Life*, 452.
13. Simone de Beauvoir, *The Force of Circumstance* (New York: Putnam's Sons, 1965), 185.
14. I indicate passages in the English edition but all translations are mine, since the English translation was inaccurate and truncated. Simone de Beauvoir, *The Second Sex* (New York: Knopf, 1971), xiii.
15. Simone de Beauvoir, *Anne ou quand prime le spirituel* (Paris: Gallimard, 2006), 27.
16. Margaret Simons, *Beauvoir and* The Second Sex: *Feminism, Race, and the Origins of Existentialism* (New York: Rowman & Littlefield, 2001), 177.
17. Beauvoir, *The Second Sex*, xiv.
18. Beauvoir, *The Second Sex*, xviii.
19. Beauvoir, *The Second Sex*, xix.
20. Beauvoir, *The Second Sex*, xvi.
21. Beauvoir, *The Second Sex*, 37.
22. Beauvoir, *The Second Sex*, 36.
23. Beauvoir, *The Second Sex*, 13.
24. Beauvoir, *The Second Sex*, 24.
25. Beauvoir, *The Second Sex*, 34.
26. Beauvoir, *The Second Sex*, 36.
27. Beauvoir, *The Second Sex*, 45.
28. Beauvoir, *The Second Sex*, 45.
29. Beauvoir, *The Second Sex*, 51–52.
30. Camille Robcis, *The Law of Kinship: Anthropology, Psychoanalysis, and the Family in France* (Ithaca, NY: Cornell University Press, 2013).
31. Beauvoir, *The Second Sex*, 53.
32. Beauvoir, *The Second Sex*, 54–55, 57.
33. Beauvoir, *The Second Sex*, 58.
34. Beauvoir, *The Second Sex*, 49.
35. Beauvoir, *The Second Sex*, 49.
36. Beauvoir, *The Second Sex*, 74.
37. Beauvoir, *The Second Sex*, 139.
38. This passage (the introduction to the second volume) was deleted in the 1952 English translation. Simone de Beauvoir, *Le deuxième sexe*, vol. 2 (Paris: Gallimard, 1976), 9.
39. Beauvoir, *The Second Sex*, 273, 278–79, 280–81.
40. Beauvoir, *The Second Sex*, 343.
41. Beauvoir, *The Second Sex*, 374.
42. Beauvoir, *The Second Sex*, 374.
43. Beauvoir, *The Second Sex*, 387.
44. Beauvoir, *The Second Sex*, 424.
45. Beauvoir, *The Second Sex*, 450–51.
46. Beauvoir, *The Second Sex*, 495.
47. Beauvoir, *The Second Sex*, 522.
48. Beauvoir, *The Second Sex*, 484.

49. Beauvoir, *The Second Sex*, 485.

50. Beauvoir, *The Second Sex*, 492.

51. Beauvoir, *The Second Sex*, ch. 24: "The Mystic," 670–78, ch. 22: "The Narcissist," 629–41, ch. 23: "The Woman in Love," 642–69.

52. Simone de Beauvoir, *Lettres à Nelson Algren: Un amour transatlantique 1947–1964* (Paris: Gallimard, 1997), 322.

53. Beauvoir, *Force of Circumstance*, 185.

54. Judith Coffin, "Historicizing The Second Sex," *French Politics, Culture, and Society* 25, no. 3 (Winter 2007): 128.

55. Martine Reid, "Anatomie d'une réception: Le deuxième sexe," in Julia Kristeva et al., eds., *(Re)Découvrir l'oeuvre de Simone de Beauvoir: Du deuxième sexe à La cérémonie des adieux* (Paris: Éditions Le Bord de l'Eau, 2008), 208–15.

56. Beauvoir, *The Second Sex*, 267.

57. Coffin, "Historicizing The Second Sex," 128–31.

58. Sylvie Chaperon, *Les années Beauvoir 1945–1970* (Paris: Fayard, 2000), 183; Coffin, "Historicizing The Second Sex," 134–35.

59. Coffin, "Historicizing The Second Sex," 135–36.

60. Chaperon, *Les années Beauvoir*, 113–14.

61. Reid, "Anatomie d'une réception," 214; Chaperon, *Les années Beauvoir*, 178–79.

62. On this, see Weiner, *Enfants Terribles*.

63. Coffin, "Historicizing The Second Sex," 124–25.

64. Carol Giardina, *Freedom for Women: Forging the Women's Liberation Movement, 1953–1979* (Gainesville: University Press of Florida, 2010), 75.

65. Giardina, *Freedom for Women*, 77, 78.

66. Giardina, *Freedom for Women*, 75–76.

67. Giardina, *Freedom for Women*, 79.

CHAPTER 5

1. Simone de Beauvoir, *The Force of Circumstance* (New York: Putnam's Sons, 1965), 302.

2. Beauvoir, *Force of Circumstance*, 365.

3. On this, see Tyler Stovall, *Paris Noir: African Americans in the City of Light* (New York: Houghton Mifflin, 1996).

4. Simone de Beauvoir, *The Prime of Life* (New York: World, 1962), 262–66.

5. Beauvoir, *Force of Circumstance*, 162–64.

6. Beauvoir, *Force of Circumstance*, 326.

7. Cited in Todd Shepard, *The Invention of Decolonization: The Algerian War and the Remaking of France* (Ithaca, NY: Cornell University Press, 2006), 6.

8. For an overview, see Shepard, *The Invention of Decolonization*.

9. Beauvoir, *Force of Circumstance*, 366.

10. Beauvoir, *Force of Circumstance*, 367.

11. Simone de Beauvoir, *Brigitte Bardot and the Lolita Syndrome* (New York: Arno Press, 1972); see also Richard I. Jobs, *Riding the New Wave: Youth and the Rejuvenation of France after the Second World War* (Stanford, CA: Stanford University Press, 2007), 185–231.

12. Beauvoir, *Force of Circumstance*, 487.

13. Beauvoir, *Force of Circumstance*, 369.

14. Simone de Beauvoir, *The Long March* (New York: World, 1958), 483.

15. Beauvoir, *The Long March*, 482, 483.

16. Beauvoir, *Force of Circumstance*, 344.

17. Beauvoir, *Force of Circumstance*, 367.

18. Beauvoir, *Force of Circumstance*, 368.

19. Beauvoir, *Force of Circumstance*, 369.

20. Beauvoir, *Force of Circumstance*, 375–78.

21. Beauvoir, *Force of Circumstance*, 326.

22. Beauvoir, *Force of Circumstance*, 620.

23. Beauvoir, *Force of Circumstance*, 382–83.

24. Simone de Beauvoir, *Tout compte fait* (Paris: Gallimard, 1972), 165.

25. Beauvoir, *Force of Circumstance*, 372.

26. Simone de Beauvoir, *Memoirs of a Dutiful Daughter* (New York: World, 1959), 382.

27. Beauvoir, *Force of Circumstance*, 471.

28. Beauvoir, *Force of Circumstance*, 407.

29. Beauvoir, *Force of Circumstance*, 396, 408.

30. Beauvoir, *Force of Circumstance*, 408, 437.

31. Beauvoir, *The Prime of Life*, 289.

32. Simone de Beauvoir, interview with *Québec* journal (August– September 1964).

33. Beauvoir, *Force of Circumstance*, 575.

34. Beauvoir, *Force of Circumstance*, 575–76.

35. Judith Surkis, "Ethics and Violence: Simone de Beauvoir, Djamila Boupacha, and the Algerian War," *French Politics, Culture, and Society* 28, no. 2 (Summer 2010): 40.

36. Judith Coffin, "Sex, Love, and Letters: Writing Simone de Beauvoir, 1949–1963," *American Historical Review* 115, no. 4 (October 2010): 1068.

37. Beauvoir, *Force of Circumstance*, 460.

38. Beauvoir, *Force of Circumstance*, 599.

39. Beauvoir, *Force of Circumstance*, 458.

40. Beauvoir, *Force of Circumstance*, 484.

41. Beauvoir, *Force of Circumstance*, 500–1.

42. Surkis, "Ethics and Violence," 39.

43. Cited in Surkis, "Ethics and Violence," 38.

44. Beauvoir, *Force of Circumstance*, 383.

45. Surkis, "Ethics and Violence," 44.

46. Surkis, "Ethics and Violence," 44.

47. Jacques Vergès, interviewed in the documentary film *L'avocat de la terreur* (Barbet Schroeder, 2007).

48. Simone de Beauvoir, introduction to Simone de Beauvoir and Gisèle Halimi, *Djamila Boupacha: The Story of the Torture of a Young Algerian Girl Which Shocked French Liberal Opinion* (New York: Macmillan Press, 1962), 9.

49. Beauvoir, *Force of Circumstance*, 575.

50. Beauvoir, *Force of Circumstance*, 587.

51. Beauvoir, *Force of Circumstance*, 596–97.

52. Beauvoir, *Force of Circumstance*, 597.

53. Beauvoir, *Force of Circumstance*, 596.

54. Beauvoir, *Force of Circumstance*, 600.

55. Beauvoir, *Force of Circumstance*, 603.

56. On this, see Shepard, *The Invention of Decolonization*.

57. Beauvoir, *Force of Circumstance*, 623–24.

58. Beauvoir, *Force of Circumstance*, 623.

59. Beauvoir, *Force of Circumstance*, 642.

60. Beauvoir, *Force of Circumstance*, 642.

61. I thank Judy Coffin for sharing her chapter on "Beauvoir's Algerian War," from her book in progress, *Sex, Love, and Letters: Writing Simone de Beauvoir.*

62. Beauvoir, *Force of Circumstance*, 658.

63. Beauvoir, *Force of Circumstance*, 653.

64. Simone de Beauvoir, preface, in Violette Leduc, *La bâtarde* (Paris: Gallimard, 1964), 10.

65. Beauvoir, preface, in *La bâtarde*, 10.

66. Her remark upon her meeting with Gisèle Halimi, in Beauvoir, *Force of Circumstance*, 450.

CHAPTER 6

1. Simone de Beauvoir, *The Force of Circumstance* (New York: Putnam's Sons, 1965), 656.

2. Simone de Beauvoir, *A Very Easy Death* (New York: Putnam's Sons, 1966), 68.

3. Beauvoir, *A Very Easy Death*, 69.

4. Beauvoir, *Force of Circumstance*, 332.

5. Simone de Beauvoir, *Tout compte fait* (Paris: Gallimard, 1972), 281–82; Danièle Sallenave, *Castor de guerre* (Paris: Gallimard, 2008), 528.

6. Beauvoir, *Tout compte fait*, 235.

7. Sallenave, *Castor de guerre*, 510.

8. Beauvoir, *Tout compte fait*, 362.

9. Beauvoir, *Tout compte fait*, 375.

10. Michael Scott Christofferson, *French Intellectuals Against the Left: The Antitotalitarian Moment of the 1970s* (New York: Berghahn Books, 2004), 50.

11. Beauvoir, *Tout compte fait*, 377.

12. Beauvoir, *Tout compte fait*, 379–80.

13. Beauvoir, *Tout compte fait*, 385.

14. Beauvoir, *Tout compte fait*, 388–89.
15. Samuel Moyn, *A Holocaust Controversy: The Treblinka Affair in Post-war France* (Brandeis: Brandeis University Press, 2005).
16. Moyn, *A Holocaust Controversy*, 5, 142.
17. François Azouvi, *Le Mythe du grand silence: Auschwitz, Les Français, La mémoire* (Paris: Fayard, 2012), 187, 188, 193.
18. Simone de Beauvoir, preface, Jean-François Steiner, *Treblinka: La révolte d'un camp d'extermination* (Paris: Fayard, 1966), 5. See also, "Preface to *Treblinka*," in Margaret Simons and Marybeth Timmerman, eds., *Simone de Beauvoir: Political Writings* (Urbana: University of Illinois Press, 2012), 305–10.
19. Cited in Moyn, *A Holocaust Controversy*, 6.
20. Moyn, *A Holocaust Controversy*, 4, 6.
21. Azouvi, *Le Mythe du grand silence*, 222.
22. Beauvoir, preface, in Steiner, *Treblinka*, 5.
23. Beauvoir, preface, in Steiner, *Treblinka*, 6; Moyn, *A Holocaust Controversy*, 48–49.
24. Beauvoir, *Tout compte fait*, 147.
25. Sylvie Chaperon, *Les années Beauvoir 1945–1970* (Paris: Fayard, 2000), 292.
26. Chaperon, *Les années Beauvoir*, 195.
27. Beauvoir, "Lettre à Jacques Lecarme (1969)," *Cahiers de l'Herne: Simone de Beauvoir*, no.100 (Paris: Editions de l'Herne, 2012).
28. Chaperon, *Les années Beauvoir*, 214.
29. Chaperon, *Les années Beauvoir*, 238–39.
30. Chaperon, *Les années Beauvoir*, 240.
31. Chaperon, *Les années Beauvoir*, 265.
32. Beauvoir, *Force of Circumstance*, 499–500.
33. Chaperon, *Les années Beauvoir*, 314–15.
34. Chaperon, *Les années Beauvoir*, 272.
35. Chaperon, *Les années Beauvoir*, 291–94.
36. Beauvoir, *Tout compte fait*, 466.
37. Max Capocardo, *Jean-Paul Sartre et Simone de Beauvoir* (1967), H-France review Judith Coffin, http://www.h-france.net/vol10 reviews/vol10no13coffin.pdf.
38. Beauvoir, *Tout compte fait*, 403.
39. Beauvoir, *Tout compte fait*, 404.
40. Beauvoir, *Tout compte fait*, 406.
41. Beauvoir, *Tout compte fait*, 406.
42. Beauvoir, *Tout compte fait*, 418.
43. Beauvoir, *Tout compte fait*, 422.
44. Beauvoir, *Tout compte fait*, 426.
45. Beauvoir, *Tout compte fait*, 428.
46. Beauvoir, *Tout compte fait*, 403.
47. Azouvi, *Le Mythe du grand silence*, 86.
48. Beauvoir, *Tout compte fait*, 443.
49. Beauvoir, *Tout compte fait*, 443, 445.

50. Beauvoir, *Tout compte fait*, 447, 448, 449.

51. Beauvoir, *Tout compte fait*, 447, 449.

52. Beauvoir, *Tout compte fait*, 459.

53. Beauvoir, *Tout compte fait*, 455, 462.

54. Beauvoir, *Tout compte fait*, 465.

55. Beauvoir, *Tout compte fait*, 588.

56. Beauvoir, *Tout compte fait*, 588.

57. Julian Jackson et al., eds, *May 68: Rethinking France's Last Revolution* (New York: Palgrave Macmillan, 2011).

58. Pierre Viasson-Pontée cited in Margaret Atack, *May 68 in French Fiction and Film: Rethinking Society, Rethinking Representation* (New York: Oxford University Press, 1999), 12.

59. Beauvoir, *Tout compte fait*, 467.

60. See Jackson, *May 68*, 5–6.

61. Beauvoir, *Tout compte fait*, 469.

62. Beauvoir, *Tout compte fait*, 468.

63. Beauvoir, *Tout compte fait*, 470.

64. Xavier Vigna, "Beyond Tradition: The Strikes of May–June 1968," in Jackson, *May 68*, 48.

65. Beauvoir, *Tout compte fait*, 468.

66. Beauvoir, *Tout compte fait*, 470.

67. Vigna, "Beyond Tradition," in Jackson, *May 68*, 48

68. Boris Gobille, "Exploitation, Alienation and the Social Division of Labour in the May–June Movement in France," in Jackson, *May 68*, 34–46.

69. Beauvoir, *Tout compte fait*, 588.

70. Beauvoir, *Tout compte fait*, 471.

71. Beauvoir, *Tout compte fait*, 476.

72. Beauvoir, *Tout compte fait*, 477.

73. Beauvoir, *Tout compte fait*, 403.

74. Beauvoir, *Tout compte fait*, 183.

75. Simone de Beauvoir, *The Coming of Age* (New York: Putnam's Sons, 1972), 13.

76. Beauvoir, *The Coming of Age*, 1.

77. Beauvoir, *Tout compte fait*, 148.

78. Beauvoir, *The Coming of Age*, 2.

79. Beauvoir, *The Coming of Age*, 2.

80. Beauvoir, *The Coming of Age*, 10.

81. Beauvoir, *The Coming of Age*, 13.

82. Beauvoir, *Tout compte fait*, 149.

83. Beauvoir, *Tout compte fait*, 149, 150.

CHAPTER 7

1. Simone de Beauvoir, *Tout compte fait* (Paris: Gallimard, 1972), 36.

2. Beauvoir, *Tout compte fait*, 10.

3. "Simone de Beauvoir interroge Jean-Paul Sartre," in *Situations X: Politique et Autobiographie* (Paris: Gallimard, 1976), 120.

4. Francis Jeanson, *Simone de Beauvoir ou l'entreprise de vivre* (Paris: Seuil, 1966), 251–56.

5. Beauvoir *Tout compte fait*, 50.

6. Beauvoir, *Tout compte fait*, 69.

7. Beauvoir, *Adieux: A Farewell to Sartre* (New York: Pantheon Books, 1984), 4.

8. Julian Bourg, *From Revolution to Ethics: May 68 and Contemporary French Thought* (Montreal & Kingston: McGill-Queen's University Press, 2007).

9. Beauvoir, *Adieux*, 4.

10. Bourg, *From Revolution to Ethics*, 66.

11. Anne-Claire Rebreyand, "May 68 and the Changes in Private Life: A 'Sexual Liberation'?" in Julian Jackson et al. eds., *May 68: Rethinking France's Last Revolution* (New York: Palgrave MacMillan, 2011), 148–51.

12. Massimo Prearo, "The 1970s Moment in Sexual Politics," in Jackson, *May 68,* 138, 144.

13. Beauvoir, *Tout compte fait*, 496.

14. Beauvoir, *Tout compte fait*, 491.

15. Michelle Zancarini-Fournel, "Notre corps, nous-mêmes," in Eliane Gubin et al. eds., *Le siècle des féminismes* (Paris: Editions de l'Atelier, 2004), 211.

16. Beauvoir, *Tout compte fait*, 492.

17. Beauvoir, *Tout compte fait*, 495.

18. Rod Kedward, *France and the French: A Modern History* (Woodstock, NY: Overlook Press, 2006), 441–44.

19. Beauvoir, *Tout compte fait*, 501, 503.

20. Beauvoir, *Adieux*, 28.

21. Beryl Henderson, *Abortion, The Bobigny Affair: A Law on Trial. A Complete Record of the Proceedings at the Court of Bobigny, November 8, 1972* (Sydney: Wild & Woolley, 1975), 4.

22. *Abortion, The Bobigny Affair,* 5.

23. *Abortion, The Bobigny Affair,* 7.

24. *Abortion, The Bobigny Affair,* 7, 159.

25. Beauvoir, Introduction, in *Abortion, The Bobigny Affair,* x.

26. Beauvoir, Introduction, in *Abortion, The Bobigny Affair,* x.

27. Beauvoir, Introduction, in *Abortion, The Bobigny Affair,* xiv.

28. Beauvoir, *All Said and Done*, 47.

29. Carlo Jansiti, *Violette Leduc* (Paris: Grasset, 1999), 447–48.

30. Beauvoir, *Tout compte fait*, 505.

31. Beauvoir, *Adieux*, 38–39.

32. For an overview, see Dagmar Herzog, *Sexuality in Europe: A Twentieth-Century History* (New York: Cambridge University Press, 2011), 156–60.

33. Danièle Sallenave, *Castor de guerre* (Paris: Gallimard, 2008), 537.
34. See www.jerusalembookfair.com/the_jerusalem_prize.html.
35. Simone de Beauvoir, "Solidarité avec Israël: Un soutien Critique," in Margaret Simons and Marybeth Timmerman, eds., *Simone de Beauvoir: Political Writings* (Urbana: University of Illinois Press, 2012), 315.
36. Beauvoir, *Adieux*, 82.
37. "Simone de Beauvoir interroge Jean-Paul Sartre," 116
38. "Simone de Beauvoir interroge Jean-Paul Sartre," 117.
39. "Simone de Beauvoir interroge Jean-Paul Sartre," 123, 132.
40. Susan Suleiman, "Introduction," in Simons and Timmerman, *Simone de Beauvoir*, 300.
41. Zancarini-Fournel, "Notre corps, nous-mêmes," 217.
42. Zancarini-Fournel, "Notre corps, nous-mêmes," 217.
43. Bourg, *From Revolution to Ethics*, 187.
44. Todd Shepard, "'Something Notably Erotic': Politics, 'Arab Men,' and Sexual Revolution in Post-Decolonization France, 1962–74," *Journal of Modern History* 84, no. 1 (March 2012): 104.
45. Zancarini-Fournel, "Notre corps, nous-mêmes," 217–28.
46. Shepard, "'Something Notably Erotic,'" 95, 101–2, 105.
47. Zancarini-Fournel, "Notre corps, Nous-mêmes," 213; Bourg, *From Revolution to Ethics*, 194.
48. Bourg, *From Revolution to Ethics*, 193–95.
49. Bourg, *From Revolution to Ethics*, 195.
50. Bourg, *From Revolution to Ethics*, 195.
51. Beauvoir, *Adieux*, 95.
52. Beauvoir, *Adieux*, 7.
53. Beauvoir, *Adieux*, 107.
54. Beauvoir, *Adieux*, 63.
55. Beauvoir, *Adieux*, 110–11.
56. Beauvoir, *Adieux*, 118–19.
57. Beauvoir, *Adieux*, 126.
58. Susan Bainbrigge, "'La Cérémonie des Adieux' and 'Le Livre brisé': Situating Sartre in the Text," *Modern Language Review* 97, no. 4 (Oct. 2002): 837.
59. Beauvoir, *Adieux*, 3.
60. Bertrand Poirot-Delpech, *Le Monde*, Nov. 26, 1981, cited in Bainbrigge, "'La Cérémonie des Adieux,'" 835.
61. Beauvoir, *Adieux*, 11, 17–18, 21, 31–34, 45–49, 54, 62, 63–65, 91, 101, 118–21.
62. Beauvoir, *Tout compte fait*, 70–71.
63. Simone de Beauvoir, *The Force of Circumstance* (New York: Putnam's Sons, 1964), 474.
64. Simone de Beauvoir, preface (presentation text to the film), *Shoah* (Claude Lanzmann, 1985), 12. See also the reprinted text in Simons and Timmerman, *Simone de Beauvoir*, 324–27.
65. Beauvoir, preface, *Shoah*, 13.

66. Beauvoir, preface, *Shoah*, 9, 13.
67. Suleiman, "Introduction," Simons and Timmerman, *Simone de Beauvoir*, 302.
68. Beauvoir, *Tout compte fait*, 42.
69. Beauvoir, *Tout compte fait*, 50.
70. Beauvoir, *Tout compte fait*, 62.

CREDITS

INDEX